RUSTLERS
and the
TEXAS TRAIL

Book One of The Christian Cowgirl Adventure Series

LAUREN K. LOTTER
ILLUSTRATED BY MONICA MINTO

Copyright © 2014 by Lauren K. Lotter

Rustlers and the Texas Trail
Book One of The Christian Cowgirl Adventure Series
by Lauren K. Lotter

Illustration Copyright © 2014 by Monica Minto

Printed in the United States of America

ISBN 9781629527925

All rights reserved solely by the author. The author guarantees all contents are original and do not infringe upon the legal rights of any other person or work. No part of this book may be reproduced in any form without the permission of the author. The views expressed in this book are not necessarily those of the publisher.

Unless otherwise indicated, Bible quotations are taken from the King James Version of the Bible, *Public Domain.*

www.xulonpress.com

The Christian Cowgirl Adventure Series

Book 1: *Rustlers and the Texas Trail*
Book 2: *Hidden Treasure and Wedding Bells* (Coming Soon)

DEDICATION

Rustlers and the Texas Trail is dedicated to my parents, Tom and Kathy, and to my siblings, Seth, Levi, and Lydia. This book would not have been possible without you.

TABLE OF CONTENTS

Meet the Characters ix

Chapter 1:   Birthday Fun.................... 13

Chapter 2:   The Capture 32

Chapter 3:   Heading Home 50

Chapter 4:   Sorting Cattle 64

Chapter 5:   Pot-S-Hook's New Hand 75

Chapter 6:   Logan's Accident and the Box 100

Chapter 7:   Arty and the Telegram 113

Chapter 8:   Preparing for the Journey
             and the Surprise 125

Chapter 9:   Heading to Texas 138

Chapter 10: Wolves and Scattered Cattle........ 152

Chapter 11: Midnight Rider.................. 164

VII

Chapter 12: Lurking Shadows 181

Chapter 13: Treasure Hunt 193

Chapter 14: The Dust Storm 209

Chapter 15: Finally There 225

Chapter 16: A Trip to Town 239

Chapter 17: Disaster in the Night. 251

Chapter 18: Adventure on the Bluff. 263

Chapter 19: The Angels Are Singing 273

Chapter 20: The Hideout Hunt 284

Chapter 21: Uncovering the Plot 301

Chapter 22: Justice for All 314

MEET THE CHARACTERS

Amy Susanna Kentworthy: A fifteen-year-old Christian girl who lives on the Bar Double Diamond Ranch in Durango, Wyoming ,during the 1920s

Clint Kentworthy: Amy's father and the owner of the Bar Double Diamond

Susanna Kentworthy: Amy's mother who died in a storm when Amy was ten years old

Daniel Kentworthy: Amy's twenty-year-old cousin

Daryl: The foreman of the Bar Double Diamond

Caleb, Ross, Ken, Gus, Cody, and **Logan**: The Bar Double Diamond's hands

Grubby: The cook

Arty: A fourteen-year-old orphan boy who is hired by Clint

Anders Archer: A fifteen-year-old neighbor boy who works for Clint from the Diamond-n-ahalf Ranch

Wyatt Archer: Anders's father and the owner of the Diamond-n-ahalf

Julia Archer: Anders's mother

Edward Archer: Anders's twenty-one-year old brother

Marianna Archer: Anders's seventeen-year-old sister

Leah Black: Amy's fourteen-year-old friend from the Pot-S-Hook Ranch

Luke Black: Leah's father and the owner of the Pot-S-Hook

Savannah Black: Leah's mother

Brian Black: Leah's six-year-old brother

Tye: A sixteen-year-old orphan boy who is hired by Luke Black

Katie West: Amy's fifteen-year-old friend that lives in town

Chad West: Katie's father and Durango's marshal

LuAnne West: Katie's mother

Roseann Henderson: A ranch girl of the Rocking H Ranch in Texas

Devon Henderson: Rosanna's father and the owner of the Rocking H Ranch

Twyla Anderson: An unsaved ranch girl of the Silver Maple Ranch

Travis Anderson: Twyla's father and owner of the Silver Maple

Jessica White: A widow living with her three children in Red River, Colorado

Tyler White: Jessica's fifteen-year-old son

Brent White: Jessica's fourteen-year-old son

Hannah White: Jessica's twelve-year-old daughter

Chapter One
Birthday Fun

Amy yawned and stretched, listening to the birds singing outside her window and watching the early morning sunlight dance across her bedroom floor.

What a beautiful day! she thought as she gazed past the ranch buildings to the open land beyond.

Suddenly she sat up. "Today is my birthday!" she exclaimed aloud. "I can't believe I forgot after I've been waiting and waiting for this day to come."

Amy kicked back the covers and went to stand at the window. *I can't believe I'm 15 years old!* she thought. *I wonder if Dad has anything special planned for the day. Maybe he'll let me take a ride on Dark Sunshine.*

Amy Susanna Kentworthy was a pretty, dark-haired ranch girl. She lived on the Bar Double Diamond Ranch in Durango, Wyoming, with her father, Clint. Her mother, Susanna, had died several years earlier.

Amy hummed as she picked out a dress, brushed and put up her hair, and pinned her white head covering on over her bun, then took the stairs two at a time.

When she entered the kitchen, she saw her dad, Clint, a tall, dark-complexioned man with brown hair and mustache, standing at the stove, flipping golden brown pancakes on the griddle.

"Good morning, Dad!" she greeted him cheerfully.

"Why, you're an early bird this morning! I guess you get the worm!" Clint said as he turned from the stove to give her a hug. "Happy birthday, Amy. The hands are going to eat with us this morning, and then you may do as you please for the rest of the day. Do you have any plans?"

"I'd like to ride Dark Sunshine to Dewey Mountain to see if I can find any mustangs," she told him.

Clint nodded. "That sounds fine," he agreed, turning back to the stove.

Amy peered around him. "Yum! My favorite! You make the best pancakes."

Clint chuckled. "Don't let Grubby hear you say that. I figured since it was your birthday it called for something special."

Amy set the table and made the coffee while Clint finished the pancakes and fried the bacon. They had just finished when the hands came in and seated themselves around the table.

There were six ranch hands: Ken, Ross, Cody, Caleb, Gus and Logan, plus Daryl, the foreman, and Grubby, the cook. Anders, a blonde-haired, blue-eyed Swedish boy from the neighboring ranch, was there also. He worked for Clint during the summer.

Amy poured the coffee, and then they all bowed their heads respectfully as Clint asked the blessing. "We ask you to bless Amy on her birthday, and I pray that she will grow in You this next year. Thank you for the food we are about to eat, and keep us safe as we go about our work today. In Jesus name, Amen."

The conversation was lively around the table.

"Where are the gray hairs, Amy?" Anders teased. "Fifteen is pretty old, you know."

Amy reached across the table and took his plate away, asking sweetly, "What did you say?"

"I said you're very young looking." Anders grinned as he rescued his plate.

"Now that you're fifteen, I think you can handle more chores. I'm sure I can think of a few for you to do today." Daryl grinned, giving Clint a wink.

Amy grinned at him. She knew that he was joking, but she asked anyway. "What kind of chores did you have in mind?"

Anders groaned. "That was a bad thing to ask!"

"Well," Daryl drawled, "I was thinking of the grain room—it can always use a good cleaning."

Amy clapped her hands over her ears, almost spilling her coffee.

"Watch it!" Clint exclaimed. "I don't need spilled coffee on the floor."

"It's Daryl's fault! He was teasing me!" Amy protested.

"Was not! I was only telling you what needed done today," Daryl insisted.

Amy shrugged. "Dad already gave me the day off."

Rustlers and the Texas Trail

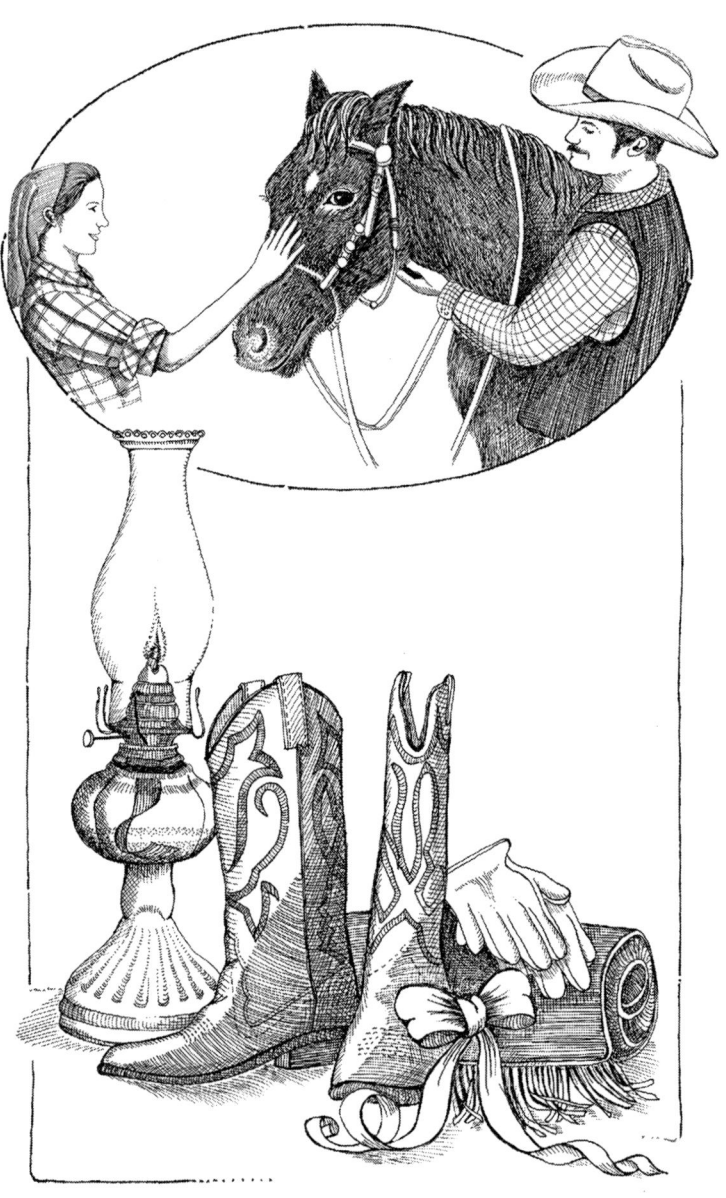

BIRTHDAY FUN

"Well, the grain room will still be there tomorrow, I guess." Daryl took another pancake and doused it with syrup.

Amy groaned, and the others laughed.

When they finished eating, Clint set a box wrapped in brown paper in front of her. "This is from all the boys," he told her.

Eagerly, Amy tore the paper away and reached inside. "New boots!" she exclaimed, holding them up for everyone to see. "Just what I needed." Slipping off one of her old boots, she tried on one of the new ones. "They fit perfectly. How did you know what to get?" she asked.

"Clint told us what you wanted," Daryl answered.

"Well, thanks everyone! This was exactly what I've been wanting."

"Let's head out to the barn," Clint said, standing up and turning toward the door. "My gift is out there."

Amy looked at him curiously, but Clint just smiled as he turned and headed for the door.

Quickly Amy pulled off her other old boot and tried to put the new one on. "Hey, there's something in my boot!" she exclaimed. Slipping her hand into the boot, she grabbed the object and pulled it out. "New gloves!" she turned them over in her hands. "Wow! These are great!"

"Those are from me," Daryl told her. "You left your old ones lying on the table in the bunkhouse the other day, and I noticed they're getting pretty worn out. I figured you could use a new pair."

"Thank you, Daryl. I almost bought a new pair when I was in town the other day, but I'm glad I didn't." Amy slipped the gloves on. "They fit great."

"Glad you like them." Daryl pushed back his chair and jerked his head toward Clint. "You'd better follow him. He's chompin' at the bit to git you out to the barn."

Amy laughed. "Well, so am I." She slipped the gloves into her pocket and followed her dad out the door.

Clint reached the barn first. He opened the door and stepped back to let her walk ahead of him.

Amy stepped through the doorway and paused, looking around and wondering where Clint's gift was.

Clint stepped around her and stopped at the nearest stall. "Here it is! Happy birthday, Amy! How do you like him?"

"Oh, Dad!" Amy squealed. "Is he mine?"

A solid black horse with a white star on his forehead stood facing them proudly. He nickered softly and stretched out his neck toward Amy.

"Yes, Amy!" Clint smiled "He's all yours. Dark Sunshine is getting small for you, so I got you a bigger mount. Wyatt Archer had him for sale. I bought him yesterday, and Wyatt delivered him last night after you were in bed. His name is Black Banner, or Bannie for short."

"Oh, Dad, he is gorgeous! I've always wanted a black horse!" Amy exclaimed. "Can I take him on my ride today?"

Clint nodded. "Sure. He's young, only four, but he's well trained, and I know you can handle him."

"Thanks, Dad. Thank you, everyone, for everything." Amy held out her hand to the gelding and stroked his velvety nose.

"Wait a minute," Anders spoke up, "you haven't opened my gift."

"I didn't know you had one for me." Amy turned around with a smile.

"Well, I do. Here it is." Anders handed her a small, soft package.

Eagerly Amy ripped back the paper and gasped." Oh, Anders! The new split skirt I've been wanting! How in the world did you get one?"

"My mom made it. So it isn't really from me," he said.

"Oh, yes, it is. It's the thought that counts," Amy told him.

"I guess so." Anders studied his boots and shifted uncomfortably.

"Amy, will you step into the tack room?" Clint asked. "The second part of my gift is in there."

Amy opened the door and stepped in. "Wow!" she exclaimed. A brand new saddle hung on the wall, along with a bridle, breast collar, and saddle blanket.

Amy fingered the soft leather as she said, "This has been a really special birthday, Dad. Thank you so much." She smiled at him, and Clint smiled back.

"I'm glad you enjoyed everything, Amy. Now I have another surprise. When I was in town yesterday, I stopped by the West and Black places and asked Katie and Leah's parents if they could go riding with you today. Leah is coming here and Katie will meet you on the ridge by 10:30. I'm also giving Anders the day off to go with you. You guys had better hurry and get ready."

"Oh, wow! Thanks, Dad! Do you think I should ride Bannie?" she asked.

"I don't think he will cause any trouble, and the sooner you start to ride him the better," Clint said. "Boys, that south fencing needs stretched today. I'll be there as soon as I see Amy and Anders off."

The hands scattered to gather their horses and tools, and Clint turned to Amy. "One reason I got Bannie for you is that I believe Dark Sunshine is in foal. In that case, you won't be able to ride her for a while."

"Oh, Dad! Really?" Amy cried. "Can I keep her foal?"

Clint chuckled. "We'll see about that when the time comes, but for now, Leah and Katie will be waiting if you don't hurry. I'll saddle Bannie while you get ready. Anders?"

"Yes, sir?"

"Get your horse and meet me at the cook house in ten minutes. Go get ready, Amy."

"Okay."

When she came out of the house a few minutes later, Anders was leading his horse, Sky Blue, out of the corral. Amy waved to him, then headed to the barn.

Clint was just leading Bannie out as she walked up.

Amy stopped and stared. For a moment she was speechless, then finally she shook her head and said, "Wow! He sure looks good in all that fancy stuff!"

Clint grinned. "He shows it off all right. Now, hop up here and we'll see how you two get along."

Birthday Fun

He held the gelding steady while Amy mounted, then pointed toward the corrals.

"Why don't you ride him in one of the corrals for a little to see how he does for you?" he suggested.

Amy rode into one of the corrals. Bannie's ears perked up at the sight of the cattle in the pasture, and he started to dance around. She gave a gentle tug on the reins, and he quickly settled down.

After riding around several times, Amy rode over to Clint, who was perched on the fence. "He's great, Dad. I don't think I'll have any trouble with him," she said, patting Bannie's neck.

"You two work great together," Anders, who had been watching from the bunkhouse, said as he walked closer. He opened the corral gate for her to ride through. "Dad bought him for Marianna, but they didn't get along. I think he knew she was scared and took advantage of that."

Amy nodded. "That makes sense. Marianna is a timid rider. Bannie started to get excited when he saw the cows, but he settled down when I got his attention back on me."

"Just remember that he's young yet." Clint told her. "He's not mature, and his training isn't completely finished. Be cautious and don't let your attention wander while you're riding."

Amy grinned. "Oh, I won't! I haven't forgotten what happened when I did that on Sky Blue!"

Anders laughed. "I told you he'd buck if you didn't pay attention, but would you listen to me? Nope!"

Clint chuckled. "I still remember what Amy looked like when she came home that day. I don't know why you switched horses."

"For the fun of it!" Amy told him, grinning.

Clint shook his head. "Kids! Will I ever understand them?"

"Probably not." Anders chuckled.

"You were one yourself not too long ago," Amy teased.

Clint shrugged. "Let's pray before you go." He and Anders removed their hats. "Dear Lord, please be with Amy, Anders, Leah, and Katie as they go on this ride together. Give them a fun, happy day. Give them your protection. In thy name, Amen. All right you guys, have a great time, and don't get into trouble!"

Amy laughed as she turned Bannie around. "I'll try. See you tonight. Don't work too hard!"

"Oh, I won't. I'll make the hands do all the hard stuff. Lucky you're off, Anders!"

"Yes, sir!" Anders grinned as they turned toward the road.

"Come on!" Amy pointed up the road. "Let's trot. I think that's Leah coming."

"I'm right behind you." Anders nudged Sky Blue with his heels, and both horses broke into a trot.

As they trotted out the lane, Amy turned to look back at Clint. In the early morning light, she could clearly see his tan face, neatly trimmed mustache, and blue, checkered shirt. *If a man ever looked like a cowboy, he sure does*, she thought to herself.

Leah met them at the end of the lane. "Hi, guys!" she greeted them.

"Hi!" Amy returned.

Leah whistled. "Is this your birthday present?"

Amy nodded. "Yep. Do you like him?"

"I'll say!" Leah shook her head. "He's a spiffy-lookin' horse!"

"Thanks." Amy leaned forward in her saddle, her eyes sparkling. "How 'bout a race?" she suggested.

"You're on!" Leah kissed to her horse, and a moment later the two girls were racing across the range.

"Come on, Anders!" Amy called over her shoulder.

"No fair! You got a head start!" he shouted after her.

"Don't be a poor sport!" Leah yelled.

"Better look out! I'm coming after you!" Anders hollered back.

Amy drew rein as they neared the river. Bannie fought her and pulled forward, stretching his neck out, still wanting to run. Amy rode him in a circle to calm him while she waited for the others to catch up.

"That wasn't a fair race!" Anders declared as he rode up beside her.

Amy grinned at him.

"Stop it!" Anders exclaimed.

"Stop what?" Amy asked.

"Giving me that silly smile!"

"Wow! Listen to that Swedish temper!" Amy laughed.

"Who said I'm Swedish?" Anders asked.

"All you have to do is look at your blonde hair and blue eyes—and your name is a dead giveaway, too—to know you're Swedish!" Amy told him.

"Huh!"

"Oh, Anders!" Leah laughed. "You are so sensitive."

"I'm not sensitive!" Anders insisted.

Amy leaned forward and peered up at him. "Your face is kind of red."

"That's spirit!" Anders kicked his horse, and they plunged into the river.

Amy and Leah exchanged looks, then burst out laughing.

"Are you coming, or do I have to wait all day?" Anders called impatiently.

"We're coming." Amy urged Bannie into the water.

"So where exactly are we going?" Anders asked after they'd crossed the river and were headed toward the mountain. He had recovered his good humor by this time.

"Well, I'd like to ride down the river and see if we can spot some wild horses," Amy said. "Then Dad asked me to ride to the north pasture to check on the stock since no one has been out there for quite a while and he can't spare any of the boys to go next week any time. How does that sound?"

"Sounds like a full day to me," Anders grumbled.

"Aw, quit bein' lazy, Anders!" Leah teased. "You're tougher than that."

The three fell silent as they began to climb the steep, difficult path up the mountain to the ridge where they were to meet Katie.

As they rode clear of the trees and the horses stepped onto the windswept ridge, Amy spotted a rider coming toward them.

"There's Katie!" Amy waved to her friend, urging Bannie into a lope.

Amy and Leah greeted Katie, then Amy told her what they planned to do, and Katie readily agreed.

"Where will we go first?" she asked.

Amy thought a moment. "I think we'll go to look for the horses first. The pasture is on our way home."

The day passed quickly as the three friends looked for the wild mustangs.

They saw several herds but couldn't get very close. The mustangs were wary and would run as soon as they caught the scent of humans.

"Well, I'd hoped to get closer, but at least we saw some," Amy said as they started home. "Let's take a quick look at the cattle and then get going."

An hour later, as they were riding at a smooth, steady trot, Amy called out to the others. "Hold on a minute, guys."

"What's the matter?" Anders asked, swinging his horse around to face her. Katie and Leah slowed their horses too.

"I heard something," she said. "It's coming from the mountain. It sounds like cattle bawling, but that isn't cattle country. There isn't any grass or water up there. What could it be?"

The four fell silent, listening.

A few minutes later, Amy exclaimed, "There it is again!"

Anders looked admiringly at her. "Good ears, Amy. That's the Indian in you. I didn't hear a thing. Suppose we ride up and take a look?"

"Well …." Amy hesitated. "Okay. Sounds as if an animal could be in trouble. Just a quick look. Will you go?" she asked the girls.

Katie agreed, but Leah hesitated. "I don't think so, Amy. I promised I would be home by four, and it is three now. I'll have to ride hard to get home on time as it is. But you guys be careful! It could be dangerous. If an animal is stuck or something, it could be crazy with fear. Will you pray before I leave you, Anders?" she asked.

"Sure, Leah." Anders removed his hat. "Dear Lord, Please protect us as we try to find out what is going on. If an animal is in trouble, please give us the wisdom to help it. Protect Leah as she travels home alone. In Thy name, Amen."

They all raised their heads as Anders finished praying and smiled at one another.

"Okay." Leah tightened her reins. "Off I go! Hope all goes well. Be sure to tell me the whole story, Amy. Bye!" She loped away, leaving Amy, Anders, and Katie by the foot of the mountain.

"All right!" Amy said. "Let's get this over with."

They rode up the steep path in silence, with Anders leading the way, stopping now and then to listen, but the noise Amy had heard was not repeated.

About halfway up, Anders suddenly veered off the path and pulled his horse up abruptly, putting a finger to his lips.

Birthday Fun

He must have heard something. Now he is the one with the better ears! Amy smiled to herself.

The three riders sat in silence, waiting.

A few moments later, Amy tensed. *"What was that?"* she wondered. She strained her ears. "Uh-oh," she murmured as she recognized the sound. *A shod hoof against rock! Either a shod horse is loose up here, which isn't likely, or someone is riding! It sounds like more than one horse.*

In a few moments, four riders appeared, and they were talking among themselves.

Amy strained her ears to hear every word.

A tall, dark-haired man was speaking. "We've got a good bunch of cattle up there. After we pick up Dan and Dave tonight, we'll head back up here and tomorrow we'll drive the cattle north, and have us a good chunk of money." He laughed and the others joined him.

"You got that right, Andy, no one is going to find out for a while. They hardly ever come out this way, so we can get away real easy!" said a young, sandy-haired boy.

The rustlers rode down the mountain path and out of sight.

The three friends sat still for a few minutes, and then Amy spoke in a low voice. "Did you hear them, Anders? They are going to leave tomorrow morning! We caught them just in time! I can't believe we found real rustlers stealing cattle!"

"But we haven't stopped them, Amy. What are three kids against six men? We need help. You and Katie have to ride back to the ranch and bring your dad and the hands. I'll stay here to watch in case something happens," Anders told her.

"But what if something happens to you? And what if those men see us? Do you think the trail is safe?" Amy asked.

"You've got a good horse. Watch him and he'll tell you where the men are. Besides, God will be with you. You need to leave right away, but we should pray first." Anders removed his hat. "Lord we need to stop these men before they hurt us or others. Help Amy and Katie as they ride home. Please keep us all safe. In Thy name, Amen."

Anders put his hat back on. "Go on, girls. Use your common sense and trust the Lord. Watch Bannie and listen to what he is telling you. See you later!" He waved his hand and disappeared up the path.

Amy and Katie were left alone.

But we're not really alone, Amy reminded herself. *The Lord is here with us.*

Taking a deep breath, she clucked to Bannie and started down the steep path.

Remembering how she had known the rustlers were approaching, she tried to avoid rocks as much as possible.

They were almost off the mountain when suddenly, Bannie froze.

Quickly the girls veered off the path and waited tensely.

After a few minutes, Amy heard voices on the trail below them. "At least we know where the men are so we can avoid them," she said quietly to Katie.

They continued cautiously down the mountain, stopping now and then to listen.

When they reached the bottom of the trail, Katie left Amy to go home.

After Katie left her, Amy urged Bannie into a gallop, heading for the south stretch of fencing where she knew her dad and the hands would be.

Half an hour later, as she neared the pasture, she spotted Clint working by himself and rode toward him. The ground was rough and rocky, making it dangerous to ride on. Bannie stumbled several times but quickly righted himself and galloped on.

Amy pulled him up sharply when they reached Clint.

"What on earth are you doing, Amy?" Clint asked anxiously. "Why are you alone? And don't you know how dangerous it is to ride that fast on that kind of ground?"

"I know, Dad, but I had to get here quickly. We don't have much time," she told him. She explained where Anders was and told him about the rustlers. "We need to get a posse together and ride up there before it gets too dark. They said they were coming back tonight."

"All right, Amy, let's ride back to the house. I've already sent the boys up, so we'll go get them and ride up to join Anders. You should ride Dark Sunshine instead of Bannie because he has already worked hard today. One more day of riding won't hurt her."

"Okay, Dad," Amy agreed.

While they were talking, Clint had mounted Renegade, his white stallion, and begun riding toward the ranch. Now they clucked to their horses and galloped the last half-mile.

As they skidded to a stop in the ranch yard, cowboys came from all directions and fired questions at them.

"What's the matter?"

"Is someone hurt?"

"Where is Anders?"

Clint silenced them with a wave of his hand and briefly explained what was going on.

The men immediately scattered to catch fresh horses and saddle up.

Clint told Amy to pack some food and get a few blankets. "It could be a long night. Better be prepared. I'll saddle Dark Sunshine for you. I wish we had time to ride for the marshal, but we don't if we want to get up there first," he told her.

"Maybe Katie will tell him and he'll come on his own," Amy suggested.

Clint frowned. "I hope he doesn't come. I want to do this without bloodshed, and in order to do that, we have to surprise the rustlers. If he comes ridin' in, it could ruin everything."

Amy nodded. "I see what you mean. I think Mr. West will figure that out on his own, though."

"I agree. Chad knows his business. I wouldn't be surprised if he was here waiting for us when we get back." Clint turned to give directions to the men and Amy led Bannie to the barn.

Moving quickly, she pulled the saddle off and hung it on a peg in the tack room. She slipped off the bridle

Birthday Fun

and turned the gelding into his stall, then hurried to the house.

She made sandwiches for everyone and packed them in her saddle bag with a jug of hot coffee. She rolled several blankets together, pulled a sweater over her head, and ran outside.

Clint had saddled Dark Sunshine for her, and the mare was tied to the hitching post. Amy slung the saddlebags over the mare's back and tied them and the blankets to the saddle. The hands were all mounted and ready to go, so Amy swung into her saddle and rode over to Clint.

After making sure everyone was ready, Clint said, "All right boys, let's pray before we head out." The men respectfully removed their hats and bowed their heads as Clint prayed. "Dear Heavenly Father, please help us as we try to capture these men and protect every one of us, and be with Anders right now and keep him safe. Amen. Let's go, men."

Chapter Two
The Capture

Clint led Amy and the men the back way to the mountain, a winding, twisting path that crossed and recrossed the river.

The sun was beginning to set as they neared the base of the mountain. A few large rocks formed a natural wall and a good place to hide.

Amy listened as Clint explained they would stay there until the rustlers came. Then she dismounted and loosened her mount's cinch.

As she pulled one of the blankets down, she saw Daryl ride around the rocks and start up the mountain.

"Where is he going?" she asked Clint.

"I sent him up to stay with Anders. It isn't time for the rustlers to be back yet from what you told me, and Anders needs someone to keep him out of trouble."

Amy laughed. "I think you're right."

"Get some sleep while you can." Clint told her. "It'll be a long night. I've got first watch."

Amy nodded and watched as he climbed one of the rocks to a spot where he could see the mountain but not be seen by anyone coming up the path. Then she spread her blanket on the ground and laid down to try to sleep.

A while later she woke with a start and looked around. It was getting dark, and a few stars were beginning to show. She shivered as she stood. The May evenings were still chilly, and the ground was damp, adding to the chill.

She folded her blanket and tied it up with the others, then went in search of Clint.

She found him standing with several of the hands. "Nothin' yet?" she asked.

Clint shook his head. "Nothin'. They're later than I thought they would be."

"Who's on watch?" Amy asked.

"Ken," Clint answered. "I expect some action any minute now."

"Mr. West hasn't showed up?"

Clint chuckled. "No, but that's okay. Besides ruining our chance for surprise, he would be endangering himself if he ran into the rustlers alone."

Amy nodded. "He sure would."

Ken's whisper, sounding harsh and loud in the still night air, interrupted them. He slid down from the rock and walked quickly toward Clint.

"Riders," he said, jerking his head toward the mountain. "Six of them. Heading up the path."

"Get your horses ready," Clint told his men. "We'll give them a head start, and then we'll follow."

Amy hurried to tighten her cinch. *I'm glad we're finally getting going,* she thought as she swung into the saddle. *I sure was getting tired of sitting around. The ground isn't exactly the most comfortable place to sit.*

The men mounted quickly and were ready to go. The horses seemed to feel the excitement in the air and pranced about eagerly.

Amy rode Dark Sunshine in a small circle to calm her while they waited for Clint's signal to start up the path.

Clint climbed back up the rock to check on the rustlers' progress.

A moment later, he stepped out of the shadows and walked quickly toward Gus, who was holding Renegade.

"They're moving fast," he said as he mounted. "I think they're far enough up the trail. Let's follow them!" He wheeled his horse and cantered away.

Amy clucked to Dark Sunshine and started after him.

After leaving the cover of the rocks, the group moved slowly and carefully, stopping often to listen. Any mistakes now, and their chance for surprise would be over. The horses seemed to sense their riders' caution and moved with their ears laid back, listening for the slightest direction.

Halfway up, Clint suddenly veered off the path. The others followed and halted their horses.

Amy rode up to him. "Hear somethin'?" she asked softly.

Clint nodded. "I think I heard horses a little way up the trail. We'll wait here a minute and let them get ahead of us more. Hopefully they haven't heard us."

After a few minutes, Clint started back onto the trail, and the other riders followed.

It was getting very dark now. Amy loosened her reins and let Dark Sunshine follow the horse in front of her. She knew that what she couldn't see, the horses could.

The night was eerily silent. Amy shivered. She had never been fond of the dark, but it was worse when the animals were silent, too.

She was relieved when the flickering light of a campfire came into view. *But that's not a friendly fire,"* she reminded herself. *That must be the rustlers' camp. Anders and Daryl would never light a fire.*

Just then, someone stepped out of the shadows and onto the path in front of her and grabbed her bridle.

Amy jumped, startled, then gave a sigh of relief when she realized it was Anders.

He motioned for her to dismount and follow him. He led her off the path into the trees, keeping the rustlers' camp in sight.

Amy tensed when Dark Sunshine stepped on a branch. In the stillness of the night, it sounded as loud as a gunshot. She glanced toward the rustlers' fire. To her relief, they didn't seem to have heard the noise. They were shouting and yelling loudly.

Probably celebrating their victory, she thought as she followed Anders deeper into the trees. *They're making so much noise, we could be a whole army going through and they wouldn't hear a thing.*

She felt a tug on the reins, and Anders whispered, "I'll take care of your horse. Go find your dad. He wants you."

Amy handed him Dark Sunshine's reins and somehow managed to find Clint in the darkness. He was tying his horse to a tree.

"Hey, Dad," she greeted him in a low voice.

"Oh, hi, Amy." He turned to face her. "I'm sending you and Anders with Logan. Do not come out into the clearing unless I call for you. Understand?"

When Amy nodded her head, he went on. "Daryl will be with me, Cody with Caleb, and Ken with Ross. I'll explain what we're going to do in minute."

"Can Anders and I watch from the edge of the woods?" Amy asked.

Clint nodded. "If things start getting hot though, you get farther away as fast as you can."

The men had finished settling their horses and gathered around to get their orders.

"We want to do this without bloodshed or violence," Clint told them. "The best way to accomplish that, I think, is to wait until just before sunrise when the men are just beginning to get going. They've been drinking. That'll make our job a little easier. When I give the signal, step out of the trees and start walking toward them. We'll work their surprise to our advantage. Now let's separate into pairs. Daryl, you come with me, Cody and Caleb, Ken and Ross, and Logan can go with Amy and Anders."

Anders had come back from taking care of the horses and joined Amy and Logan as they searched out a good vantage point.

As they walked, Anders turned to Amy with a grin. "How'd I get stuck with you?"

Amy swatted him playfully. "You know I'm as tough as any boy, Anders Archer!"

"Yeah, sure, and almost as smart, too!" he returned.

Amy chuckled. "You always have to have the last word, don't you?"

"Can't let you win all the time."

As they settled down on the ground, Logan moved a few feet away and pulled his hat over his face. "Let me know if anything exciting happens," he told them.

Amy pulled one of her extra sweaters over her head. The night wasn't getting any warmer. She watched the rustlers in the dim flickering light of their fire.

"Why would anyone want to do that?" she said after a few minutes of silence.

"Do what?" Anders turned around to look at her.

"Drink. It ruins so many lives. Not just of those who actually drink it, but their families, too."

Anders nodded. "It sure does. I wouldn't touch the stuff for all the money in the world. Our bodies are the temple of God. We are supposed to take care of it. You're right. It doesn't just affect the ones who drink it."

Amy shook her head sadly. "I'm glad my father doesn't drink."

"Me, too," Anders agreed.

"I'm going to get some sleep," Amy told him a minute later. "Wake me up if anything happens."

"You think I'm gonna stay awake?" he asked.

"You're too excited to sleep," Amy told him.

"Huh!" Anders snorted.

*****

As soon as the first ray of sunlight streamed in her window, Amy bounded out of bed. Dashing to the closet, she pulled a dress off its hanger and pulled it over her head. She snatched up the hair brush off the dresser and yanked it through her thick locks of hair and quickly braided it. Then she flung open the bedroom door and hurried down the stairs, nearly colliding with her mother, Susanna, as she rounded the corner.

"Whoa! Hold your horses!" Susanna laughed. "You seem to be in a hurry! I wonder what could be going on today." She tapped her chin thoughtfully.

"Mom! It's my birthday!" Amy exclaimed.

"Why, so it is! I'd almost forgotten!" Susanna's eyes twinkled merrily. "I can't believe you are ten years old already! Why, it seems no time at all since you were just learning to walk!"

"Well I think I am past the learning-to-walk stage!" Amy giggled.

Just then Clint entered the room. "Well, the birthday girl is up and about already, huh?"

"Good morning, Dad!" Amy cried, launching herself up to give him a hug.

"Well, don't strangle me now! You won't want me weak from lack of oxygen when you hear my plans!" he teased.

"What is it, Dad? What is it?" Amy jumped up and down in her excitement.

"How would you like to go on a ride with your mother and me to Dewey Mountain?"

"Oh, Dad! Really?" Amy cried excitedly.

"Yes, really, Amy, but I need my grubs first. I smell sausage. Let's storm the kitchen!"

Amy laughed and darted ahead of her parents into the kitchen, "Whoopee!" she shouted. "Flapjacks and sausage, maple syrup, and strawberry shortcake! Yummy!"

"Well, I guess I won't have to force you to eat breakfast this morning, will I?" Susanna chuckled.

"No ma'am!" Amy said emphatically as she slid into her place.

As soon as they finished eating, Amy prepared for her ride while Clint and Susanna did the dishes. Amy had gotten out of dishes because it was her birthday.

"Ready, Amy?" Clint called from the doorway.

"Almost, Dad. Who am I riding?"

"Oh, I don't know. We'll see when we get out there," he answered vaguely as he walked out the door.

Amy thought that the way he answered was strange but didn't give it much thought.

Clint and Susanna were standing on the porch when Amy walked outside. "There you are, Amy. Let's head to the barn," Clint said, leading the way. He opened the barn door with a bow and a flourish.

Amy giggled at his dramatic actions.

Susanna led Amy to the nearest stall.

Amy stopped and stared. In that stall was the most beautiful horse Amy had ever seen, a small but sturdy-looking dark bay mare with soft, intelligent eyes.

"Surprise!" Clint and Susanna shouted together.

Amy gasped, too overcome for words. Her dream had always been to have a horse of her own.

"*Is she mine?*" she finally squealed, looking at Susanna.

"Yes, honey. She is yours. We think you are old enough to have your own horse. Do you like her?" Susanna asked.

"Oh I love her, Mom. Thank you so much!" Amy smiled happily.

"You're welcome! What are you going to name her?"

"Did you even have to ask? Dark Sunshine, of course!" Amy had always said she would name her first horse that if it was a bay mare.

"If you would like, you may ride her today," Clint suggested.

"I wouldn't think of doing anything different!" Amy laughed.

"So we thought." Clint chuckled. "Well let's not burn any more daylight. Susanna, why don't you help Amy get saddled up and get your horse ready, too? I need to tell the boys a few things; then I'll get Renegade."

Clint strode towards the bunkhouse and Susanna turned to Amy. "Okay, Amy. Let's get her out and tacked up."

Amy grabbed a lead rope and opened the stall door. Dark Sunshine eyed her a bit nervously, but Amy spoke softly, and the mare settled down. Amy snapped the lead rope onto her halter and led her out of the stall.

Susanna stepped up and fed her a treat. "Lead her outside, Amy, and tie her to the hitching post and get your tack. I'll go get Mitzie."

The Capture

Amy tied Dark Sunshine up and headed back in for her tack. Susanna brought her horse out and then helped Amy tack up. Dark Sunshine behaved beautifully.

"Now why don't you ride her around the yard to see how you get along?" Susanna suggested when they had both horses saddled.

"Okay, Mom, but I'm sure we'll get along just fine," Amy said as she swung into the saddle.

"I'm sure, too." Susanna smiled.

Amy rode around for a few minutes and was thoroughly convinced that Dark Sunshine was the sweetest horse around.

Clint had joined Susanna by the time Amy rode back to the barn. "Well, how's it goin'?" he asked.

"It's going great! Are we ready to go?" Amy patted Dark Sunshine's neck.

"Sure we are. Let's get mounted!"

The hands waved as they loped out the drive.

Amy grinned with eager anticipation as they turned toward the mountain. "This is going to be a great day!" she thought. Little did she know what lay ahead.

They rode almost all day. They spotted several mustang herds and other wildlife. Amy and Dark Sunshine worked well together. The little horse was patient and gentle, carefully choosing her footing and listening to Amy's commands.

About noon they stopped and ate the picnic lunch Susanna had packed, leaving the horses ground tied with their nosebags on. Amy ate hurriedly.

"Slow down, Amy, this isn't a race!" Susanna chuckled.

"Sorry." Amy smiled. "I just can't wait to start riding again!"

"I understand, but we've got all day," Clint told her.

They rode for several more hours, exploring areas of the ranch where they seldom went. Amy was enjoying herself very much.

At three o'clock, Clint announced that it was time to head home.

As they rode toward the ranch, Clint noticed dark clouds forming in the west. He said nothing because he didn't want to alarm Amy.

A few minutes later, Susanna caught his eye, then glanced at the rapidly advancing clouds.

He nodded and said, "Amy, it looks like there is a storm coming up. Let's let the horses canter a while."

Clint was getting more and more concerned. This storm was big and coming up fast. He realized they weren't going to beat the storm home.

Suddenly the storm was upon them! The wind whipped around them, stinging their skin with flying sand. The rain was coming down in sheets, and Amy couldn't see a thing. Dark Sunshine was fighting for her head, and Amy clung to her desperately.

Through the gloom, a running horse appeared beside Amy. At first, she couldn't see who it was, but soon, as they drew closer, she saw it was Susanna.

As Amy rode along side, the mare seemed to stumble, then disappeared from view, taking Susanna with her. Amy screamed and pulled Dark Sunshine in their direction.

Clint rode up beside her and grabbed her bridle. "Come on!" he yelled. "Don't go near there!" His voice sounded panicked.

As Clint led her away, Amy had the distinct feeling that she would never see her mother again. She looked up at Clint and saw grief and despair written in every line of his face.

"What happened?" she cried.

"They fell into an arroyo ..." Clint's voice broke, and he could not go on.

A sob tore at Amy's throat as the reality of what had happened struck her like a blow.

She knew, as every ranch child does, that arroyos were dry river beds that could be transformed in a matter of seconds into a swollen, raging flood. She also knew that few people ever returned from a flooded arroyo alive.

In that moment, she knew she would never see her mother alive again.

*****

Amy felt someone shaking her. She opened her eyes and in the dim light saw Anders bending over her.

"Are you awake?" he asked.

When she nodded, he handed her his bandana. Amy took it and wiped the tears off her cheeks.

"Are you okay?"

Amy nodded again.

"Dreaming about your mom?" he asked.

"Yeah, thanks for waking me up." She drew a shaky breath.

He nodded and put a finger to his lips. "I'm sorry, Amy. I can't imagine what that must feel like."

"It's okay." Amy handed his bandana back. "What time is it?"

He pulled his watch out of his pocket. "5:30. Should be seeing some action before long."

They both fell silent, enjoying the peaceful dawn. After a while, the men beside the fire began to stir. One man began to make coffee and bacon.

Anders caught Amy's eye and made a face, rubbing his stomach.

Amy giggled and reached into her saddle bags, pulling out a sandwich. He took it and gave her a thumbs up as he began eating.

Amy woke Logan up and gave him one, too.

By the time she turned back to Anders, his sandwich was gone.

"Did you inhale it or what?" she asked.

"Got any more of those?" he asked, his eyes fixed on her saddle bags.

"You pig!" she teased.

"Not for me!" he protested. "I was thinking of the other guys. They'll be hungry too."

"I was just thinking of that, too." Amy stood and picked up her saddle bags.

"Let me carry those," Anders offered.

"Thanks." Amy flashed him a smile.

"How 'bout you tie some up in your sweater, and I'll do half and you can do half," Anders suggested.

The Capture

Amy nodded and pulled her sweater off.

Anders left her, and she walked as quietly as she could through the trees.

She gave Ken and Ross their sandwiches, then moved on to Clint and Daryl.

"What are you doing, Amy?" Clint asked when he saw her.

"Bringing you some supper, or I guess its breakfast now!" She grinned.

"Thanks. I'm so hungry I've been dreaming about food!" Clint took the sandwich she handed him. Amy sat with them for a few minutes until Anders arrived.

"You better hurry back. We'll be goin' any minute now. Check on the horses on the way back," Clint told them.

"Okay." As Amy turned to walk away, she bumped into Logan. "Oh, Logan! You scared me!" she gasped.

"I thought you were taking a little longer than you should have, so I came to look for you," he explained. "I'll go with you to check on the horses."

After checking on the horses, making sure their lead ropes weren't tangled and their feed bags were filled, Anders walked over to the edge of the cliff.

Amy saw him stiffen. "What is it?" she asked.

"Come look." His voice was low and tense.

"What?" She and Logan walked over to join him.

"Look down there!" He pointed.

A lone rider was making his way up the steep path.

"It must be another rustler! We hadn't counted on this." Logan frowned. "Anders, you run and tell the boss. Amy, you come with me. Anders will be able to go faster without us."

Anders took off and disappeared into the trees.

"What will Dad do?" Amy asked as they walked back toward the clearing.

"Probably capture them before he gets here. His arrival will probably speed things up," Logan answered.

They were almost back when Anders appeared, out of breath from running. "The boss said to get ready," he told Logan.

Logan nodded and hurried ahead of them. Amy and Anders ran after him.

"Slow down, would you?" Amy panted. "You've got longer legs than me."

"I can't help it that you're short!" Anders retorted.

"Smart alec!" Amy shot him a grin as they dropped to their knees next to Logan.

"Shhh!" Logan held a finger to his lips.

Amy turned her attention to the rustlers.

They were standing by the corral with their horses, discussing something, but Amy couldn't make out the words. She caught a movement out of the corner of her eye, and turning quickly, she saw Clint step out of the woods.

All around the clearing, the men followed his lead and stepped out from behind the trees.

Amy stood cautiously to her feet so she could see better.

Suddenly, Clint's voice broke the silence. "Don't move! Stay where you are!"

The rustlers froze. Slowly they raised their hands.

Clint walked up behind them and jerked their guns from their holsters and handed them to Daryl.

"Put them down somewhere," Amy heard him say. "We won't be needing them. Let's get these boys trussed up in the woods and wait for the other one."

"That was easy," Amy remarked to Anders.

"It's not done yet. Listen. I can hear the horse coming," he told her.

Amy waited tensely.

The man they had seen on the trail rode into the camp a few minutes later. *He's not much more than a boy,* Amy thought in surprise.

She watched as he dismounted and scanned the clearing with a puzzled look on his face.

He hesitated a moment, then called loudly. "Dan? Sandy? Where are you?" He walked over to the shack and looked inside. "I know you're here." He started to turn around.

"Hold it right there!" Clint leaped out of the woods.

The boy froze, fear written plainly on his face. "Wh-what's going on?" he stammered.

"You're game's up," Clint told him. He pulled the boy's gun out of his holster and motioned toward the trees where the rest of the men waited. "Walk into the trees, young man."

The boy walked meekly in the direction indicated. His shoulders slumped dejectedly when he saw the others.

Ken came over to him and gently pushed him to the ground before tying him up.

"Poor fellow," Amy murmured.

"What do you mean?" Anders asked.

Amy hesitated. "Well, I don't know. He's just so young, and he doesn't look like the bad type. Maybe he isn't. Maybe he's an orphan or something and just got involved with these guys so he could have friends and something to eat every night."

Anders nodded. "It could be. Lots of men get into trouble that way."

Logan spoke up. "That's a good point. You start hangin' around bad company and you're likely to get hung up in stuff you never intended to. Choose your friends carefully and remember, the Lord will provide. We don't have to steal. He'll always take care of us. Hopefully a little time in jail to think things over will do him good and he'll make wiser choices when he gets out."

Amy was surprised by this flow of words from the normally quiet cowboy.

After a minute she said, "You're right, Logan. The Lord will take care of us, and we should pick our friends carefully. Even if you think you can help the other person, a lot of times, it's their bad habits that rub off on you instead of the other way around."

"In that case, maybe you shouldn't be hangin' around me!" Anders grinned.

Amy chuckled. "I think you know what kind of habits I was talking about."

"Yeah, I was just kiddin' around."

Just then Clint called, "Amy! Anders!"

"Coming!" Amy called back. She and Anders hurried over to him.

"Can I look around?" Amy asked when they reached him.

Clint nodded. "Sure. Coming Anders?"

"Sure thing!" Anders's blue eyes sparkled eagerly.

Chapter Three
Heading Home

As they strode out of the trees, Amy looked around eagerly, "I've never been in a rustlers' camp before," she remarked to Clint.

"No, I guess you never would have been. We haven't had anything like this happen since you were a baby."

They started toward the corral, and Daryl met them partway.

"What's the matter?" Clint asked him.

"They aren't all Bar Double Diamond cattle," Daryl informed him.

"I'm not surprised," Clint said. "Rustlers don't usually stick to one ranch."

Daryl nodded. "Right. At least most of them are from ranches close by. Might be hard to find the owners of those others."

"We'll cross that bridge when we come to it," Clint told him.

The two men continued on to the corral together.

As Amy followed her dad and Anders to the corral, she realized how tired she was. She struggled to keep up and stifled a yawn. She joined the men by the corral gate and looked over the cattle while listening to Clint give instructions.

"Well, men, our first job is to get the men and cattle down to the ranch. We'll get the marshal out to take care of the men, then we'll work on finding the owners of the cattle. Daryl, you and Ken rope the horses together and take the men down. The rest of us will herd the cattle. Let's get going. These cattle haven't had anything to eat or drink in several days by the looks of them. We'll need to take it slow down the mountain."

"Shouldn't someone go for the marshal?" Cody asked.

Clint shook his head. "I think Chad will be at the ranch waiting for us, and I need all my men."

He gave some instructions to the other hands, then turned to Amy. His eyes held a mischievous twinkle. "Maybe you should go down with Ken and Daryl," he suggested.

"Are you serious, Dad?" Amy groaned.

He laughed. "No, of course not! You can stay. I was just foolin' you."

"Good!" Amy smiled. "I wouldn't miss this for anything!"

"Well, now that you've gotten your way, how 'bout gettin' Dark Sunshine and tell Anders to bring Renegade here, please?"

"Okay." Amy turned and headed for the woods.

She spotted Anders riding back to the clearing as she walked down a narrow game trail. "Hey, Anders!" she called. When he caught sight of her, he waved and turned Sky Blue. "What now?" he drawled as he drew alongside.

"Dad wants you to bring Renegade to him," Amy told him.

"And I suppose you're going after Dark Sunshine?" he asked.

Amy nodded.

"Want a lift then?"

"Do you think I could pass that up?" Amy laughed. Anders kicked his foot out of the stirrup, and she grabbed hold of the cantle and pulled herself up.

"I thought you said you were tired," Anders remarked as he started Sky Blue back through the trees.

"What do you mean?" Amy asked, puzzled.

He grinned. "In my opinion, if you can still joke, you aren't tired enough!"

Amy laughed. "Then I guess I'll never be truly tired by your standards!"

When they reached the horses, Amy slid down with a groan. "All that sitting in the cold made me stiff and sore."

Anders spoke over Renegade's back. "Aw, quit whinin', Amy. I sat just as long as you and I ain't sore."

Amy ignored him. *If I say something, he'll just think of something smart to say back*, she thought. Instead she approached Dark Sunshine, who nickered softly. Her breath hung in a small, white cloud in the frosty air.

"These spring mornings are still chilly, aren't they girl?" Amy said softly as she tightened the cinch.

"You talkin' to that horse again?" Anders called.

"At least she can't talk back," Amy called back, laughingly.

She swung lightly into the saddle and then rode up behind Anders, who was bending over and checking Renegade's hooves for rocks. Amy urged Dark Sunshine forward until the mare's nose bumped Anders's back.

He jumped, startled, then sputtered, "Could you watch where you're going?"

Amy laughed and pulled the mare away. "Hurry up. I'll ride back to the clearing with you."

When they entered the clearing, Daryl and Ken were just about ready to head to the ranch with the rustlers.

"Just open the east pasture gate as you ride by," Clint was saying as Amy and Anders rode up.

"You bet, boss." Daryl nodded. He lifted the reins, and his horse started off.

"Here's your horse, Mr. Kentworthy," Anders said, riding forward.

"Thanks, Anders." Clint took the reins and, after checking the cinch, swung into the saddle. "Okay, boys, gather 'round!" he called.

The hands dropped what they were doing and waited for Clint to give them directions.

"Amy and Anders, I want you and Logan to ride drag. Once we get down on the range, I want Cody and Anders on the left, Amy and I right, Ross and Logan drag. Remember, these cattle are weak from lack of water and food, and there are a good many of them.

Move quietly and slowly, and don't raise your voice unless you have to. Now let's get these dogies out of here. Amy and Anders, drive them out."

Daryl opened the corral gate and Amy slipped inside, followed closely by Anders.

Slowly Amy worked Dark Sunshine around the edge of the corral, gently pushing the nervous cattle toward the open gate. Once the cattle saw it, many of them lunged forward. The cowboys on the outside of the corral slowed the cattle down and guided them down the tree-lined path.

Once all of the cattle were out and on their way down the mountain, Amy shut and latched the gate, then followed the herd.

As they crept along, keeping to a pace that wouldn't be too much for the weakened cattle, Amy had time to think.

God works in such amazing ways! If it hadn't been my birthday, and if Dad hadn't given me the day off to go riding, and if God hadn't given Anders the wisdom to know what to do, we wouldn't have gotten back our stolen cattle or caught the rustlers! Thank you, Lord, for protecting us all and giving us the wisdom to catch these men.

She was jolted back to the present by a shrill cowboy yell. The skittery cattle began to circle nervously, a dangerous act on the narrow mountain trail.

"What's wrong?" she heard Clint yell over the noise of the herd.

"A cow went over the edge!" Ross yelled back. "Looks like she's gone already."

Heading Home

"Logan, you go down and check her out. The rest of you, move slower," Clint instructed.

Amy could barely see Clint through the dust, gently urging the cattle forward.

It was long after lunch before the cattle were safely penned in the east pasture. The starved, dehydrated animals fought for a place around the water trough, jostling each other around. Some of the younger, smaller cattle were in trouble in the milling herd. The riders rode through the herd, spreading the cattle out until the panic died down.

When the cattle had quieted down and spread out to graze, Amy looked around for her dad. She spotted him sitting quietly on his horse, scanning the grazing herd, his battered hat pulled low over his forehead.

Amy smiled to herself as she rode toward him. *Once a cowboy, always a cowboy. No one will ever be able to take that away from him.*

"Ready to head home?" she asked as she rode up beside him.

Clint smiled. "I reckon. They're settled in. Let's go."

"Good work," Clint told the exhausted hands as they rode out the pasture gate and headed toward the ranch. "As nervous and weak as that herd was, I call losin' only one cow a job well done."

"Well, I'm glad that part is done, and I'm ready for a hot meal!" Amy commented.

"Yeah!" Anders cheered. "Those words are music to my ears!"

As they rode along, the men laughed and joked among themselves, relaxed now that the strenuous job was over.

Sweaty, dust stained, hungry, and tired, they were looking forward to a hot meal and comfortable beds. As they were untacking their horses at the barn, Clint said, "I think we've done enough today, and the cattle need to rest. We'll sort them tomorrow. I recognized Black's, Archer's, and Anderson's brands in addition to the Bar Double Diamond cows, but that fifth one I don't. They must have been rustled a ways from here."

Anders spoke up. "There used to be a big Circle H outfit in California, but I think that dried up a long time ago."

Clint stroked his chin thoughtfully. "Hm. I remember hearin' about that. There has to be another Circle H ranch somewhere. I'll have Chad do some checking around. Oh, here he is now. Looks like you were right, Amy!"

Amy laughed. "He sure timed it right." Amy liked Chad West for more than one reason. He was a Christian, the father of one of her best friends, and one of her dad's closest friends.

"Howdy, Chad!" Clint called as the marshal pulled his lathered team to a halt.

"Howdy, yourself. Hello, Amy. Had a birthday yesterday, didn't you?" Chad gave her a grin as he swung down from the wagon.

"Hi, Mr. West. Yes, I did, but how did you know?" Amy asked with a smile.

"Well as the marshal, I'm supposed to know things, aren't I?" He gave her a wink and explained. "First, your dad told me when he asked if Katie could join you yesterday. Second, I remembered from last year. And third, Katie told me about half a dozen times!"

Amy laughed. "That's quite a list, Mr. West."

Chad chuckled. "You could say so." He turned to Clint. "I hear you're doin' my job for me. We get many more men like you around here and I'll be out of a job!"

Clint laughed. "I'll be sure to call you next time. The boys are by the corral. Why don't you pull around there and we'll help you load 'em up?"

"You're the boss." Chad climbed back onto the wagon seat and clucked to the horses.

Ten minutes later the rustlers were loaded in the marshal's buckboard and headed for town.

"Come 'n get it!" Grubby called from the cookhouse.

Anders rode up to Amy on Sky Blue as she crossed the yard to the house.

"Where are you going? Aren't you eating with us?" she asked.

Anders shook his head. "Mom'll be worried, and I have to stop at Black's and Anderson's to tell them about their cattle. Grubby gave me some sandwiches. I'll be back tomorrow to help sort. See you then!" He turned his horse and started out the lane.

"Bright and early!" Amy called after him.

"Amy!" her dad called from the cookhouse. "We'll eat with the hands tonight. Come on!"

"Coming," she called back.

The cookhouse was unusually quiet that night. The usual joking and kidding around was missing. The hands talked quietly among themselves, and there was an undercurrent of weariness in their conversation.

As soon as she was finished eating, Amy headed for the house. After washing up and changing clothes, she joined Clint on the porch.

Seating herself in the rocking chair, she smiled at him. "Busy day, wasn't it?" she remarked.

He nodded. "Sure was. Bet that's the last time anything like this happens for a long time."

"But we're not done yet," Amy reminded him.

Clint nodded. "Reckon you're right."

"I hope we don't find the owner to those cattle for a while." Amy stared out across the ranch and looked up a moment later to find Clint staring at her.

"Did I hear you right?" he asked.

Amy nodded. "If we don't find the owners for a while, it'll make it more interesting. Like a mystery we have to solve or something."

Clint chuckled. "You know, Amy, you are so much like your mother. Sometimes I forget it isn't her. That is exactly what she would have said."

"Nights like this make me think of her," Amy told him. "I've never been able to figure out why."

Clint took a deep breath. "Nights like this were her favorite. She would sit on the porch for hours, enjoying the beauty of the night. She never knew it, but I used to pull back the curtain and watch the shadows play across her face and listen to the wind whisper through her hair."

He paused for a moment, and Amy saw tears in his eyes. Though Susanna had died five years earlier, the loss was still very fresh to both of them.

"She loved this ranch." Clint went on. "Did you know that her father, your Grandpa Ed, first came to this ranch as a hand?"

Amy shook her head.

Clint went on. "Yep, he came here as a hand and ended up buying it when the owner died. Then he met your Grandmother Marie. They had three children, but only your mother lived. Then when Susanna and I got married, Ed gave the ranch to us as a wedding gift. Marie died shortly after that, and your grandpa left here. He couldn't bear to stay where everything reminded him of her. I guess it was different with me somehow. I needed to see things that would remind me of Susanna. I wanted you to love the things she loved." Clint looked at Amy. "Don't ever forget what a wonderful woman your mother was."

"I won't." Amy's voice was soft.

For a long time Clint stared into the distance, the deepening shadows playing across his face.

Amy knew how much he had loved her mother, how hard they had worked together to make it on the ranch.

Finally Clint turned to her with a gentle smile. "Well, it's late, young lady, and even a fifteen-year-old needs her sleep." He gave her cheek a playful pinch. "If you'll get me my Bible, we'll have our devotions so you can get to bed."

"Okay, Dad." Amy hurried into the house and picked up Clint's Bible from where he kept it beside his chair in the living room. Back out on the porch, she handed it to him and sat down beside him.

"I think we were on chapter 22 of Proverbs, weren't we?" he asked as he thumbed through the pages.

Amy nodded. "I think so."

"Ah, here it is." Clint read the first verse aloud. "A *good* name is rather to be chosen than great riches, and loving favor than silver and gold." He paused, then asked, "What do you think this verse is talking about, Amy?"

Amy thought a moment. "Well, I guess you could apply this to the rustlers. They were seeking silver and gold rather than doing what's right and seeking a good name."

Clint nodded. "Yes, that's right. You could apply this to questionable business deals also. Now verse two: 'The rich and the poor meet together: the Lord is the maker of them all.' I think this verse means that we are not to be prejudiced or look down on anyone because they are poorer than us. You could also say this applies to people of a different nationality than us or of a different color skin. The Lord made them all, and therefore we are all equal in His sight."

Amy nodded in agreement. "It makes me so sad to see people taking advantage of others or mocking them. They don't seem to care or to realize that they could have so easily been in the other person's position. And also, the Bible tells us that we never know when we could be entertaining angels unawares."

"Very true." Clint stroked his chin. "We should always treat others with kindness and consideration."

They read through the rest of the chapter, discussing the verses as they read them. After they finished reading, Clint prayed and thanked the Lord for His protection that day and asked His blessing on the coming days.

When Clint finished, Amy stood to her feet. "Night, Dad."

"Goodnight, Amy. I love you." Clint gave her a warm smile.

"I love you, too." She opened the house door and stepped into the hall. Once inside, Amy lit a lamp and slowly climbed the stairs to her room. She loved her little room under the eaves. Susanna had painted the walls and ceiling a bright yellow with scattered wildflowers.

Amy set the lantern down on her dresser, and walked over to a shelf; she picked up a little black book.

It was her mother's Bible. Clint had given it to her shortly after Susanna's death. Amy treasured it and read from it every day. Gently she turned the pages and selected a chapter to read. Then she settled down in her rocker to read.

When she finished reading, she took down her hair, brushing the long dark waves and thinking about the things her dad had told her and about everything that had happened since yesterday morning.

I never dreamed that all this would happen between then and now. I'm so glad Dad told me those things about Mom. It makes her seem closer. She put the brush back on her dresser and braided her hair for the night.

A few minutes later, Clint called up the stairs. "Goodnight, Amy."

"Goodnight," she called back.

I'm so wound up I don't know if I'll be able to sleep, she thought as she laid her clothes for the next day over the back of a chair. *I'm really tired, but I know I won't be able to relax and go to sleep for a while.*

Just before she slid into bed, she leaned down to blow out the lamp, and her eyes rested on a plaque her mother had given her.

If you can't sleep,
Don't count sheep,
Talk to the Sheppard.

As she slid into bed, she began to pray for her friends, family, and neighbors.

It worked, and soon she was fast asleep.

Chapter Four
Sorting Cattle

Amy woke early the next morning. Yawning and stretching, she walked to the window. A gray mist hung over the ranch.

She glanced at the clock. Its luminous hands showed 6:00 AM. She rubbed the sleep from her eyes. *Time to get movin'*, she told herself. *We've got a lot of work to do today.*

Swiftly she got dressed, made her bed and headed down the stairs. When she entered the kitchen, she spied a note on the table. Picking it up, she read it aloud.

Dear Amy,

I'm outside. There's a sandwich on the table for you.
Come out as soon as you can.

Love you!
Dad

SORTING CATTLE

Amy ate the sandwich and quickly washed the few dishes that were on the table.

On her way out the door, she grabbed a couple pieces of jerky and stuffed them in her pocket for later.

The yard was empty and quiet as she walked to the barn, but she could hear shouts in the distance.

Bannie nickered as she opened the barn door. "Hey, boy," she greeted him. She rubbed his forehead and gave him a carrot, then stood a moment, letting him play with her hair.

"Come on, sleepyhead!"

Amy jumped and whirled around, her heart pounding, to see Clint standing there, hands in his pockets, leaning against the wall with a grin on his face.

"Dad! You scared me!" Amy sagged against the stall door.

Clint chuckled. "Come on. The men are bringing the cattle in from the pasture to the corral. I'll help you saddle up."

Clint got her saddle while Amy led Bannie out and brushed his already gleaming coat. As she slipped the bit into his mouth, she heard shouts and bellowing cattle.

"I'll go open the gate for them," Clint said as he swung her saddle over Bannie's back. "Meet us by the corral."

"Okay." Amy nodded.

Clint went out the barn door, and a few minutes later, Amy followed him. The cattle were filing into the large corral as she swung into the saddle.

A night's rest has done them a world of good, she thought. *They look a lot better than they did yesterday.*

She urged Bannie into a trot, and they crossed the yard to the corral. Anders was helping push the cattle through the gate and waved as she rode up.

Clint began assigning the men their tasks. "A few of the Bar Double Diamond calves in here aren't branded yet, so we'll brand them before we turn them loose. Caleb, you tend the fire. Daryl, you help brand. Logan will help Amy cut, and the rest of you will help manage the gates and the branding pen."

Daryl opened the gate and Amy rode in. Bannie pricked up his ears and danced excitedly as they rode into the herd. "Easy, boy," Amy murmured, rubbing his neck soothingly. "By the end of the day, you'll be sick of cattle. Better save your energy for workin'." Bannie quieted down, and she expertly guided him through the herd.

Clint had given instructions to cut out the Bar Double Diamond cattle first so the calves could be branded. Amy spotted a cow with the Bar Double Diamond brand and a young calf by her side and locked her eyes on them. Bannie seemed to sense which cow she was after and picked up his pace. Amy lifted her reins and guided him around the cow. The cow did not want to leave the others and darted first this way, then that way. Bannie kept up, dodging other cattle, and gradually he and Amy pushed the cow and calf through the gate. A cheer went up as Bannie nipped the calf playfully as it dodged into the other pen.

Anders gave Amy a thumbs up. "Nifty work!" he called.

Amy grinned. "Thanks!"

Two hours later, Amy had just cut out a calf that needed branded, pushed it through the gate into the branding pen and was turning back to the herd when a shrill yell split the air.

She looked up just in time to see Ken riding the back of the husky calf she had just cut out, and it was heading for the gate, a single pole placed across the opening between the pens about chest high. The calf's mother was on the other side, bawling.

As the calf charged under the gate, the pole caught Ken on the chest and flipped him over backward.

With a yell, Amy dug in her heels and Bannie surged forward. As he slid to a stop at the gate, she swung to the ground and ducked under the pole.

Clint was already kneeling beside Ken when she reached him. Ken's face was distorted with pain.

"What hurts?" Clint asked.

"My chest." Ken tried to sit up, but fell back with a groan.

"Don't do that," Clint said. "You could hurt yourself worse. Are you having trouble breathing?"

Ken shook his head. "No, it hurts to breathe, but I'm not having trouble."

Clint ran his hands down Ken's chest and gently probed with his fingers. A few minutes later, he sat back on his heels. "Looks like you busted a few ribs, Ken. Nothing serious. We'll carry you up to the bunkhouse and wrap it up."

"Don't you think we should get the doctor?" Amy asked.

Clint shook his head. "I've patched up I don't know how many busted ribs. No reason to get the doctor."

The men formed a crude stretcher from some saplings and an old blanket and gently rolled Ken onto it. They tried to be careful and not jostle him as they carried him to the bunkhouse, but by the time they reached it, Ken's face was white and he gritted his teeth as they moved him from the stretcher to a bunk.

Clint knelt on the floor beside him. "Amy, go get a sheet from the house," he instructed. "We'll need it to wrap these ribs so they'll heal."

"Yes, sir." Amy dashed out the door.

When she returned a few minutes later, Daryl and Ross were helping Ken sit up. Clint took the sheet from her and began ripping it into wide strips. "Go find Grubby and ask him to give you the bottle of laudanum he keeps in the storage cupboard. Stay with him until I call you."

Amy got the laudanum from Grubby, then waited impatiently for Clint to call her. Finally, she heard someone call her name. "Coming," she called back, and she snatched up the laudanum and hurried out to the bunks.

Ken was lying down again, and what remained of the sheet was on the floor beside him. Clint took the bottle from her, poured some laudanum into a spoon, and gave it to Ken. "That should help with the pain," he said, screwing the cap back on. "Are you comfortable?"

Ken made a face. "As comfortable as I'll get I guess."

Clint stood to his feet. "Try not to move too much. Get some sleep."

Ken nodded. "Don't reckon I'll sleep much for a while, but I'm certainly not gonna try to move around."

Amy picked up what was left of the sheet and folded it as she asked, "How'd the calf get away?"

"Daryl was tryin' to get it down, and it knocked him down, then took off for his mama, and Ken just happened to be in the way," Anders explained, laughing.

"Shhh!" Amy scolded him. "It's not funny. Ken got hurt."

"It's all right. It must have looked funny. I never was so surprised in my life!" Ken chuckled, then grimaced.

"We'd better get back to work. Do you think you'll be all right alone?" Clint asked him.

Ken nodded. "Yeah, I'll be fine."

"Okay. I'll have someone check on you in a little while." Clint motioned for the others to leave the room.

Anders started laughing again as they walked outside.

"You shouldn't be laughing," Amy scolded him, but she was laughing too.

Clint chuckled. "The result of the incident isn't funny, but you have to admit, the look on Ken's face was amusing. Let's hope the rest of the sorting goes smoothly."

Bannie was standing by the gate, right where Amy had left him.

"Good boy," she praised him as she gathered her reins and stepped into the saddle. "Gotta get back to work now."

Bannie tossed his head and eagerly pushed his way into the herd.

When they stopped for lunch a few hours later, Amy slid gratefully to the ground and tied Bannie to the hitching post. After putting on his nosebag, she hurried into the house to make something for lunch.

She was just about to settle for cold sandwiches when Clint stuck his head in the door. "We're eating in the bunkhouse, Amy," he told her.

"Oh, good!" Amy stepped into the hall. "It will certainly be better than sandwiches." She pulled on her boots and followed him outside.

Clint checked on Ken before they started eating. "How are you doing?" he asked.

Ken shrugged, then grimaced as the movement shifted his ribs. "Okay."

"Do you want something to eat?" Clint asked.

Ken shook his head. "No, thanks. I couldn't eat anything."

"All right. Just holler if you need anything." Clint and Amy joined the others at the long tables and helped themselves to the delicious food Grubby had prepared.

"What are you going to do with the cattle that we don't know whose they are?" Amy asked Clint.

"I guess we'll keep them in one of the pastures for now. I'll try to find the owner. We'll just have to wait and see what happens." He turned to Anders. "Your dad said he would come for your cattle about six, right?"

"Yes. Black's and Anderson's said they could come about then, too," Anders answered.

After she finished eating, Amy started for the door, ready to get back to sorting.

She opened the bunkhouse door and started to step out, then stopped abruptly. Anders, who had followed her out, nearly bumped into her.

"Why'd you stop?" he asked as he peered around her.

"Where's Bannie? I left him at the hitching post." Amy looked around with a puzzled expression.

"Oh, yeah!" Anders laughed. "I guess Dad forgot to tell you. He's a great escape artist. There's only one knot he hasn't figured out how to untie ...*yet*. Come on. I'll show you how to do it after we find him."

Amy shook her head as she followed Anders around the bunkhouse to look for Bannie. "He is such a silly horse."

As she rounded the corner of the building, she nearly ran into the black gelding.

He was standing there quietly, placidly eating his oats, and he gave her a "what did I do?" expression.

Amy laughed and picked up his lead rope. "Come along, little mischief maker! You won't get away after this."

Anders chuckled. "I wouldn't be too sure. He's smart." He showed Amy the knot and made her practice it until she got it right. By the time the men were coming out of the bunkhouse ready to go back to work, Amy had it down.

Anders left to get his own horse while she pulled Bannie's nosebag off and tightened the cinch.

After she swung into the saddle, she rode over to the cattle pens and through the gate Daryl held open for her. It took the rest of the afternoon to sort the cattle and finish the branding. Amy had just herded the last cow into the correct pen when she saw riders coming up the road.

"Riders coming!" she called to Clint.

"Well, we finished that just in time, didn't we?" he grinned. "Go help—" His voice was drowned out as someone shouted.

Anders, who had been helping the men with the branding, stood up slowly, holding a hand to his face.

"What now?" Amy asked as she rode toward him.

Daryl grinned. "The calf kicked him. Just a bloody nose, I think."

Anders pulled out his bandana and held it to his nose.

"Do you need me to doctor you?" Amy asked with a grin.

"No way!" Anders shook his head.

Amy laughed. "I figured I knew the answer to that one."

The riders Amy had seen on the road were turning in the ranch lane as she turned her horse and rode out of the corral.

Clint caught up to her and finished what he had been saying. "Go help Logan and Ross drive our cattle and the unknown cattle to the east pasture," he instructed.

Amy nodded. "Okay."

Caleb opened the corral gate, and Ross and Logan drove the cattle out. Amy helped herd them between the ranch buildings and down the river path.

As they filed down the path, a yearling steer broke from the herd and tried to run back to the ranch yard. Bannie whirled without any direction from Amy and expertly drove the steer back where he belonged.

"Good boy," Amy praised him.

When they reached the pasture, Logan opened the gate. The cattle seemed to know that grass and water awaited them and gave no trouble.

When the last cow had entered the pasture, Amy rode over to the water tank and let Bannie drink.

"I sure wonder where those cattle came from," Logan said thoughtfully.

Amy shrugged. "I don't know. Sure would be interesting to know."

As they started back to the barn, Amy noticed a lone rider coming toward them. "Looks like the Black girl," Caleb commented.

"It is Leah!" Amy dug in her heels, and Bannie shot ahead.

"What are you doing here?" Amy asked breathlessly when she reached her friend.

"I'm here to invite you to spend the night with me," Leah told her with a smile.

"Really?" Amy asked eagerly. "I'd love to if Dad will let me!"

"I'm dying to hear what happened last night, and as far as I could see, this is the only way to find out without waiting until Sunday. What was wrong with Anders? I saw blood on his face as I rode past," Leah remarked with concern.

"I'll tell you as we ride to the house." Amy told her about Ken's accident and Anders's incident with the calf.

Leah laughed gaily at her vivid description of the scene. "I wish I could have seen Anders's face! He must have been so surprised."

"He was. I offered to doctor him, but he would have none of it," Amy told her.

"I certainly can't imagine him accepting it." Leah chuckled. "If your dad says you can come, seeing as tomorrow is Saturday, I thought we could do some shopping tomorrow morning in town."

"That would be fun! I don't think Dad will have an objection to your plan," Amy said.

When they reached the house, Amy dismounted and tied Bannie to the hitching post, then went to find Clint.

She found him by the barn mending a bridle. "Hey, Dad."

"Hey, Amy. What's Leah doing here?" Clint asked.

"She wants me to go spend the night with her tonight and then go shopping in Durango tomorrow."

Clint thought a moment. "All right. I need some things from town, so I'll ride in tomorrow afternoon and accompany you home."

"Thanks, Dad." Amy started for the house, calling over her shoulder to Leah. "I'll pack a few things and be right out."

Chapter Five
Pot-S-Hook's New Hand

Amy ran into the house and let the door slam behind her. She ran lightly up the stairs. In her room, she quickly packed the few things she would need in her saddlebags, then took the stairs two at a time.

Dashing into the kitchen on her way past, she wrote a note to Clint.

> Dear Dad,
>
> Thank you so much for letting me go to Leah's. If you don't want to eat with the hands, there is some soup in the icebox you can warm up.
> See you tomorrow!
>
> Love,
> Amy

She placed the note on the table and hurried out the door.

Bannie nickered when he saw her coming.

"Easy boy." Amy flung the saddlebags over his back. Stepping into the saddle, she turned Bannie around and nudged him into a trot.

"See you later, Dad!" she called over her shoulder.

"Have a good time, and stay out of trouble!" Clint shouted after her.

Amy laughed. "I'll try!" She lifted her reins, and Bannie tossed his head and sprang into a lively canter.

Leah was waiting for her at the end of the lane. "I thought you'd never come!" she laughed when Amy reached her.

"Sorry!" Amy grinned. "I packed as fast as I could."

Leah glanced over at Bannie. "He sure is a spunky thing," she remarked.

Amy nodded. "He sure is. It's definitely a change after having ridden Dark Sunshine for so long, but after all, he's only four."

"Really?" Leah raised her eyebrows. "He looks more mature than that."

"Well, he was left a stud until six months ago," Amy told her.

"Oh." Leah nodded. "That would explain it."

Bannie chose that moment to skitter sideways, dancing and bobbing his head excitedly. "Hold on there!" Amy exclaimed as she struggled to regain control. "Would you please keep two feet on the ground at once?"

Leah laughed. "Maybe he isn't so mature after all. He just looks like it."

Amy flashed her a grin. "I think you've got that right. Maybe we should run a mile or two, let him get his excess energy out."

"Sure!" Leah lifted her reins.

Leaning forward in her saddle, Amy squeezed her legs against Bannie's sides, and the big gelding leaped ahead.

Leah let out a cowboy yell that spurred the horses on, and Bannie started bucking.

"Hey!" Amy shouted. "You tryin' to get me piled?"

Whooping and shouting, the girls raced on down the road.

A few miles later, Amy pulled Bannie down into a walk. "Boy, that was fun," she commented.

"Sure was." Leah agreed.

After chatting for a few minutes, Leah asked, "Are you going to come to school this year, Amy?"

"You know how Dad feels about school, Leah." Amy answered. "I like doing it at home, and Dad doesn't want me to have to travel so far in the winter. No, I'm not coming to school."

"But wouldn't you like to go to school?" Leah persisted. "It seems like it would be lonely with just you and your dad."

Amy shook her head. "If we get lonely or bored we just go out to the bunkhouse. It's never boring out there!"

Leah shrugged. "Well, I'm glad I can go to school, and it would be a lot more fun with you."

Amy didn't say anything. They lived too far out of town for her to go to school if the weather was bad, and

Clint didn't want her going to school with the town kids. She knew Leah knew that, so she didn't argue.

When they arrived at the Pot-S-Hook Ranch a few minutes later, the ranch yard was empty.

"Where is everyone?" Amy asked as they dismounted. "It's so quiet."

"I think they left to get the cattle from your ranch. They must have taken the back way, otherwise we would have passed them on the road."

"Oh."

Leah flashed her a grin over her horses' backs. "I'm warning you, you're gonna have to tell me everything about yesterday or else!"

"In that case ..." Amy laughed, pretending to remount.

Leah lunged for her and dragged her back down. "No, you don't!" she laughed.

"All right, all right!" Amy freed herself and grabbed Bannie's reins. "Show me where to put Bannie, and I'll tell you every last thing!"

After unsaddling the horses, the girls headed for the house.

"I see you succeeded in stealing her away!" Savannah Black, Leah's mom, greeted the girls.

"Yes, she's holding me hostage!" Amy told her.

"Oh, Amy!" Leah wrinkled her nose.

Mrs. Black chuckled. Handing them a plate of cookies, she said, "Head on up to your dungeon, Amy, and enjoy the cookies."

"Thanks, Mrs. Black." Amy took the plate and followed Leah up the stairs to her bedroom.

"I wanted to have Katie over, too, but it didn't work out. They were having company," Leah told her as she opened the door and stepped inside.

"Oh, that's too bad. Not that they have company, but that she can't be here." Amy quickly explained.

The girls had just seated themselves on the bed when the door opened a crack and a boyish face appeared. "Hi, Amy!"

"Hi, Brian!" Amy smiled. "How's the Tornado today?"

Brian's grin widened. "Just fine!"

Brian was Leah's six-year-old brother, nicknamed "The Tornado" because he created a whirlwind of activity wherever he went.

Leah went to the door and handed Brian a cookie. "Run along, Brian. Amy and I are talking.

Slowly, Brian backed out of the room, munching his cookie. When he was gone, Amy laughed. "He gets real quiet with a cookie in his hand."

Leah grinned. "Sure does. He'll do just about anything for a cookie or some sort of treat. Now I want to give you your birthday gift. I was going to do it yesterday, but things got kind of crazy." As she spoke, she pulled out a bag from under her bed and handed it to Amy.

"Should I be afraid to put my hand in there?" Amy asked.

Leah laughed. "No, it's perfectly safe. You felt the need to ask that?"

Amy chuckled. "Yep. You have a reputation, you know!" She slid her hand in and felt something soft.

Pulling her hand out, she saw it was a woven leather nosebag with the Bar Double Diamond brand burned into the corners. "Oh, Leah, it's beautiful!" she exclaimed.

"They're a lot better than burlap ones, they last a lot longer, and they're nicer looking." Leah told her. "One of the hands showed me how to make it."

"Thank you so much, Leah. I'm sure I'll get a lot of use out of it." Amy put it back in the bag.

Leah stretched out on the bed. "I'm making one for Katie, too. Why don't you help me? You can tell me all about yesterday while we work."

"Sure. I talk better when my hands are busy."

By the time Mrs. Black called them down to supper, the girls had finished Katie's nosebag and started on another.

"I can't believe all that happened without me," Leah said as they walked down the stairs.

"Well, it did, so you'll have to depend on my story-telling ability," Amy told her.

"I'm not sure I trust that!" Leah teased as they slid into their seats at the table.

"Can you two stop talking so Dad can pray?" Brian asked impatiently.

"I was thinking of suggesting that myself," Luke Black, Leah's dad, said goodnaturedly as he took his seat.

After thanking the Lord for the food and the recovery of the stolen cattle, the conversation resumed.

"Your dad told me that it was your birthday yesterday, Amy," Mr. Black said as he passed her the potatoes. "And Leah tells me that it was your sharp ears that detected the rustlers."

"Oh, they would have heard it in another minute," Amy replied modestly.

"Well, several of the ranchers around here are indebted to you. If you hadn't heard anything, they would be losing a lot of money," Leah insisted, reaching for a biscuit.

"Amy must be a hero!" Brian declared.

"Heroine," Mrs. Black corrected him. "And I agree."

Amy was embarrassed. "It was really nothing," she protested. "I'm glad I could help the ranchers out."

"We're thankful to you anyway," Mr. Black told her.

Much to Amy's relief, the conversation soon turned to other things. When they finished eating, Amy helped clear the table and stack the dishes.

"You girls run along," Mrs. Black told them. "Brian can help me with the dishes."

"Aww, Mom!" Brain pouted. "I want to go with the girls!"

"No, son." Mrs. Black told him firmly. "You are going to help me with the dishes."

"Thanks, Mom." Leah started for the door. "There was a new foal born last night," she informed Amy as they stepped out onto the porch. "Want to see it?"

"Do I ever!" Amy laughed. "Dad says that Dark Sunshine is pregnant and I might be able to keep the foal. That's why he got Bannie for me, 'cause I won't be able to ride her much longer."

Rustlers and the Texas Trail

"That's great! I wish I had a mare. Here's Josie's stall." They had reached the barn while they were talking, and Leah opened the stall door and stepped in.

"Oh it's so cute!" Amy exclaimed, catching sight of the tiny foal. "Is it a colt or a filly?"

"A colt," Leah answered. "Dad says this one looks promising already. He's from some of our best lines. Dad might keep it and let me train it. By the time it's fully trained, Brian will be old enough to have a horse of his own, and Dad said he might let him have it."

The colt was the color of gold, and his creamy mane and tail made his coloring stand out. He had a small star on his forehead and large, dark eyes. He stood on his still wobbly legs and stretched his nose out toward Amy inquisitively. "What are you going to name him?" she asked.

"Brian wants to call him Nugget, and Dad seems to like that. If he turns out to be good enough, Dad might keep him as a stud to use for breeding," Leah told her.

The girls played with the foal for a while, and then Leah showed Amy some of the other broodmares and their foals. The Blacks were known for their line of palomino stock horses and had over fifty breeding mares and several stallions.

After a while, they headed back to the house.

Mr. Black looked up from reading the paper as they walked in. "Let me guess where you two have been: in the barn with the foal."

"That was too easy, Dad." Leah laughed.

"Well, when there's a baby of some kind and two girls on the place, you're right, it is easy! Now run along to bed. It's getting late."

When they entered Leah's room, Amy sat down on the floor with her back against the footboard and reached into her bag to pull out her Bible.

"Let's do our devotions together," Amy suggested.

"Sure," Leah agreed. She set the lamp she had carried up with her on the dresser and started to pick up her Bible off the nightstand. Suddenly, she froze, her eyes glued to the window. "Amy? Did the curtain just move, or did I imagine it?" she asked, her voice shaking.

Amy glanced at the window. "I think it's open, Leah. It was probably the wind. I wouldn't worry about it," she told her.

Leah shook her head. "I closed it when we went down for supper."

Amy stood up. "Well, let's see what it is." She grabbed the curtain and yanked it back.

A shadow darker than the rest leaped out. Leah screamed and jumped back, falling over the bed. Amy yelped, then relaxed as Brian appeared in the circle of light.

"I scared you! I scared you!" he cried triumphantly.

"You little rascal!" Leah caught him by the collar and marched him out of the room, shutting the door firmly behind him while Amy collapsed onto the bed, shaking with laughter.

"You wouldn't think it was so funny if you had a little brother that did stuff like that all the time." Leah scowled. Then she grinned. "I guess it was kind of funny."

"I think that is just what a person needs before going to bed! That was hilarious!" Amy declared when she caught her breath.

"I should have known it was him." Leah shook her head as she seated herself on the bed. "Usually he is still sitting by Dad when I head up here. Remember what Brian said about you earlier? He said that you were a heroine, and now I agree with him!"

"Oh, Leah!" Amy groaned. "Don't bring that up again."

"I will, and what's more, you'll hear me!" Leah insisted. "I never would have had the courage to pull that curtain back. I would've run downstairs and got Dad to come up here."

"Can we have our devotions now?" Amy jiggled her Bible impatiently.

"Of course." Leah opened her Bible. "What do you want to read?"

"Dad and I have been studying Proverbs. We could read something from there," she suggested.

"Sounds good to me."

They read a chapter together and prayed, then undressed and settled down for the night.

"Boy, am I tired." Amy yawned as she snuggled down under the quilt.

"Yeah, me, too. Must've been listening to your exciting tale got me all wore out!" Leah chuckled.

Amy laughed. "Glad it was interesting. Well, goodnight. Sleep tight and ... don't let the bed bugs bite!" they finished together.

Amy lay awake for a long time, thinking over the last two days. She grinned into the darkness. *It is so much fun to ride Bannie. I'm so glad Dad got him for me. And I'm really glad we were able to stop the rustlers and get all the cattle back. I hope we can find the owners to all of them. Little Nugget is so cute! I hope Dark Sunshine's foal looks like that.*

Long after Leah's steady breathing told Amy that she was asleep, Amy lay wide awake. *Come on, brain, go to sleep!* she told herself.

Finally, she slid out of bed, being careful not to wake Leah, and walked to the window. Sitting on the sill, she rested her head on the cool glass and let her thoughts wander back to the days when her mother, Susanna, had been alive. *I'm happy with Dad, but I miss having a mother. There's something missing in our home. I like to have a mother again, but it would be an adjustment getting used to someone else running things. I wonder if Dad will ever marry again. He hasn't said anything, but I think he's lonely. I'd like to have a brother or sister someday.*

How long she had been sitting there, she didn't know, when she saw a movement by the barn. She shook her head to clear her thoughts and looked again. A moment later, she saw it again. A dark shadow slid down the barn wall toward the door. *Am I imagining things?* she wondered.

She waited a minute, and soon the shadow moved out from the wall and took shape. *Hm. What is a man doing wandering around this time of night?* Amy wondered. *It isn't one of the hands I don't think.* As she watched, the man stepped farther out from the building, and the moonlight fell on his face. "It's only a boy!" she exclaimed in surprise.

Standing up, she walked over to the bed. "Leah!" she called softly. "Wake up."

Leah mumbled something in her sleep, but did not wake up.

"Leah!" Amy shook her friends shoulder.

"Huh? Amy? What's going on?" Leah sat up, rubbing her eyes.

"Leah, there's somebody sneaking around your barn, and I don't think it's one of your hands."

Leah was instantly wide awake and throwing back the covers. She followed Amy to the window.

"Do you see him?" Amy whispered.

"No." Leah shook her head.

"Right there, by the barn. He just stepped back into the shadows" Amy told her.

"I think I see him." Leah stepped away from the window. "I'm going to get Dad. Stay here, but don't let him see you."

"Okay." Amy kept her eyes on the spot she'd last seen the boy.

A few minutes later, Leah returned, followed by her dad.

"Where is he?" Mr. Black asked Amy in an undertone.

Amy pointed. "I can't see him now, but that's where he was, and I've been watching here since Leah left to get you, and I didn't see anything move."

"Hm." Mr. Black stroked his chin. "If he's as young as you say, I doubt he's up to anything much. Probably just looking for somewhere to stay the night. I'll go down and have a look around."

"Can we come if we stay by the house?" Leah asked.

Mr. Black thought a minute. "All right," he finally agreed. "But keep quiet."

Amy followed Leah through the dark kitchen and out the back door. They crouched by the steps while Mr. Black stepped behind a tree and waited.

As they watched, the barn door slid open slowly, then shut again. Amy and Leah stayed hidden, while Mr. Black strode quickly to the barn. Breathlessly, Amy waited. The seconds ticked slowly by.

Just when it seemed she couldn't wait any longer, Mr. Black appeared in the barn door. A tall, thin boy followed him.

"Leah, go get your mom," he said quietly, walking quickly to the house. The boy followed silently.

"Yes, sir." Leah raced into the house and up the stairs, Amy following.

When Mrs. Black appeared, she took in the situation at a glance. "Go back to bed," she said to the girls who had followed her downstairs.

Leah started to protest, but a look from her dad quickly changed her mind.

As they left the kitchen, Amy glanced over her shoulder and saw the boy's face highlighted in the glow

Pot-s-Hook's New Hand

of the lamp Mr. Black had lighted. She was shocked at how pale and thin it was.

"I wonder who he is." Amy voiced the question they were both thinking as they got back into bed. "Got any ideas?"

"No." Leah shrugged. "Did you notice how tired and thin he looked? And his clothes were all torn like he'd had to walk through a lot of brush."

"Uh-huh." Amy agreed sleepily. "I wonder what he was doing out here by himself."

"Guess we'll find out in the morning. Goodnight ... again." Leah rolled over and pulled up the covers.

"Goodnight." Amy snuggled down on her pillow and was soon asleep.

*****

Both girls were up bright and early the next morning in spite of the night's adventure.

Mrs. Black greeted them when they entered the kitchen. "Good morning, girls. Did you sleep well, Amy?"

"Yes, I did," Amy answered as she seated herself at the table.

"Where's Brian?" Leah asked as she placed bowls on the table. "He usually beats me downstairs."

"He's out looking at the colt," Mrs. Black replied. "He loves that critter."

A few minutes later, Brian came running into the house. "What's for breakfast, Mom? I'm starved!"

"Oatmeal, Brian," Mrs. Black answered, setting a bowl in front of him.

After the girls' bowls were filled and they had asked the blessing, Mrs. Black joined them at the table.

"What happened with the boy?" Amy asked.

Mrs. Black glanced at Brian, but he was busy drawing pictures in his oatmeal with his spoon.

"Well," she began, "His name is Tye, and he is fourteen years old. It's a sad story. His father was killed in a riding accident about a year ago, and just a few months ago, his mother died of pneumonia. He's been on his own ever since."

"But doesn't he have any relatives or somebody that will take him in?" Amy asked.

Mrs. Black nodded. "He does have a rich, old uncle, but he will have nothing to do with Tye because Tye's father married against his father's wishes. So Tye has been wandering around, looking for work. He was going to sleep in the barn last night." Mrs. Black finished.

"So where is he now?" Leah asked, taking a bite of toast.

"He slept in the bunkhouse last night, and that's where he'll be staying for the time being. We'll give him some work to do, and if he works well, we'll hire him." Mrs. Black told them. "He seems like a nice boy, responsible and trustworthy."

"I want to show Amy the colt!" Brian exclaimed just then.

"You can show it to her while Leah helps me with the dishes," Mrs. Black told him, standing up from the table. Leah made a face.

"Leah!" her mother scolded.

"Sorry, Leah," Amy called over her shoulder as Brian dragged her out the door.

"Dad says I can have the colt for my own," he informed her as they walked to the barn.

"That will be nice." Amy reached for the barn door as she spoke, then stumbled back in surprise as the door swung open in front of her.

When she regained her balance, she saw Tye standing in the doorway.

"I'm sorry," he said quickly. "I didn't know you were there."

"Oh, it's all right." Amy assured him hastily. "I was just surprised when the door opened right in front of me."

Tye gave her a small smile and started to walk away.

"Wait a minute." Amy called after him.

Tye turned around and waited.

Brian disappeared into the barn as Amy hurried to catch up to Tye. "You must be Tye, right?" she asked.

He nodded. "That's right."

"And you're going to stay here?"

"Yes. At least for a while." Tye ducked his head and wouldn't look at her.

Amy held out her hand. "Well, I'm Amy Kentworthy of the Bar Double Diamond ranch. It's just down the road a few miles. There's a couple other kids that get together and go for rides and such. Leah, she's the girl that lives here, comes with us a lot. You'd be welcome to join us, too."

Tye shook her hand. "Thank you. I might do that," he said. "If Mr. Black doesn't need me."

"Great!" Amy smiled. "See you later, Tye."

"See ya." Tye disappeared with a wave of his hand.

"Amy!" Brian called impatiently from inside the barn.

"Coming!" Amy slipped through the open door. *He doesn't talk like a common country boy*, she thought as she made her way down the row of stalls. *You can tell his father was cultured man.*

"Amy!" Brian hollered again.

"I'm coming!" Amy called back, laughing at his impatience.

After admiring the colt with Brian, Amy was heading over to Bannie's stall when Leah caught up with her.

"I saw you talking to Tye out the window," Leah said as Amy led Bannie out of his stall. "What's he like?"

"He's really nice." Amy tied Bannie to a metal ring in the wall and picked up a brush, running it over his back. "I told him he could join us when we go on rides. He'd be really lonely just hangin' around here. Then again," she laughed, looking out the door, "Brian might not let him get lonely!" Brian was following Tye around as he did the chores Mr. Black has assigned him.

"Where is your dad?" Amy asked as she hoisted the saddle onto Bannie.

"He left for town early this morning," Leah replied as she led her gelding in from the corral. "Oh, and Mom said Tye could come with us into town."

"Good. I'm glad," Amy said. "Does he know yet?"

Leah shook her head. "Uh-uh. Mom said for us to tell him. Would you tell him? I'm kind of nervous about talking to him."

"Sure." Amy finished saddling her horse, then crossed the yard to where Tye was standing next to the corral with a bucket of grain in his hand, feeding Mr. Black's prize cowhorse.

"Would you like to go with Leah and me into town?" Amy asked him. "Our friend, Anders, from the Diamond-n-ahalf will be there. You'll like him."

Tye looked doubtful. "I'll have to see if it's all right that I leave."

"Mrs. Black said you can." Amy told him.

"All right then, I'll come. Just got a few things to finish up, then I'll be ready." He set the bucket down and grabbed a pitchfork.

"How 'bout I help you? You'll get done sooner," Amy suggested.

Tye looked at her curiously, then shrugged. "Sure."

It did not take them long to get the chores finished and saddle a horse for Tye.

A short time later, they were headed out the lane. Mrs. Black waved from the porch. Brian, much put out that he could not come with them, was nowhere to be seen.

They covered the five miles to town rapidly, the horses being fresh and lively, and half an hour later, the town came into sight.

"So this is Durango, huh?" Tye looked around with interest as they rode into the outskirts of the town.

Amy nodded. "Yep. Not much to it, but you couldn't find a friendlier group of people anywhere."

"There's Anders!" Leah cried a moment later.

Amy turned just in time to see Anders go into the general store.

"Let's take the horses to the livery stable, then we can join him," Amy suggested.

After stalling the horses, Amy hurried ahead of Tye and Leah to find Anders. She found him in the tool section of the store and quickly told him a little about Tye.

"Oh, so what you're saying is I'm supposed to be nice to him?" he asked with a twinkle in his eyes.

"Yes," Amy said emphatically. "And none of your smart stuff either!"

Anders laughed. "You know me too well."

"That knowledge has saved you more than once," Amy reminded him.

Leah joined them just then with Tye and Amy introduced them.

The boys hit it off right away, and Amy left them to do her shopping. Leah went to get her family's mail while Amy looked at the material. Clint had told her she could get some to make herself a dress.

She had just picked out the pattern she wanted and was about to head up to the counter when someone grabbed her shoulders and spun her around. She gasped with surprise, struggling to free herself.

"Don't you recognize me?" a teasing voice asked.

"Why, Daniel Kentworthy!" she exclaimed. "What in the world are you doing here? I thought you were in Ohio working."

"I was." he leaned against a barrel, grinning down at her. "Boss let me go."

"In other words, you got fired. Were you naughty or what?" Amy asked, smiling.

Daniel was the only son of Clint's late brother Phil, and Clint loved him like a son. They had not heard from him for a while, and Amy was very surprised to see him.

"No, I wasn't naughty." Daniel replied, answering Amy's question. "Business has been down, and he didn't need all of us. Thought you might need some help on the ranch until I find something else."

"I'm sure we can find something for you to do. We're just getting into the spring branding, and Dad doesn't want Daryl to work so hard this year. He's not been feeling the greatest," Amy told him.

"Good." Daniel nodded. "I was hoping I could stay with you. We've got a lot of catching up to do. But what are you doing in town this early?"

Amy explained briefly about the rustlers, staying at Leah's, and Tye.

"Whew! Sounds like you've had a busy couple days! Happy birthday by the way." Daniel gave a little tug on her covering.

"Thanks." Amy smiled.

Daniel grinned. "For wishing you a happy birthday or yanking your covering?"

Amy rolled her eyes. "The former. If I started thanking you for yanking my covering, you'd never stop doing it!"

"Very true, cousin." Daniel chuckled.

After she had paid for the material, she led Daniel to where Anders and Tye stood talking just outside the store.

"Hey, Daniel!" Anders exclaimed when he caught sight of them. "When did you get here?"

Daniel explained, then Amy introduced Tye and turning to Anders asked, "Where did Leah go?"

"She went to get Katie, said to meet her in front of the ice cream parlor when we got through here," Anders told her. "Is she going to treat us or is Daniel?"

"Neither," Amy said firmly. "You can't pretend you're poor because I saw Dad pay you last night."

Anders made a face. "See how she treats me?" he asked the others.

Amy ignored him. "Will you come with us, Daniel?"

Daniel shook his head. "I'll come out to the ranch tomorrow after church. I've got some things to do in town yet."

"Okay. I guess we'll see you then."

"Sure thing." Daniel waved as he crossed the street.

Leah and Katie were already at the ice cream shop when the three arrived. Tye and Katie were introduced, and a few minutes later, they were all busy eating their ice cream.

The bell above the door jingled, and Amy looked up to see who was coming in. She groaned inwardly when she saw who it was. Twyla Anderson was known around town for being snooty, and no one really liked her. Amy always tried to be kind to her, but it wasn't easy.

"Hello, Twyla," she said pleasantly as the girl passed their table.

POT-S-HOOK'S NEW HAND

Twyla looked the other way and said nothing.
Amy shrugged and turned back to her ice cream.
Anders looked disgusted. "What kind of manners was that?" he asked.

"None at all." Amy answered wryly, then she gasped. "Anders! Tip your bowl up! You're dripping ice cream all over your lap!"

"Oops!" he chuckled, quickly tipping his bowl up and wiping up his drips with a napkin. "Say, Amy, do you know Philip Bender? He's walking by right now."

"Yes." Amy nodded, glancing out the window. "What about him?"

Anders leaned back in his chair. "Well, you know how he's afraid to ride any horse except that old one of his dad's because he got bucked off when he was little?"

Amy nodded. "What about it?"

Anders grinned. "His name means 'lover of horses'!"

Amy laughed, almost choking on her ice cream. "And when did you take up the study of names?"

"I didn't," Anders protested. "Marianna has a name book, and last night she was reading it out loud."

"Twyla's name must mean 'rude,'" Leah said as she stood up.

"Oh, Leah, that's not kind," Amy said quickly. "We should be nice to her. Have you ever thought how lonely she must be?"

"No, I didn't. I'm sorry," Leah said with a sigh. "Sometimes she gets on my nerves."

"I didn't know you had any." Anders grinned at her.

"Apparently you don't either," Leah shot back. "Doesn't anything ever get you rattled?"

"Sure." Anders nodded. "Amy is an expert at it."

"Let's go to the harness shop," Amy suggested, ignoring Anders. "I'd like to look around."

"I have to pick up something for Dad there, so that suits me." Anders agreed.

They spent the rest of the day visiting friends, catching up on the news, wandering through the stores, and enjoying their day off. As they came out of the drug store, Katie glanced at her watch. "Did you realize it's four o'clock?" she asked. "I promised to be home at five, and I still have an errand to run for Mom."

"And we'd better head for the livery stable." Amy said. "Dad was going to meet us there at five, but knowing how things usually go, we'll get stopped by something, or someone, about ten times before we get there."

Pot-S-Hook's New Hand

Chapter Six
Logan's Accident and the Box

True to Amy's prediction, they were stopped several times on the way to the stable. They reached it just as Clint was riding up.

"Hi, Dad," Amy greeted, staring at him in bewilderment. Finally she found her voice. "What is that?" she asked, staring at a black and white wiggly bundle sitting in front of Clint's saddle.

Clint laughed. "*That* is Rio. He's a border collie working dog. He'll be useful around the ranch and company for you. I got him for you."

"Really? Thanks Dad!" Amy reached up to pet Rio. "I've always wanted a dog." Rio licked her hand. "He's got a good cow dog name," she commented.

Clint dismounted and set Rio down. "The main reason I got him is because I don't like you going places alone. From now on I want you to take him with you," he told her.

Logan's Accident and the Box

"Okay," Amy agreed. She knelt down beside the dog and giggled as he licked her face.

Standing up, she asked, "Do you need anything else in town?"

"Nope. I'm ready to go if you are. Where did your friends go anyway?" he asked, looking around. "And who was that other boy with you? I didn't recognize him."

"They probably went to get their horses. I'll explain about Tye on the ride home. I'll get Bannie, then we can—whoa!" Amy exclaimed as she turned around and bumped into Anders.

He grinned down at her. "Walk much?" he asked.

"I guess not!" Amy shook her head as Anders handed her Bannie's reins. "Thanks for saddling him up."

He shrugged. "Don't mention it."

With Rio running alongside, they quickly covered the miles that separated them from home. Leah and Tye left them at the end of their lane, and soon after, Anders left to cut across the pastures to his home.

Once they were alone, Amy told Clint about Tye.

"The Blacks will give him a good home," Clint said when she finished. "It's good of them to give him another chance in life."

Amy nodded. "I can't imagine losing both parents, then not having anyone, especially family, take me in."

Clint nodded, but remained silent.

Soon they were riding in their own lane. "What's going on?" Amy asked as they rode toward the house.

"I'm not sure." Clint's voice trailed off as he studied the activity in the ranch yard.

Men and horses were milling around, and Amy could hear loud shouts. The hands huddled in a group near the bunkhouse, looking at something on the ground.

Clint was alarmed. Amy could see it on his face. He urged his horse into a gallop, and Amy followed.

As they rode into the yard, Amy pulled back on the reins, and Bannie slid to a stop. Throwing his reins over the hitching post, she followed Clint to toward the men.

She followed him as he pushed through the crowd, and when she reached the center of the circle, she gasped.

Logan was sitting with his back against the wall. His shirt was covered in blood. His face was pale and drawn with pain.

"Cody, ride for the doctor!" Clint commanded as he knelt beside the injured man. "Ken, help me lay him down. Daryl, get a blanket. Amy, get water."

Amy leaped to her feet and whirled around, rushed to the house, and filled a bucket with hot water from the tea kettle.

Hurrying back outside, she watched as Clint gently washed the wound in Logan's shoulder with the water and bandaged it with strips of cloth. Even though the day was fairly warm, Logan was shivering violently. Clint covered him with the blanket and took the cup of coffee Caleb brought him. Holding it to Logan's lips, he encouraged him to drink. Logan took a few swallows, then Clint pulled the cup away. "That's enough for now. Let's carry him up to the house."

Carefully, the men rolled Logan onto a blanket and carried him into the house. Amy hurried ahead of them and pulled the blankets back on Clint's bed.

Logan's Accident and the Box

Clint made Logan as comfortable as possible, and then everyone settled down to wait for the doctor.

"Is it bad?" Amy asked Clint as the men gathered in the living room.

Clint shook his head. "Not too bad. It's in his shoulder, and he lost a lot of blood. He'll be laid up for a while, but I think he'll be fine. We don't want to take a chance with infection; that's why I sent for the doctor." He turned to Daryl. "How did it happen?"

"Well, we were ridin' along by the river," Daryl began, "looking for a couple steers that had broken out, when a boy came galloping out of one of those little box canyons. He started yelling and firing his gun. Logan was hit. I shot above the boy's head and told him to drop his gun. When he did, I took his gun away and told him he had to come talk to you to get it back. He said something about some men that stole from him or something. He wasn't talkin' straight. I think he thought we were them."

Clint frowned. "I wonder ..." he began, but he was cut off as someone called out from the porch that the doctor was riding in.

Clint met the doctor at the door and led him into the bedroom.

Amy walked out to the kitchen and poured herself a cup of coffee. She was thinking about the boy who had shot Logan when a knock at the door startled her. She hurried to open it, wondering who it could be.

To her surprise, she found Anders standing there.

"Anders! I wasn't expecting to see you." Amy stepped back and opened the door wider.

"What's going on?" he asked, stepping inside. "I saw Cody and the doctor go by at top speed."

"Logan got shot by some kid," Amy told him.

"Is he going to be all right?"

Amy nodded. "Dad thinks so. It's just a flesh wound he says."

"That's good." Anders took a deep breath. "Had me worried for a minute. Will you come outside a minute?" he asked. "I've got something I want to show you. Marianna rode over with me. Mom told her to get out of the house."

An understanding grin passed between them as Amy followed Anders outside. It was commonly known among the young people that Marianna did not like to be out in the sun or get dirty. She much preferred to stay in the house and sew or cook.

Amy followed Anders to the barn where Marianna was waiting with the horses, and as they approached, she noticed a wooden box sitting beside the hitching post.

"What's that?" she asked curiously.

"Guess!" Anders grinned.

"I can't guess," Amy told him.

"Guess!" he insisted.

"I told you, I can't guess."

"Please, Amy, guess!"

"Well—" Amy began.

"It's a box!" Anders broke in.

Amy stared at him. "You tell me to guess, then you tell me anyway? And I can see that it's a box!"

Anders grinned sheepishly.

Marianna chuckled. "Just tell her your brilliant idea and be done with it."

"Well," Anders said. "I thought we could put this in a hidden place and you, me, Leah, Katie, and Tye could write notes in code to each other. It'd be our own secret thing."

"That's a good idea," Amy said. "You could do it with us, too, Marianna."

"Thanks, but no thanks." Marianna smiled.

"How about coming with us to find a place to put it. It'll help pass the time until the doctor is done with Logan," Anders suggested to Amy.

"From the look on your face, you already have a spot picked out," Amy observed. "Let me tell one of the hands where I'm going, then we can go."

They were gone several hours. Anders had found a hidden spot on his family's ranch just off the road that had rock walls on three sides, forming a small, sheltered canyon. They put the box under a rock ledge, and Amy was assigned to write copies of their code.

"I feel kind of silly," Amy remarked as they started back to the ranch.

Anders chuckled. "Maybe it is kind of childish, but hey, who said we can't have fun?"

"Just so it's the right kind of fun," Marianna said quietly.

Amy nodded. "Right. What some people consider fun is just plain wrong."

"Well, since this will keep us *so* busy, we won't have time to get into the wrong kind of fun!" Anders joked.

It was almost dark when they returned, and Clint was standing on the porch waiting for them.

Amy slid out of the saddle, ground tied Bannie in front of the bunkhouse, and hurried to the porch.

"How's Logan?" she asked.

"He's resting right now," Clint told them. "The doctor said the bullet didn't do a lot of damage. He'll be laid up for a while, but he'll soon be good as new."

"That's wonderful! The Lord protected him," Amy said reverently.

Anders, who had followed Amy to the porch, nodded. "He sure did. I'm glad he's all right. We'd best be getting home. It's getting late."

Clint nodded. "See you both tomorrow."

Amy waved as Anders and Marianna rode out the lane, then hurried to unsaddle Bannie and do her chores. Because Logan was hurt, everyone would have extra work to do. After feeding the sheep and the horses, she headed inside, eager for some time alone with Clint.

Clint was just coming out of the bedroom as she stepped into the hall. "He's sleeping," he said in answer to her unspoken question. He seated himself at the table while she began preparing supper. "Tell me about your day, Amy."

"What a day!" she laughed.

Clint chuckled. "It seems that adventure and excitement seek you out ... or do you seek them out?"

"Probably both." Amy shook her head.

She told him about seeing Daniel and his need for a job and about the box.

"That box reminds me of something I did as a boy." Clint's eyes had a faraway look in them. "Remind me to tell you about it after supper," he told her.

Several of the hands came to the house after supper was finished, and they passed the evening talking and eating cookies in between checking on Logan. The doctor had given him something for pain, so he was sleeping most of the time.

When the clock struck nine, the hands left for the bunkhouse, leaving Clint and Amy alone.

As the door shut behind Daryl, Clint picked up his Bible. "Proverbs 23 tonight, I believe." He read the first three verses aloud. "When thou sittest to eat with a ruler, consider diligently what is before thee: And put a knife to thy throat, if thou be a man given to appetite. Be not desirous of his dainties: for they are deceitful meat."

"Those are some good verses," Amy commented.

Clint nodded. "They sure are. What do you think the first verse is talking about when it says, 'consider diligently what is before thee'?"

Amy thought a moment. "I guess it could be talking about the unclean things the children of Israel were not to eat."

"It could mean that," Clint agreed. "Don't you think it could also mean strong drink?"

Amy nodded. "Yes, it could."

"And verse two, I think this verse is saying we should not be gluttonous. The Lord tells us here to put a knife to our throats if we be given to appetite. That's pretty serious."

"It sure is," Amy agreed.

"What about verse three?"

"I think it means we shouldn't be covetous," Amy said promptly.

"That's what it seems to indicate." Clint nodded in agreement.

They finished the chapter and prayed together, then Amy told Clint goodnight and headed to her room.

During her own devotions, she thanked the Lord for leading Tye to the Blacks and for keeping Daryl and Logan safe, and she prayed for Logan's recovery.

When she finished, she blew out the lamp and a few minutes later was fast asleep.

*****

When she awoke the next morning, the sun was already up.

What a beautiful Sunday morning! she thought as she flung back the covers.

Quickly she dressed in chore clothes and hurried downstairs. Clint's bedroom door was open, and she peeked in at Logan. He was sleeping peacefully.

Quietly she tiptoed down the hall and stepped out onto the porch.

Rio was lying beside his food dish, eating nosily. He woofed happily as she opened the door.

"Dad must have fed you already, huh, boy?" Amy observed, giving him a quick pat as she slipped on her boots.

She was halfway across the yard when Clint stepped out of the barn and shut the door behind him.

"Sleepy head!" he teased. "All your chores are done, so run along inside and get dressed. Grubby is going to stay with Logan so we can go to church. I'll have breakfast ready when you're finished." It was their tradition that Clint fixed breakfast on Sunday.

"Okay. Thanks." Amy turned and hurried back to the house.

Back in her room, Amy slipped into her favorite blue dress, brushed her hair, pinned on her covering, and picked up her Bible. The spring mornings were still chilly, so she put on a sweater before heading down to the kitchen.

When she reached it, Clint had breakfast on the table. "Eat fast," he told her. "We'll be late if we don't hurry."

When she pushed back her plate fifteen minutes later, Clint shook his head. "You eat as much as a boy! I don't know how you can eat so much and stay thin."

Amy laughed. "I don't either."

Hastily she stacked the dishes and followed Clint out the door.

Daryl had hitched the horses to the wagon, and the hands were sitting on the makeshift seats in the bed made out of boards.

Amy climbed up onto the wagon seat beside Clint and drew a blanket over her lap. Clint started the horses, and they set off at a brisk pace. This Sunday, church was to be held at the Archers' home.

Soon they were pulling into the ranch yard, which was already crowded with wagons, and the corral was filled with saddle horses.

"Looks like quite a crowd," Amy remarked to Clint as he helped her down from the wagon.

He nodded. "Looks like. You run along inside. I'll help the boys unhitch and be right in."

"Okay." Carefully, she unwrapped the cake she had brought for the meal after the service and carried it to the kitchen.

She greeted several people and looked around for Daniel, but before she could spot him, it was time for the service to start. Amy slipped into her seat beside Leah just as the first song was announced.

"What's this about Logan getting shot?" Leah whispered as she picked up her song book.

"Later," Amy whispered back.

After the service, she hurried to help the women get the food ready for the potluck. She was carrying a plate of cookies out to the tables when a hand reached over her shoulder and snatched one. "Daniel!" she scolded when she saw who it was. "You're not supposed to eat dessert before your meal, and when did you get here? I looked but didn't see you."

"I got here a little late, so I sat in the back. I heard you had some excitement last night," he said, munching his cookie.

Amy nodded. "Who told you?"

"Anders. I just got done talking to him."

"Are you coming back to the ranch with us?" Amy asked.

Daniel nodded. "I'm planning on it."

"Good! Now I'd better go." Amy flashed him a smile and hurried away.

Logan's Accident and the Box

After setting the cookies on a table, she joined Leah, Katie, Anders, and Tye.

Anders was telling them about the box. He turned to her as she walked up. "Do you have the copies of the code?" he asked.

Amy nodded and handed out the copies she'd made the night before.

"I feel like I'm six again!" Katie laughed. "Secret canyons, a wooden box, codes." She rolled her eyes.

"But it'll be fun," Amy said. "I don't think you ever get too old to have fun like that."

"You're right," Katie agreed.

"Did you tell them about Logan?" Amy asked Anders.

He nodded. "Yep."

The afternoon passed quickly, and all too soon it was time to head home.

As Amy climbed on to the wagon seat, she asked Clint, "Where's Daniel? I thought he was coming home with us."

"He is." Clint picked up the reins and clucked to the horses. "He's visiting with Edward right now. He'll ride out in a little while."

Amy looked puzzled. "He has a horse?"

Clint nodded. "He bought a nice-looking mare in town yesterday. Figured he'd need one if he was going to be staying on the ranch."

"So he's staying?" Amy probed. "I told him I thought we'd have work for him, with Daryl not feeling well."

"My, you're full of questions today!" Clint teased.
"Yes, I told him we could use the help. He'll stay until he finds work."
"Oh, good." Amy nodded. "I hope he finds something closer than his last job."
The rest of the day was quiet. Amy spent the afternoon and evening on the porch with a book while Clint talked to Logan who was in some pain, but otherwise felt fine.

Around five o'clock Amy took him his supper and was glad to see his appetite was as good as ever. She and Clint ate with him in the bedroom.

At nine o'clock, Amy and Clint had their devotions. It was their custom to discuss the morning service as their devotions on Sundays. Clint asked Amy what the theme of the message was and they discussed it.

When they finished, Amy told Clint goodnight and headed to her room.

After doing her devotions, she opened the window to let the cool, night breeze in and got into bed.

She lay awake for a while, thinking and praying. *Thank you for sparing Logan's life, Lord. Please help him to recover quickly with no complications. Thank You for the wonderful sermon we heard today and for the sweet fellowship we enjoyed. Please help me to grow in You and reflect Your love to others. Help me to be a testimony, Lord. Thank You for giving us Your Word that we might know how You want us to live. Thank You for the gift of life. In Jesus's name, Amen."

Chapter Seven
Arty and the Telegram

I'm so bored, Amy thought to herself as she sat on the porch one sunny afternoon in June, three weeks after Daniel had come to stay with them. *There's nothing to do. I'm all caught up on the gardening and housework, all my friends are busy, and Dad and the hands except Logan are all away.* With a sigh, she got to her feet and went into the house. After getting a drink, she went into the living room where Logan was sitting, reading.

He looked up with a smile as she came in. "Why the long face?" he asked.

"I'm bored." Amy flopped into a chair.

"Bored? Don't you think I should be the one complaining about being bored?" he asked with a grin. Then he sobered. "You know, for the first week or so I was laid up, I fretted about not being able to work, and I began to feel sorry for myself. 'Everyone else is out enjoying the spring sunshine and here I am stuck in bed.' Then the Lord got a hold of me. 'Logan,' he said, 'instead of feelin' sorry for yourself, why don't you do find something you can do and do it?' Then I knew what I could do, I could pray. It got my thoughts off myself and onto others."

Amy was quiet a minute. "Thanks, Logan. I was being pretty self-centered, and I think I know what I'll do." She stood to her feet with a smile. "I'm going to check the box, if you'll be okay without me, and while I'm riding down there, I'm going to do some praying."

"Sounds like a good idea. I won't be needing anything for a while. Stay out as long as you like. You've been cooped up too much lately," Logan told her. "I'll tell your dad where you are when he gets back. And you know, even though the Lord helped me learn to be patient, I sure am glad I'll be able to move out to the bunkhouse in another day or two."

Amy chuckled. "I suppose Dad and I are rather tame compared to your usual companions."

Logan shook his head. "Come on, Amy, you know that's not it. I'm just ready to work again, and the doctor said my shoulder is well enough for me to do simple chores. As a matter a fact, I could have moved out to the bunkhouse quite a while ago, but I was enjoying your good cookin' so much, I wanted to delay the move as long as possible!"

"You're a flatterer, Logan." Amy chuckled. "But thanks for the compliment. Dad and I have enjoyed having you stay in here with us."

Amy packed a sandwich and a canteen of water in her saddlebags, then headed to the barn. "It's too hot to use a saddle, she said to Bannie as she led him in from the pasture.

Bannie bobbed his head. "So you agree with me, do you?" she chuckled. Throwing a saddle blanket over his back, she hopped on and rode out the lane.

The box was situated about a half-mile down the road, and as the gelding plodded along, Amy had plenty of time to pray. She arrived at the little canyon feeling mentally refreshed, and her spirits had lifted.

Bannie stopped in front of the box. Amy slid down, opened the box, and reached inside. Her fingers closed around a small piece of paper, and she seated herself on a rock to read the short note from Katie. She had almost finished reading when Bannie suddenly snorted and pawed the ground nervously.

"What's the matter, boy?" Amy asked, slipping the note into her pocket and standing to her feet.

Bannie snorted again and stared steadily at the canyon rim behind her.

"You see something, Ban?" As Amy turned to look, a rock fell to the ground.

Bannie whinnied and backed away. Amy grabbed his reins to stop him and waited in silence.

A moment later, a frightened boyish face appeared from between the bushes. The boy's eyes wandered over the canyon, then, as they rested on her, he drew back quickly.

"Wait!" Amy cried.

She flung herself across Bannie's back and snatched up the reins, and she guided him out of the canyon.

A moment later they were standing where she had seen the boy from below, but she was not surprised she could not see him now. *Anyone who ducks back and takes off when they know you've seen them has a reason for not wanting to be seen,* she thought.

Amy rode back and forth, patiently searching carefully for any sign of the person she had seen. *The land here is flat, with only scattered brush. Even if he was on horseback, he couldn't have gotten away that fast,* she told herself. *And there would be tracks somewhere.*

Finally she spotted him, a young boy trying to hide behind a small bush.

She dismounted and left Bannie ground tied, and walked up to him. Even from a distance, she could see that his ankle was very swollen, and he looked thin and dirty.

"Who are you?" she asked when she came in speaking distance.

The boy said nothing.

"What's your name?" Amy persisted.

"Arty," he said sullenly.

"My name is Amy," Amy introduced herself. "You look like you could use some help. I live about a half-mile from here. If you come with me, we'll get that ankle patched up"

Arty was silent for a moment before saying, "I can't walk that far." He seemed to be searching for excuses not to accept her offer.

"You can ride Bannie. He's gentle." Amy took the sandwich out of her saddlebags and offered it to him while she tied her bandanna around his ankle to support it.

When she finished, she helped him to his feet and managed to hoist him onto Bannie's back, trying not to jostle his ankle, but as she drew back, she saw his face was white with pain, and he was gritting his teeth.

"Are you okay?" she asked him.

Arty nodded. "Yeah. I'll be fine."

"Okay." Amy took hold of the reins and started walking. She tried to choose the smoothest path, but glancing back every few minutes, she could see Arty's face was filled with pain, and he was biting his lip.

"Can you make it?" Amy asked him.

"I'm no sissy," Arty said forcefully.

"I didn't say you were," Amy quickly assured him. "I just thought I'd ask."

As they rounded a curve in the road and the ranch came into sight, Amy was relieved to see Clint standing by one of the buildings. *He'll know what to do.*

She had started to hurry Bannie along when a sound from Arty caused her to look back. He was gripping the gelding's mane with both hands, and his face was so white, Amy thought he was going to faint.

"I'm so sorry, Arty!" she exclaimed. "I didn't mean to jostle you."

"Forget it."

Amy started Bannie again with a tug on the reins and turned in the lane.

Clint was waiting for them when they reached the house.

"This is Arty, Dad," Amy told him. "Looks like he hurt his ankle pretty good."

"I see that." Clint helped Arty off the horse, set him gently on the ground and bent to examine his ankle.

Arty winced as Clint's fingers touched the bruised flesh.

"Are you the boy that shot Logan?" Clint asked.

Arty nodded, his head bowed.

"Where's your horse?"

Arty jerked his head in the direction of the mountain. "Under the rockslide."

"Is that how you hurt your ankle?"

Arty nodded. "Yeah."

Clint straightened up. "This needs a doctor. Bring the team around, Daniel."

Arty was gently helped into the wagon bed, and Clint picked up the reins. "Be back later tonight," he said to Amy as he started the horses.

As soon as the wagon was out of sight, the hands surrounded Amy, demanding an explanation.

"How'd you catch him?" Anders asked eagerly.

Amy explained, then laughed as Anders exclaimed. "Aw, how come stuff like that always happens when I'm not around?"

After preparing the spare bunk in the bunkhouse, Amy went into the house.

"I heard everything from the window," Logan told her. "So you don't have to repeat it."

Amy smiled. "Good. Are you going to have a problem with him staying here?"

Logan shook his head. "He needs some looking after and some of your good cooking. I don't think he'll try anything like that again. He didn't have anything against me, just against the person he thought I was."

"My thoughts exactly," Amy told him.

A few hours later, Amy flew outside when she heard the wagon roll in.

Arty was wearing a cast and using crutches. She waited while Clint and Daniel helped him into the spare bunk and then returned to the house with Clint and Daniel.

"Is supper ready?" Clint asked as they stepped into the hall.

Amy nodded. "Yes. I'll serve it up, and then you can tell us about Arty."

"All right." Clint went into the living room to talk Logan.

"So what was wrong with his leg?" Amy asked after Clint had asked the blessing.

"He broke his ankle. The doctor said it wasn't a bad break. I don't know much about him. He was hurtin' pretty bad, so I figured it would be better to wait to talk to him. The doctor gave him something for pain, and that made him drowsy. I told him I wanted to talk to him tomorrow. He did say he's been on his own for several years. I'm thinking about hiring him if his story is satisfactory. That is, if you don't object, Logan. He could use a family."

Logan shook his head. "No objection here."

"Then he'll stay. I'll have him tell his story tomorrow," Clint said, closing the matter.

*****

The next morning, after breakfast, Clint helped Arty to the house, and Amy and the others gathered on the porch to hear his story.

"I lived in Montana before I came here. We lived miles from anyone, trying to make a living at farming. When I was twelve, there was an epidemic of smallpox. We all got it, but Ma, Pa and my little sister died. Why I lived I don't know. I was as sick as the rest of them."

Arty paused for a moment, and Clint said, "Maybe the Lord has a special plan for you."

Arty shrugged. "Maybe. Anyway, I don't have any relatives, so I struck out on my own. I knew I couldn't make it on the farm. I've been wandering around for three years doing odd jobs when I could get them."

"Why don't you tell us what happened the day you shot Logan?" Clint suggested.

Arty ducked his head, and his voice was low and ashamed. "I was tired and hungry from a long ride that day. I had been out of work for a long time, and I was pretty desperate. I stumbled onto the camp of some rough-looking characters. They invited me to eat with them and spend the night. I was fool enough to agree. They must've drugged my food or something because it was very late the next day when I woke up and all my supplies were gone, along with the guys. I'm really sorry about what happened. I think the drug must have messed up my brain or something. I don't usually go around shooting at people." He looked apologetically at Logan.

"It's all right, Arty. No harm done," Logan told him.

Arty looked relieved.

"Well, son, I believe you are sorry for what you did, so as soon as your leg heals, I'm going to offer you a job. You're welcome to stay as long as you like," Clint told him.

"Thank you, Mr. Kentworthy." Arty smiled shyly.

Clint stood to his feet. "For now you can stay in the house with Amy and Logan." He winked at Amy. "They'll offer plenty of entertainment, I'm sure."

"Dad!" Amy shook her head at him, smiling.

Clint started down the steps. "Come on, Daniel. We've got work to do."

It was baking day, and Amy was busy making all sorts of good things. Her hands flew as she put together rolls, bread, cookies, and pies.

While she worked, Logan and Arty sat at the table, snitching tidbits.

"If you are going to eat everything, you have to help make it," Amy told them.

"Dish out the work." Logan laughed. "As long as I can do it with one hand, I suppose I don't have anything else to do. Might as well help, right, Arty?"

"Right." Arty picked up another roll and flashed Amy a smile.

Amy could already see the difference a family atmosphere had made on Arty. He was more relaxed and willing to talk, and he seemed to be enjoying himself. He set to work rolling out cookie dough willingly while Logan cut the cookies out and Amy kneaded the bread.

She had just slid a tray of cookies into the oven when there was a knock at the door. "I wonder who that could be," she murmured as she dried her hands on her apron.

Rustlers and the Texas Trail

She opened the door to find a courier standing on the porch.

"Telegram, ma'am," he said, handing her a yellow envelope.

Amy signed for it and paid him.

"Who's it from?" Logan asked as she shut the door.

"I don't know." Amy searched the envelope for a clue. "It says it's from Texas, but we don't know anyone there. It's addressed to Dad, so we'll have to wait 'till he gets home to find out what it's about."

Logan shrugged and reached for another cookie. "Curiosity killed the cat. These are really good."

"Both of you are going to get sick if you eat any more," Amy scolded.

When Clint got back that evening, Amy gave him the telegram. He tore it open, and Amy watched his face closely as he read, but it revealed nothing.

"Who is it from?" Amy asked as he folded the paper and put it in his pocket.

"A rancher in Texas, Devon Henderson of the Rocking H Ranch. He says his ranch was raided several months ago, and he lost quite a few animals to the thieves, and when he heard that a large number of cattle that bore the Rocking H brand had been found in this area, he thought they might be his. Looks like they are."

"But why would the rustlers drive the cattle all the way up here?" Amy asked. "Mexico would have been a lot closer."

"Because they weren't heading for Mexico," Clint told her. "They were taking them to the railroad and shipping them to the East."

"Weren't they taking more of a risk that way?"

Clint shrugged. "Maybe, maybe not. I'm not sure. Anyway, Mr. Henderson wants to know if he could hire us to drive them down there to him. He also may be interested in buying some cattle from us."

"I wonder how he heard about the cattle all the way down there."

"Chad sent out a report to a lot of towns across the country in hopes the news would eventually reach the owner," Clint informed her.

"Oh, I see." Amy nodded. "So what are you going to tell him?"

"Well, I haven't thought it all the way through yet, of course. If I can get a few extra men I might do it. I have some cattle I was planning on selling anyway." Clint stroked his mustache thoughtfully.

After a few minutes, he said. "I want to pray about it first, but I think we can start preparing for the journey!"

Chapter Eight
Preparing for the Journey and the Surprise

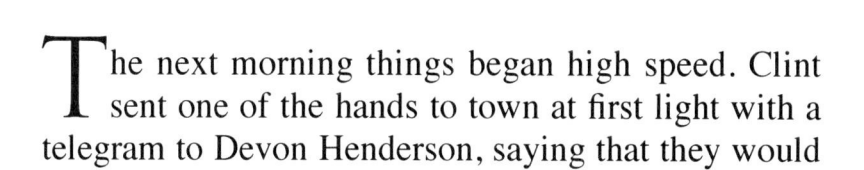

The next morning things began high speed. Clint sent one of the hands to town at first light with a telegram to Devon Henderson, saying that they would drive the cattle to him.

Amy and Clint discussed it over breakfast.

"I prayed about it and feel that this is what we should do," he told her. "Not only does it provide an opportunity to sell some of those cows, but I miss the cattle drives. Ever since that railroad was put in things haven't been the same. Cattle drives used to be a huge event and a chance to meet new people and catch up with old friends." Clint stared unseeingly out the window for a moment, then looked back at Amy. "I want you to see how it used to be before all these new-fangled inventions, how things like this brought people together and united them in a way that all these modern conveniences cannot do. The old way that brought man and God closer. It let man experience God's creation. No, it isn't always the easiest, but I think it's the most rewarding." He paused, then went on. "So today I am going to ride to the Diamond-n-ahalf and the Pot-S-Hook to see if they can spare some men. I think I'll leave Ken, Ross, and Logan here to look after the ranch while we're gone."

"Who are you going to get to help?" Amy asked, taking a sip of coffee.

"I'd like to get Anders and Tye for sure, I'm not sure who else yet. I figured Tye would enjoy coming along, and I'll need Anders to look after you." Clint said the last with a straight face.

"I can take care of myself," Amy retorted, laughing. "And you'd better not tell that to Anders. He doesn't need any encouragement."

Clint chuckled. "He does seem to take pleasure in watching out for you, though I would say he does it so he has more chances to tease you!"

Amy shook her head. "Probably. What about Arty? Are you going to leave him here?"

"I think we'll take him. He can ride on the chuck wagon with Grubby 'till his leg heals. It'll be good for him to be part of this. Well, I'd better get going if I plan on getting anything done today." Clint got to his feet. "Good breakfast, Amy."

Amy stood up, too. "What should I do today?" she asked as she began to clear the table.

"You can pack whatever you think you'll need, and I don't mean your whole room. Then you can ask the men where they need help the most. Be sure to clean and

Preparing for the Journey and the Surprise

oil your tack. Oh, and we are taking Rio. He'll come in handy with the cattle."

"Okay, do you want another cup of coffee?"

"No, thanks. I told Daryl to get you when they are ready to gather the cattle from the pasture," he called over his shoulder as he headed out the door.

"All right," Amy called back.

After she finished the dishes, Amy packed a bag with extra clothes and found her bedroll. She dug her old pair of boots out of her closet and added them to her bag, and then she went outside to see what she could help with.

Daryl and Cody were struggling with the wagon cover. "Here, Amy, give us a hand," Daryl called when he spotted her.

Amy caught the corner that Daryl tossed to her and helped pull it over the wooden hoops. After they had tied it down, Daryl turned to her. "I was just about to come get you. We're ready to round up those yearlings. We'll bring them up to the holding pen. There's some two-year-olds that need sorted out. We'll sort them after we bring Devon's cattle up."

Amy nodded. As she started for the barn, she thought, *Daryl doesn't look as pale as usual. Going to the doctor must have helped.* She chuckled as she remembered the heated discussions between Clint and his foreman. Clint had noticed Daryl had seemed run down and tired and suggested he go to the doctor. Daryl had immediately fired up and insisted doctor visits were for weaklings. Daryl had finally given in and gone to the doctor but refused to tell even Clint what the doctor had said.

"Meet us by the rock," Daryl called as she opened the barn door.

The rock was a large boulder set near the river. It was said that it used to be an Indian altar where they sacrificed to their gods. Amy felt burdened for the people who did not know the one true God. *Maybe God will call me to tell people about Jesus*, she often thought.

As she entered the pasture where Bannie spent most of his time with the other riding horses, Dark Sunshine came over to greet her.

"Hurry up and have that baby," Amy told her, though she knew it would be almost a year before the foal would be born. "I'm eager for a sweet, cute foal to cuddle."

The mare rubbed her head on Amy's shoulder, and Bannie immediately trotted over and pushed her away.

"Jealous, are you?" Amy laughed. She slipped his bridle on and led him to the barn.

Bannie stood quietly as she saddled him, but as soon as she mounted and turned toward the river, he began to prance impatiently.

Amy loosened the reins, gave him a nudge, and leaned forward as he broke into a smooth gallop. They flew along the river, the pounding of Bannie's hooves on the packed ground accompanied by the sound of rushing water.

When the others came into sight, Amy pulled Bannie in and walked the rest of the way. The gate was already open, and Amy trotted through. Caleb closed it behind her. Daryl separated them into three groups. One was to ride the left fence, one the right fence, and the third

Preparing for the Journey and the Surprise

was to ride the back fence and flush the cattle out. Amy was assigned to the third group.

Cantering briskly, she headed for the back fence, and when she reached it, she turned and rode back in a zigzag pattern the way she had come, gathering cattle as she went. Whenever there was a cow nearby, Bannie always let her know.

By the time she caught up to the hands, she had gathered quite a number of cattle. They bunched the cattle and pushed them through the gate and up the trail toward the corral by the barn. Amy rode on ahead of the rest and opened the gate. As the cattle drew near, Amy helped by blocking the space between the house and corral and turning the cattle into the gate.

Amy patted Bannie's neck as the last steer ran through the gate. "Good boy," she told him.

It took the rest of the morning to gather Devon's cattle from the east pasture and sort the two-year-olds out of the bunch Clint was selling.

Amy offered to drive the two-year-olds to their pasture and check on the newly branded calves. Daryl agreed, so she set off.

The cattle were nervous and jumpy from being separated from their friends, and it took all of Amy's skill to keep them bunched and moving smoothly along the trail. Twenty minutes later she had driven the cattle through the pasture gate and was on her way back.

When she got back to the ranch yard, she found a beehive of activity. Ken was greasing the wheels of the chuck wagon; Grubby was hauling sacks of beans; coffee, flour, and cornmeal out to the wagon; Anders was loading up sacks of oats and corn for the horses; Arty was helping Caleb repair saddles, bridles and lariats; Daryl and Daniel were leaving for town to buy supplies; and Cody was shoeing the riding horses.

As Amy rode up, everyone began shouting orders.

"Come hold this grease can."

"I could use some help carrying boxes."

"Grab this sack."

"I need some more wire."

"I need some leather oil."

Amy dismounted and tied Bannie to the corral fence. "Do you think I've got eight arms? I can't do everything at once."

"Then just help me," Anders suggested.

"You've got the easy job." Amy laughed. "I think I'll help Cody shoe the horses.

Anders groaned, then grinned mischievously. "Hey, Amy, your dad said he's going to ask my dad if I can go along to look after you."

"Dad told you that? I told him not to!" Amy held up her hands in mock despair.

Anders chuckled. "You'll have no end of teasing about that from me now," he warned her.

"What horse is going to be my extra?" Amy asked Cody as she led a horse out for him.

Cody shrugged. "Pick whatever one you want."

Amy looked over the horses milling in the corral. "I guess I'll take Buck. He's the closest temperament to Bannie," she decided.

After helping Cody for a while, Amy went in to make lunch, and half an hour later, Clint rode in just as she put it on the table.

Amy met him on the porch. "Who'd you get?" she asked eagerly.

"Hold your horses! Let me at least get in the door," Clint told her.

"Sorry! I want to know who my travelin' partners are going to be!"

After Clint had thanked the Lord for the food, he told her about his morning. "I got Bo and Tye from the Pot-S-Hook and Derek and Anders from the Diamond-n-ahalf. With the men I'll take from here, I think that's plenty."

"You'll have me, and I'm always a big help," Amy added slyly.

"Oh, sure." Clint laughed. "Maybe I'll leave you at home."

Amy shrugged; she knew he was joking. "So what's our route?" she asked.

"I know the general route, but I haven't worked out all the details," he told her, biting into his sandwich.

"Will we go through Cheyenne?" Amy asked. "I've always wanted to go there."

Clint nodded. "Probably so you can brag to your friends, eh? Yes, I was thinking of hitting Cheyenne on the way back."

"That's not very nice." Amy frowned.

"What?" Clint looked puzzled.

"You said we'd hit Cheyenne." Amy replied, trying not to smile.

"What do you ... oh, very funny, Amy!" Clint chuckled. "You certainly inherited your mother's humor."

Amy grinned as Clint stood to his feet. "Come on," he told her. "We've got lots of work to do. I'd like to leave a week from today. Oh, Katie was at Leah's when I got there, and they said to ask you to come over for a little this afternoon. You've worked hard this morning, so you can go if you like."

"Thanks." Amy began clearing the table. "I've been wanting to see Katie. Is there anything I need to do first?"

Clint shook his head. "You can go right now. Be back by bedtime." He disappeared into the living room.

Amy stacked the dishes and ran outside, whistling cheerfully.

"What are you so happy about?" Anders asked from his perch on the hitching post.

"Wouldn't you like to know?" Amy laughed as she opened the barn door.

"Aw, come on, Amy. You're goin' somewhere, aren't you? How come you always tease me?" he asked.

"'Cause I haven't got any brothers or sisters so I have to take it all out on you," Amy told him as she lifted the saddle onto Bannie's back. "But I'll tell you where I'm going. Katie and Leah invited me to spend the afternoon at Leah's. Aren't you jealous?" she teased.

"Naw ... well, maybe a little. I couldn't go even if I had been invited. My dad says I have to go somewhere with him this afternoon. See you tomorrow." he finished with a shrug as Amy swung onto Bannie and began riding away.

When Amy arrived at the Pot-S-Hook a short time later, Katie came running out to meet her. "I'm so glad you could come, Amy. We are going to ride to the lake and Heather's Garden. Leah is in the barn."

It only took a few minutes for Katie to saddle her horse, and then the girls were on their way.

"Are we going to the lake first or the garden?" Amy asked as they started out.

"I was thinking we could go to the lake first. One of the hands was back there last week and he said there were a lot of duck nests," Leah said.

"I think we should go to the garden first," Katie disagreed. "We don't have a lot of time, and Heather's Garden is a long ride. I was really hoping to see it."

"Okay. If Amy wants to we'll go to the garden first, and if we have time we'll go to the lake," Leah consented.

"I'd like that," Amy agreed. "I haven't been there in a long time." They turned the horses and headed for the garden.

Heather's Garden was a beautiful spot set in the only group of trees for several miles. The entrance was a rose-covered arbor. The garden was surrounded by a split rail fence and was filled with stone walks, flowers, and rustic benches. It was a quiet, peaceful spot.

As they approached, Amy suggested they leave the horses and walk the rest of the way. Leah and Katie agreed, so they hobbled the horses and left them to graze.

The three of them had seen the garden many times before, but it still awed them every time they saw it.

Amy sat down on one of the benches. "Did you know that my dad proposed to my mom here?" she asked.

"Really?" Katie looked surprised.

"I wonder how long this garden has been here," Leah said thoughtfully.

"Well, it was here when Amy's dad was young," Katie observed.

"Oh, then it must be really old!" Leah laughed.

They all chuckled.

"Wouldn't it be fun to have a tea party here?" Amy asked.

"Oh, yes, an elegant tea party with fancy dresses, and remember to hold your pinky out!" Katie joked.

They spent quite a while in the garden, and then the girls checked on some freshly branded calves, took a quick look at the ducks at the lake, and headed back to the ranch.

As they rode past the barn, Amy stared in bewilderment. "What is all this?" she asked, puzzled.

The corrals were full of horses, and men, women, and children filled the yard, porch, and barn.

"Surprise!" Katie and Leah shouted together.

"It's a going away party for you," Leah explained. "Did we surprise you?"

"You certainly did! I had no idea!" Amy shook her head incredulously.

As she dismounted, she spotted Anders walking toward her, grinning broadly. "Anders!" she exclaimed. "What are you doing here?"

"I guess we both got duped, eh, Amy? This is where I had to go with Dad, though I didn't know it." He grinned.

"Looks like half the town is here," Amy commented.

"Of course. I'm a very popular person." Anders joked.

Amy rolled her eyes at him. "Don't I know it!"

"Seriously, though, it's been a long time since anyone did anything like this my dad says." Anders went on. "Quite an event, wouldn't you say?"

Amy nodded, then pointing, she asked, "Is that Twyla Anderson?"

"Yep." Anders shook his head. "If she hates us so much, why would she come tonight?"

Amy shrugged. "I sure don't know. Maybe just for the socialization."

"Did you hear she's going on a trip to England?"

"Really?" Amy was surprised. "What for?"

Anders shrugged. "Not really sure. I think she's going to some fancy school near some relatives she has over there. From what I heard, she'll be gone about a year. She's probably glad to get out of the uncivilized West!"

Amy chuckled. "That wouldn't surprise me at all." She started to lead Bannie to the barn, but Anders held out his hand.

"I can take him," he offered.

"Sure, thanks." Amy flashed him a smile as she handed him the reins.

As she started toward the house, someone spoke behind her.

"How's your evening going?" She turned to see Clint standing there with folded arms, grinning down at her.

"You knew all along, didn't you?" Amy playfully accused him.

His grin widened. "Sure, I did. It was nice of our friends to plan this spur of the moment. I guess Ken stopped at all the ranches on his way to town this morning to spread the word. Mrs. Archer had Anders tell him. Have a nice time." He left her to join the men by the barn, and she continued on inside.

A delicious aroma greeted her as she entered the kitchen where the ladies had gathered. "My, it smells good in here!" she exclaimed.

"Hello, Amy. Did you have a good time on your ride? Are you enjoying yourself?" Mrs. Black asked, giving her a hug.

"Oh, yes, we had a lovely ride. I certainly am enjoying myself, and thank you so much for hosting a party on so little notice."

Mrs. Black laughed. "I figured I had to do it now if I was to manage it at all. Before long, you'll all be so wrapped up in preparations that you'll hardly stop to eat, let alone attend a party!"

"That's probably true." Amy laughed. "And I suppose the ride was to keep me from guessing what the invitation was really for?" she asked archly.

"Exactly!" Mrs. Black smiled. "Now run along and enjoy yourself."

Amy joined the group of young people on the porch. Most of them were ones she knew from church, but a few were kids from the town that she had come to know. They spent the time until supper discussing as only young people can, laughing and chatting about the upcoming trip and saying how lucky Amy and the others were to be going along.

The ladies had worked hard on the meal, and it was delicious. There was lots of talk and laughter around the table.

The party lasted late, and Amy was tired and ready to go by the time the last person had left. She had thoroughly enjoyed the evening but was ready for some peace and quiet.

She was quiet as she and Clint rode home together in the moonlight.

"Cat got your tongue?" Clint asked after a while.

Amy smiled and shook her head. "I was just thinking. It was so nice of everyone to give a going-away party. I really appreciate the wonderful friends God has given me. Did you ever think what it would be like without them?" She could barely see Clint nod his head in the darkness.

"Yes, I have Amy. The more I think about it, the more thankful it makes me for my friends and for my daughter." He flashed her a smile. "We will always hold this night in our hearts, and when we get weary on the trail, we'll remember the people we have waiting for us. Are you ready to go?"

Amy nodded. "Yep. I'm ready to ride."

"Good. We'll leave in two days. We have just a few more things to do, and then we'll be heading to Texas!"

Chapter Nine
HEADING TO TEXAS

Amy woke to raindrops pattering on her window the next morning. She slipped out of bed and walked to the window.

Though it was raining, she could see the hands working outside, their yellow slickers warding off the rain.

I wonder if this will delay us. I sure hope not because I'm eager to get started, she thought as she turned from the window.

She dressed swiftly and hurried downstairs to the kitchen where she found Clint slicing a loaf of bread.

"Is this liquid sunshine going to set us back?" she asked as she poured herself a cup of coffee.

Clint shook his head. "It shouldn't. What still needs to be done can be done inside I think."

Just then the back door opened and Anders stuck his head in. "Hey, Amy!"

"What?" Amy stepped into the hall. "

"Do you think it will rain today?" Anders grinned at her and winked, then slammed the door.

Amy stepped back into the kitchen, shaking her head and chuckling. "A typical Anders joke," she remarked to Clint.

Clint laughed. "Yep. And I have to admit, it was funny!"

Amy chuckled. "It was."

They were both silent for a moment, then Clint asked, "What are you going to do today?"

Amy made a face. "Mending. You boys wear out your clothes so fast!"

Clint chuckled. "I think I'll be outside all day!"

Amy laughed. "Yeah, I might be tempted to hand you a needle!"

After she had washed the dishes and tidied the kitchen, Amy settled down in the living room with her pile of mending.

With a sigh, she threaded her needle and picked up a shirt that was missing a button. Mending was not her favorite job, but it had to be done.

It was midmorning when Amy heard the door slam and looked up to see Anders, Daniel, and Clint standing in the doorway. Water streamed off their clothes.

"You're soaked!" Amy exclaimed, standing up quickly. "Why weren't you wearing your slickers?"

"We were in the barn and thought we'd come in and get warmed up. We thought we could make it across the yard without getting too wet, but I guess we were wrong." Clint shrugged his shoulders under his wet shirt.

Amy pulled some blankets out of the closet and handed them out. Then she hurried to the kitchen, saying, "I'll get some coffee."

When the coffee was hot, she carried it to the living room and handed them each a steaming cup.

"How lucky you are!" she said, sitting down and picking up her sewing again.

"Lucky?" Anders stared at her.

Clint chuckled and Anders shot him a puzzled look.

Amy grinned. "Uh-huh. You get to work outside while I have to do all this awful mending," she said, frowning at the pair of pants she was holding.

Anders shook his head. "I'd say you were the lucky one, working inside while we're out in the rain and cold."

"We could trade jobs," Amy suggested, winking at Clint.

"No way!" Anders exclaimed. "I'm not about to become a seamstress!"

Amy laughed. "You sure fell for my little trap, Anders. I didn't think you would agree to a trade though. How 'bout you, Daniel?"

Daniel shook his head emphatically. "Count me out! I'll take the rain any day!"

"Well, I tried." Amy grinned.

"Amy tried to get me this morning," Clint told them. "She's a slick one!"

"I think I'm dry enough!" Anders grinned. "It's safer outside!"

Amy spent the rest of the day mending, stopping only long enough to prepare lunch.

Someone should invent a material that doesn't rip, she thought as she laid aside a hopelessly torn shirt. *I'm so tired of sewing.*

Stop it, Amy Kentworthy! she scolded herself as she stood to her feet and started for the kitchen. *Be thankful you have clothes to mend. Some aren't even that fortunate. I'll start supper. Dad and Daniel will be in soon, and that will keep me busy to I won't have time for negative thoughts.*

That evening, after supper, she and Clint sat in the living room listening to the rain pounding on the roof. Daniel had gone out to the bunkhouse to play checkers with Ken, so they were alone.

"Amy, I want to tell you how pleased I was with your attitude today. I know you don't like mending and would have much rather been helping us outside, yet you remained cheerful and pleasant. Your mother would have been proud," Clint told her.

"Thanks, Dad. I knew it had to be done and that I could be miserable and unhappy about it or I could choose to be happy. I wasn't cheerful all the time, but whenever I started to feel blue, I just thought of the verse in Proverbs, 'A merry heart doeth good like a medicine but a broken spirit drieth the bones.'"

Clint nodded. "That's the way to think." He reached for his Bible. "Let's do our devotions now so you can get to bed." He thumbed through the pages. "Proverbs 26 tonight." He read the first two verses aloud. "'As snow in summer, and as rain in harvest, so honour is not seemly for a fool. As the bird by wandering, as the swallow by flying, so the curse causeless shall not come.' What do you think the first verse is talking about?" he asked.

"Well, I think its saying that just as it would be odd to have snow in the summer, a fool should not have honor," Amy said.

Clint nodded. "I agree. And the second verse seems to say a curse will not come upon us without cause. Meaning, maybe, if there is a curse, it comes with a reason."

They finished the chapter, then prayed together. Clint set his Bible down and gave Amy a kiss. "Off to bed now! We've got a long couple days."

*****

The next two days were busy ones in spite of the rain as they finished last minute repairs and packing.

The day they were to leave dawned bright and clear. Clint woke Amy early, just as the sun was beginning to rise. "Get up, Amy. We're leaving today," he called as he knocked on her door.

Amy was instantly wide awake. "Be right down," she called back, scrambling out of bed.

Her fingers flew as she buttoned her dress, pulled on her socks, brushed her hair, pinned on her covering, and picked up her saddlebags. She flew down the stairs to the kitchen. She had just barely enough time to stuff some jerky and hardtack in her saddle bags before the hands all gathered in the living room.

Caleb, Derek, Cody, Bo, Tye, Arty, Anders, Daryl, Daniel, and Grubby were going with them while Ken,

Ross, and Logan stayed behind to look after the ranch with the help of some of Clint's rancher friends.

Clint was giving instructions as she slid breathlessly onto the sofa next to Anders. "Grubby and Arty will start out in the chuck wagon on the road until they get to Wilson's Fork, then they'll leave the road. We'll meet them with the cattle a mile west of there at Cattle Creek." He gave a few more instructions, then said, "All right boys, I think that's all. Let's hit the trail!"

They filed out of the house and stepped off the porch into the crowd that had gathered to see them off. Amy threaded her way through the crowd to Katie and Leah, who were waiting by the barn with Bannie. They had groomed him until he shone and saddled and bridled him.

"Thanks for saddling Bannie, girls." Amy threw her saddle bags over his back and buckled on her spurs, talking as she worked. "I'm glad you could come see us off. We won't see each other for a couple of months, I guess."

"Probably not." Leah sighed. "It won't seem like the same old Durango without you around."

Amy laughed. "Sure it will. I doubt the stores will close or people move away or ranch work stop just because little, insignificant me isn't around."

The girls laughed, and Katie and Leah hugged Amy goodbye, then she swung into the saddle and rode over to Clint. He was talking to Wyatt Archer and Luke Black. They were going to be helping look after the ranch while they were gone.

When he finished talking to them, he mounted his white stallion, Renegade, and waved to the crowd. "We're off, folks!" he cried.

A shout went up as the riders wheeled their horses and rode past the barn and out of sight of the house. Amy cantered over to Anders. His blue eyes sparkled with excitement as he grinned at her. "So we're off at last. Can you believe we're actually going on a cattle drive all the way to Texas? Sure hope Dad doesn't change his mind at the last minute!"

"Oh, I don't think he'll do that," Amy assured him. "I can hardly believe we're on our way either."

They reached the pasture as the bawling cattle were being pushed toward the gate by the other riders. There were four hundred head of Devon's that had been stolen plus the three hundred he was buying from Clint.

Amy whistled to Rio and stationed herself to guide the cattle along the river as they filed out the gate. It was very dry, and the seven hundred head of cattle kicked up a lot of dirt. Small eddies of wind sent in swirling over the cattle's backs, and Amy pulled her bandana up to cover her mouth and nose.

As the cattle started heading south, Rio yipped, and Amy turned to see what was wrong. A big steer had broken from the herd and was trying to return to the pasture. Amy wheeled Bannie around and went after him, but the steer was determined.

The rest of the herd got farther and farther ahead as Amy struggled to turn the stubborn steer around. Every time Bannie tried to head him off, the steer would turn as if to rejoin the herd, then dash around the gelding.

Daniel saw her predicament and came to help. Together they were able to turn the steer around and get him started in the right direction.

Heading to Texas

As the steer joined the herd, Daniel gave Amy a thumbs up. "Great work, Amy. If Bannie had been a little more experienced, he would have known what to do."

Amy nodded. "Yep. A more experienced cowhorse would have guessed the steer's game and been ready for him. As it was, I couldn't cue Bannie fast enough to keep up with the steer's movements."

Rio ran alongside, his tongue lolling out of his mouth, and wagged his tail. "Good dog!" Amy praised him.

It didn't take long to reach Cattle Creek. Cattle Creek wasn't really a creek. It was an old waterhole that dried up in the summer, but right now it was full from the spring rains.

They did not stop to water the cattle because they had just started out; they pushed them on past the water hole. As she rode past, Amy spotted the chuck wagon. She spotted Arty perched on the wagon seat and waved. He saw her and waved back.

Several hours later, Anders loped over to Amy. "Here's your lunch," he said, handing her a bag. "You were in such a hurry this morning you forgot it on the table. Thought I'd grab it for you."

"Thanks. I had forgotten it until just a few minutes ago. I put some jerky and hardtack in my saddlebags, but that's pretty poor fare." Amy hungrily bit into a sandwich.

Later that afternoon, the sun was shining brightly , and Amy was slouched sleepily in the saddle, relaxing. For once Bannie was plodding steadily along without his usual antics, and the cattle were walking quietly.

Suddenly she gasped in surprise. Choking back the urge to scream, she turned around quickly to find Anders doubled over with laughter. "Anders Archer!" she cried. "You poured water down my back!"

"Yep," he said, looking pleased with himself.

"And it was cold!" Amy continued. "How did you get cold water?"

Anders grinned. "There's a fast-flowing creek over there." He motioned with his hand. "Nice, cold mountain water. Want some?"

"Sure, if you don't pour it down my back again!" she tossed him her canteen.

When he came back, he said, "The cattle are moving along well, so your dad told me to keep you company."

"What?" Amy asked, cupping her hand around her ear.

"I said your dad said to keep you company," he repeated.

"What?" Amy asked again, leaning closer to him.

"*I said*, your dad said ... Amy Kentworthy!" he exploded.

Amy laughed. "Got ya! You're not the only one who can play good jokes!"

Anders shook his head. "Dad said I'd never meet my equal in that respect, but I guess he was wrong!"

Amy chuckled, then pointed to the chuck wagon. "Arty's waving!"

She and Anders waved back, then Amy looked at her watch. "It's five o'clock. We should be making camp any time. Dad said he didn't want to push the cattle too hard until they get used to walking. Who's on night watch?"

"I think Bo and Daryl have first watch, Caleb and Derek on second, and Cody and Daniel on third. We get to sleep tonight." Anders grinned.

Tye loped up just then. "Mr. Kentworthy said for you two to help Grubby set up camp. The rest of us are taking the cattle to drink at the river, then out to graze."

Anders looked after him for a moment as he loped away, then turned to Amy, shaking his head. "Well, since I'm stuck babysitting you, and being chore boy, I might as well make the best of it."

"Anders! You are *not* babysitting me! I'm only a month younger than you and quite capable of taking care of myself," Amy informed him.

Anders chuckled but made no comment.

They caught up with the chuck wagon and dismounted. Grubby stopped in an open spot and stiffly climbed down from the wagon seat.

"You picked a good place for a camp, Grubby," Anders said as he tied his horse to the wagon.

Grubby nodded. "Thank ye, laddie. So the boss sent ye to help me, eh? And ye, too, lassie," he added as Amy joined them.

Amy nodded and smiled. *Grubby's accent is so interesting to listen to*, she thought.

For the next hour, Amy was kept busy gathering brush, hauling water and being generally useful. Arty sat on the wagon tongue with his leg propped up, talking to Anders as he rubbed down the mules and cleaned the harness.

By the time they were nearly finished setting up camp, all the boys except Caleb and Tye, who were herding the cattle until later that night, began coming into camp. Anders saddled a fresh horse and took the cavvy out to graze.

Amy greeted Clint as he rode in.

"How's the food comin'? I'm about starved!" He grunted as he slid to the ground. "Boy, am I stiff! Must be getting old!"

Amy helped him unsaddle Renegade, then as Clint turned him loose with a slap on the rump, they joined the others around the fire.

Amy leaned against the wagon wheel and listened to the boys talk as Grubby dished up.

"We lost one cow today, boss," Daryl informed Clint.

"That so? What happened?" Clint asked.

"She broke from the herd and headed for the river. She was an old one and knew where to find water. I tried to head her off, but before I could get to her, she stepped in a gopher hole. Broke her leg clean in half. I had to shoot her."

"Well, it can't be helped. I wonder if I should put three men on watch tonight." Clint looked thoughtful. "The cattle did seem to get a little edgy as we approached the river."

"Might be a good idea," Daryl agreed.

"I can help," Amy offered.

"Not tonight, Amy." Clint shook his head.

Amy was disappointed but did not protest as Clint went on giving instructions. "I'll take first watch, Tye can take second, and Anders can take third."

"Let's have a song or two," Daniel suggested a while later. He got his banjo, and Amy got her guitar. The music blended with the night sounds and produced a soothing melody.

Later, after devotions, as Amy settled down under the wagon in her bedroll, she thought how fortunate she was to have a Christian father and friends. She lay listening to the low murmur of voices and the sounds of the cavvy, Tye, and Caleb returning to camp. She picked up bits of Caleb's conversation with Clint.

"We saw some shadows. Not sure what it is. ... Cattle are restless, might be wolves. Gotta watch the young calves. ... Already warned the boys."

"Keep a sharp watch. ... Wolves might follow. Keep your guns loaded. ... I'll ride out and check," she heard Clint say, then all was quiet.

Please keep the men and cattle safe tonight, Lord, Amy prayed as she fell asleep.

Heading to Texas

Chapter Ten
WOLVES AND SCATTERED CATTLE

"What on earth?" Amy sat up suddenly, bumping her head on the bottom of the wagon.

It was still dark, but she could hear shouts and gun shots and faintly see moving shadows she recognized as men and horses. Scrambling out from under the wagon, she yanked on her boots and ran toward the shadowy figures gathered around the horse corral.

"Saddle up, Amy!" Anders shouted when he caught sight of her. "Wolves attacked the cattle and they scattered; we've got to help round them up." He touched the reins to Sky Blue's neck, and the gelding swung around and galloped off into the night.

Amy raced back to the wagon, gathered her tack, and ran back to the cavvy's makeshift corral of rope. Amy ducked under it and whistled for Bannie.

A few minutes later she was galloping toward the noise and lantern light.

Wolves and Scattered Cattle

As she pulled Bannie up sharply, she looked around. The night was dark, with neither moon nor stars to give any light, but some of the men held lighted lanterns, and in the dim light she could see the bodies of two yearling steers and several young calves. Three wolves lay on the perimeter of the herd.

The men were discussing what had happened, and she rode closer to listen.

"We had been watching the cattle closely and keeping them bunched." Daniel was saying as she joined the group. "I noticed a slinking shadow to my right, then as I looked closer, I saw dark shapes all around. I fired into the air but they kept coming. Then they broke and charged. We killed the three you see here and injured a few more I think. The cattle scattered at the first shot. They headed that way." He indicated the general direction with a wave of his hand.

"Well, we've got to round them up. It's pretty rough country that way. It may take a while. Let's get the cattle that are here bunched again. We'll have to wait until it's lighter to go after the others. It's too dark to do much right now," Clint said when Daniel had finished.

The cattle were nervous and edgy and kept rolling their eyes fearfully and trying to run away from the smell of blood. Amy helped gather them up and take them to the water hole to drink. After the cattle had drunk their fill and had calmed down some, the men herded them back to an open area to graze.

The sun was just coming over the horizon as they headed out to look for the missing cattle, leaving a few of the men with the remainder of the cattle.

Amy pulled some jerky out of her pocket and ripped a piece off with her teeth, wishing for a warm breakfast. Grubby had pressed the jerky into her hand as she rode from camp.

At least I have something to eat, she thought.

Anders, who was riding in front of her, turned his head and said, "First full day out and already we've got trouble."

"Yep. Good thing the boys were paying attention or we might have lost a lot more cattle," Amy replied.

Anders nodded. "I noticed the cattle were getting a little more restless when I heard Daniel's shot. A minute later, a huge wolf ran right in front of Sky Blue and grabbed a calf." He grinned. "I shot that one."

Amy chuckled. "And I suppose you're gonna skin it and keep the hide?"

"Maybe." Anders grinned. "I might even sleep under it. Let me guess what you're about to say: gross!"

"How smart you are!" Amy laughed. "You can have all the skins you want. I'll leave them hanging on my wall. Or better yet, on the animal!"

"Guess you'd better take off your boots then," Anders told her. "They're made of leather, which comes from a cow, in case you didn't know."

"Thanks for that valuable information. I think I'll keep my boots," Amy told him laughingly.

"Suit yourself!" He grinned.

Tye, who had been listening, chuckled. "You two are about the funniest pair I've ever met. Are you ever going to grow up?"

"If by growing up you mean stop joking and having fun, I guess not." Anders said.

"That goes for me ,too." Amy agreed. "If you stop joking and havin' fun, well, it's just not any fun!"

"Well said, Amy." Daniel rode up beside her. "While you've been laggin' behind here, we've been doin' some trackin'. Looks like most of the cattle headed into a box canyon while about thirty headed up that ridge."

"Oh, great!" Amy groaned as she surveyed the rough trail leading up the rock strewn ridge.

"Oh, great is right." Daniel nodded. "And we get the honors of trailin' them. Uncle Clint is taking the other men with him into the canyon while you three come with me."

"This should be interesting." Amy winked at him. "I can't believe Dad would trust us on a mission like this."

"Uh-huh. Funny, Amy." Daniel rolled his eyes. "Come on. We've got a long ride ahead of us."

They started up the steep trail, and Amy leaned forward in her saddle to help Bannie along.

The rocks did not hold a trail well, but occasionally Amy saw a track or two. When they reached the top of the ridge, they stopped to rest the horses while Daniel studied the terrain below them.

"Where do you think they are?" Amy asked him.

He shook his head. "I can't say. I guess the best thing to do is to keep following the tracks. I think they'll lead down into that ravine, but I'm not seeing any sign of the cattle below." He shrugged and started his horse down the trail again.

The trail was narrow so they rode in single file. Daniel first, then Amy, Tye, and Anders. Amy leaned back in her saddle and tugged slightly on the reins to steady Bannie on the downhill. It was very steep, but there was more dirt, which gave traction and held more tracks. Daniel's horse moved along quickly.

When they reached the level, Daniel veered sharply to the left.

Amy thought she knew what he was doing. From the top of the ridge, she had seen a large water hole. The cattle would be thirsty and would head for water. Instead of tracking them, Daniel was heading straight for the water hole and hoping to pick up tracks from there.

"You headin' for the water hole?" Tye asked just then.

Daniel nodded. "Yep. They haven't had any water since last night, and this is the only water around."

The ground they were riding on now was rough and uneven. The horses moved slowly, picking their footing carefully.

Amy gave Bannie his head and concentrated on the ground, watching for tracks.

"Here's some tracks!" Tye called a few minutes later. "Looks like you were right, Daniel. They're headin' for water, all right!"

Sure enough, the tracks led them straight to the water hole. They watered the horses, then scouted around.

Anders picked up the trail leading away, and the others followed.

They stopped to rest in the shade of a mesquite bush a short while later. Amy dismounted, pulled out her canteen, and took a long drink.

Bannie bumped her gently and nickered. "You just had a drink!" she told him. "Can I borrow your hat, Anders?"

"What for?" he asked suspiciously.

She held up her canteen. "To give Ban a drink."

"You spoil that horse, Amy!" Anders shook his head as he handed her his hat. "Pretty soon he'll have you spoon feeding him!"

"I'm not that crazy!" Amy laughed. She poured some water into the hat, and Bannie slurped it up nosily.

Soon they were back on the trail. Daniel looked anxiously at the sun. "This is taking longer than I though,." he muttered, wiping the sweat from his face. "They sure covered a lot of ground fast."

The tracks were getting fresher now, and the weary group urged their horses on.

"There they are!" Amy shouted as they rounded a bend in the old cow path. The cattle were standing under a rock outcropping that offered some protection from the burning sun.

"Yeah!" Anders cheered.

Daniel looked relieved. "You three hold them. I'm going to climb that rock and find the best way out of here. It'd be mighty hard to take them out the way we came in." he said. He tied his horse to a bush and hurried up the slope.

The cattle were dozing contentedly under the rock outcropping, so Amy rode over to the boys and handed them each a few pieces of jerky.

"Save some for me!" Daniel hollered from above.

"We will," Amy called up to him.

Anders and Tye promptly settled down in the shade with their hats over their faces to rest, so Amy busied herself checking the horses for cuts, scratches and bites.

When Daniel returned, he said. "There's an opening just beyond those rocks." He motioned with his hand. "From what I can see, it should come out right where we want to be."

"Let's go then." Amy picked up her reins. "I'll drive them out."

Expertly she drove the reluctant cattle out of the shade of the outcropping. As they rode toward the opening Daniel had seen, the cattle moved along at a steady pace, giving Amy time to talk.

"I can't believe something like this happened on our first day out," she said.

"Well, I wish it hadn't happened," Daniel said sullenly.

"I think it was kind of fun," Amy told him.

"What?" Daniel exclaimed. "You thought this was fun?"

"Sure!" Amy grinned. "Adventure! Sounds like something out of a book when you think about it, wolves killing cattle, a scattered herd, cowboys—and cowgirls, of course—taking chase into remote areas. Sounds pretty good, huh?"

"Oh, just dandy, Amy. I'd want to do all that on my summer vacation." Daniel rolled his eyes.

"Thank you!" Amy laughed.

"If all girls are like you, oh, brother!" Daniel groaned.

"Aw, Daniel," Amy protested.

"I'm kidding, I'm kidding!" He gave an exasperated sigh.

"I bet your wife will be just like Amy," Anders broke in.

"Oh, no, she won't be! I can't take two of them!"

The four laughed together.

They were nearing the river, and Amy strained her eyes to catch the first glimpse of the camp.

Then she heard someone shouting and turned to see Daryl galloping toward them from the river.

He drew rein as he reached them. "I was just coming to look for you," he said. "The boss was getting worried since you were gone so long. We got the cattle from the canyon and they went on ahead, left me here to meet you. I'll help you drive them to catch up."

It was mid-afternoon when they caught up to the rest of the herd. The two groups quickly merged back together, and Amy went back to riding drag.

She was tired, having gotten little sleep the night before, and the sun was warm, making her sleepy. Bannie was doing his job, so she closed her eyes and dozed in the saddle.

Suddenly, her head came up with a jerk, and with a yell she grabbed for the saddle horn, missing completely. She tried to regain her balance, but it was no use. Bannie was headed one direction, and she in another.

She flew through the air and landed hard. "Ow!" She sat still for a moment, then stood to her feet slowly. "I'll be one big bruise," she said to herself.

She heard someone laughing and turned around to see Daniel leaning over his saddle horn, grinning down at her.

"Now that was the funniest thing I've ever seen! What were you doin', tryin' to fly?" He shook his head with a chuckle. "You okay?"

"Sure. I'll be sore, but nothin' broken." Amy brushed herself off. "What happened anyway?"

"Calf broke from the herd," Daniel said as she swung up behind him on his horse. "Bannie went after it. Can't blame him none. He was just doin' his job."

He turned his horse toward Bannie, who was sedately following the herd.

When they reached him, Amy slid down and whistled.

The gelding nickered and trotted over, tipping his head to one side to keep from stepping on the reins.

Amy gathered them up and stepped into the saddle. "Thanks for giving me a lift," she told Daniel.

"Don't mention it." He tipped his hat with a mock bow before riding away.

Amy grinned wryly to herself. *I'll probably be the talk of the camp tonight*, she thought grimly. Then she chuckled. *I must have looked funny, though, flyin' through the air!*

By three o'clock, Amy was completely exhausted. She had gotten up very early, and it had been a long day. She sat wearily in the saddle. Clint had told them they would be traveling late to make up for lost time that morning.

Bannie seemed to be tired, too. This was his second day of hard riding. Clint had warned Amy to be easy on Bannie and had reminded her that he was still young and not ready for as much work as an older horse.

"Sorry, boy. I wasn't thinking this morning when I saddled you up." Amy patted Bannie's neck. "I'll give you the day off tomorrow."

It was already dark when Clint finally called a halt.

Amy had never been so eager to stop at the end of the day. Wearily, she unsaddled Bannie and took him to drink at the nearby waterhole.

She stood watching him for a moment as he splashed and pranced about, thinking how nice it would be to have so much energy at the end of the day, and then she turned him loose with the cavvy and walked slowly toward the wagon.

Amy had just slipped off the gelding's halter and started toward the wagon when she heard a chuckle and turned to see Anders and Tye grinning at her.

"We heard you tried to fly today." Anders bit his lip to keep from laughing.

"I didn't *try* to fly. I guess Bannie decided I needed a lesson in aviation," Amy retorted.

The boys roared with laughter.

"Daniel said you looked like a rag doll," Tye snickered.

"I'm sure I did. And of course, Daniel had to tell everyone." Amy rolled her eyes.

"He couldn't keep it to himself. It was too funny." Anders grinned. "You'll be the talk of the camp tonight."

"Thanks for reminding me," Amy said dryly.

They joined the others at the fire, and Amy seated herself beside her dad after filling her plate.

After a few minutes, Daniel spoke up. "Amy decided to try to fly today."

A few of the men snickered as Daniel related the story in detail.

By the time he had finished, Amy was red with embarrassment.

"So what suddenly made you want to fly?" Daryl asked with a smile.

"Maybe we should ask Bannie," Bo suggested. "It seems to have been his idea."

"You'll never hear the last of this," Cody told her.

"It's okay, Amy." Caleb came to her rescue. "We've all experienced that. I could tell a few stories about you boys." He glanced around the circle of faces with a meaningful look.

The men grinned but remained silent. They understood what Caleb was implying.

"Thanks Caleb." Amy gave him a grateful smile.

After supper, the men went to their separate tasks, and Amy and Clint were left alone.

Amy rested her arms on her knees and stared into the fire.

"Tired?" Clint asked.

Amy looked up briefly and nodded. "I'm not used to riding that many miles in a day."

Clint chuckled. "I know what you mean. I can remember the first time my dad agreed to let me come on a drive." He made a face. "I realized it wasn't all fun, but a lot of hard work. It made me appreciate my father and the hands more."

Amy nodded. "I guess it made me realize how hard my ancestors had to work. We really have a lot to be thankful for."

"We sure do," Clint agreed. "I'm glad you realize that. A lot of young people today take too much for granted. We need the youth to realize how this nation was won: by hard work, sweat, and most importantly, with the Lord's help." He gave her a warm smile. "Let's do our devotions, then you can get to bed. We have to get an early start tomorrow."

They read Proverbs 28 together, and then Amy crawled under the wagon and slid into her bedroll. Rio snuggled close and licked Amy's face.

"Cut it out, Rio!" Amy giggled. She pulled him under the blankets, grateful for his warmth.

Thank you, Lord, for keeping the cattle safe and helping us to find them. Keep us safe on our journey. Thank you for the lessons You are teaching Dad and me through Your word. Amen.

Chapter Eleven
Midnight Rider

Amy sat up quickly, bumping her head on the bottom of the wagon. She rubbed the top of her head. *What woke me up?* she wondered.

They had been on the trail a week. Things had gone smoothly, and no more cattle had been lost. Now, in the quiet of the night, Amy strained her ears for any unusual sound.

After a few minutes of silence, she noticed a commotion near the horse corral. Quietly she pulled on her boots and crept out from under the wagon. The soft ground muffled her footsteps, and she kept to the shadows as she made her way toward the corral.

As she got closer, she dropped to the ground and wiggled forward on her stomach.

She stopped when she reached the fence, watching and listening. The horses were all alert with ears pricked. Amy noticed that they were all staring toward a small grove of trees. She strained her eyes. A moment later, she saw something move.

Amy lay perfectly still, eyes and ears alert.

A few minutes later, she saw it again, and the horses in the corral moved restlessly.

As she watched, the head of a horse appeared out of the trees and she could faintly see the indistinct form of a rider. After a moment, they disappeared as suddenly as they had come. Amy lay still, waiting.

Suddenly, a hand was placed over her mouth. She gasped and fought desperately to free herself.

"Stop kicking, will you?"

Amy sagged with relief as Clint took his hand off her mouth and whispered grimly, "I hope you haven't scared our visitor away."

"Sorry," Amy murmured. "I didn't know it was you. Why didn't you say something?"

Clint lay down beside her. "I figured you would have screamed or something. What did you see?" he asked.

"A horse and rider in the trees." Amy told him. "The horse didn't look like one of ours. How did you know I was out here?"

"I was coming back from getting a drink at the creek when I saw you heading over here, so I followed. I was just about to come up to you when I saw something move. I thought it was a horse and rider, but I wasn't sure," he explained.

The horses moved again nervously. "Someone is certainly out there," Clint said in a low tone. "Let's hope it's just some passerby."

"At 2:30 in the morning?" Amy asked.

She felt her dad shrug. "Maybe."

They lay silently side by side for a long time but saw nothing. The horses were still alert and restless, but nothing presented itself.

"Looks like you scared whoever it was away." Clint got slowly to his feet. "Let's hope they're gone for good. You get back to bed. I'll ride out and see what's going on at the herd. Maybe the boys heard something out there. Goodnight."

"Goodnight. Be careful." Amy could barely distinguish her dad's face in the darkness.

He nodded and walked swiftly away. Amy stood looking after him for a moment, then she turned and walked toward the wagon.

She was walking quickly and had almost reached the wagon when suddenly she tripped over something soft and fell to her knees.

"What's the big idea?" someone sputtered.

"Uh-oh!" Amy's shoulders shook with silent laughter. She recognized the voice. In the darkness, she had not seen Anders where he was sleeping on the ground. His voice was slurred with sleep as he sat up and looked around in bewilderment.

"Sorry." Amy bit her lips to keep from laughing.

"Amy? What are you doing wandering around this time of night? Stop laughing! It isn't funny." Anders shoved his blanket back disgustedly.

"I beg to differ with you," Amy said, laughing.

Tye, who had been sleeping nearby, sat up yawning and rubbing his eyes sleepily. "What's going on?" he asked.

"That's what I'd like to know!" Anders stared at Amy. "Why did you wake me up like that?" he demanded.

"Sorry," Amy said again. "I didn't mean to."

"Oh, sure!" he said sarcastically.

"I didn't!" Amy protested.

"Well, if you didn't, explain what you were doing out here in the middle of the night."

Anders and Tye listened wide eyed as Amy explained.

"Are you sure you weren't dreaming?" Anders asked when she finished.

"I'm sure. If you don't believe me, ask Dad in the morning," Amy told him.

"Well, this looks like adventure for you, Amy." Tye grinned.

Amy smiled. "Good. Keeps life interesting. But we'd better get back to bed. We've got a long day tomorrow."

"Yeah, chasing a dream." Anders scoffed.

Amy shrugged. "It wasn't a dream." She turned and walked away, being very careful not to step on anything else.

As she stretched out on her blankets under the wagon, she heard a horse coming into camp. She watched Clint dismount by the fire, then glanced at her watch. *Three o'clock*, she thought. *Almost time to get up.*

Two hours later, Amy rolled out of bed. The sky was just starting to turn pink as she splashed cold water on her face from the bucket that hung on the wagon side.

Grubby was already fixing breakfast, and some of the men were riding out to relieve those on watch.

After she washed up, she went to find her dad. He was saddling Morgan by the corral when she found him.

"What happened last night?" she asked.

Clint slipped the bridle on as he replied, "There certainly was someone out there. The men said they thought they'd heard something too. The cattle were restless and wouldn't settle down to graze." He frowned. "And Rio stayed with them all night."

"That's strange." Amy ran her hand over Morgan's shoulder. "I did notice that he was missing. He usually stays with me."

Clint nodded. "I thought it was strange, too. If it was someone just passing by, they sure hung around. As far as who this person is or what they're doing, " he shrugged, "that's something for you to figure out: the case of the mysterious midnight rider!"

Amy grinned. "Detective Amy Kentworthy!"

Clint chuckled. "Well, come on, detective. It's time for my breakfast. Seriously though, I want you to keep Rio with you at all times until we figure this thing out. We'll post extra men around the cattle, too, just to be sure."

He left her to talk to Daryl, and she hurried to saddle Buck. She put on his nosebag, tied him to the wagon, and walked over to the fire.

Grubby was just serving up. She filled her plate with his delicious bacon, biscuits, and eggs and found a seat.

"Hello, Detective Kentworthy!" Anders appeared beside her.

"I think you've talked to Dad." Amy laughed.

Anders grinned. "I'm still sore from you kicking me in the ribs last night."

"Your reaction was funny, Anders," Amy told him, chuckling.

"Well, it was a very painful experience. I thought I was being attacked by wolves or something."

The men within hearing chuckled, and Amy knew that Anders had already spread the story around.

"Rest assured, Anders. There was only one wolf in camp last night, and she isn't generally very ferocious!" Clint said, chuckling.

"Well, I wouldn't be too sure about that." Anders made a face as he rubbed his side.

When the men finished eating, Clint gave them their instructions. "Keep an eye out for anything unusual. It's probably nothing, but it never hurts to be careful." He grinned at Amy. "I'm afraid that means no snoozing or flying lessons!"

There was a general chuckle as the men got to their feet.

Amy smiled. "I won't ... if I can help it!" She faked a yawn.

"Go ahead and snooze while we're workin'." Daniel told her. "It got you back yesterday."

"It sure did." Amy rubbed her shoulder and made a face.

Amy gave her empty plate to Grubby, put her bedroll in the wagon, then mounted Buck and loped out to the herd.

"You may be a good horse, but you can't hold a lantern to Bannie," she told him.

Buck tossed his head proudly.

"Gonna disagree with me, huh?"

Buck tossed his head again and nickered and Amy laughed as she patted him on the neck.

"Are you so lonely that you've taken to talkin' to your horse?" Daniel and Anders rode up beside her.

"Well, without you two homely fellows to talk to, I most certainly am." Amy laughed.

"Man, I sure hope my wife isn't like you," Daniel declared, shaking his head. "With you on one side and her on the other, I don't think I could stay a sane man!"

Anders laughed. "I hope my wife is just like Amy. It'd take someone like her to keep up with me and be able to laugh at my ever-ready jokes."

Amy chuckled. "Thank you for the complement, Anders. Daniel, you'll be hard pressed to find a girl to suit you in our community. Most of the girls I know are just like me."

"Just my luck," he groaned.

They laughed together. The cattle were beginning to move out, so Amy left them and took her position.

Amy managed to stay awake all day and was constantly on her guard. Several times she thought she saw movement among the rocks and bushes, but upon closer scrutiny, nothing appeared, and she laughed at herself for being so jumpy.

It was late afternoon when Anders rode over to her.

"Your dad wants me to ride near you," he told her. "Daniel found the tracks of a lone horse not far into those rocks. Someone is following us. I'm going to ride off a little, but I'll have my eye on you. So will Daniel. Keep Rio close." Without waiting for her to reply, Anders wheeled his horse and rode a short distance away.

Amy halted Buck and whistled to Rio. He came bounding over, his tongue lolling out of his mouth, a happy, contented look on his face. As he drew close, she waved her hand, and the dog leaped up in front of her. She chuckled to herself. "I'll bet this wasn't what Anders meant when he said to keep you close, boy, but it'll work just the same."

Half an hour later, Amy felt eyes watching her. Nervously, she glanced around, but saw no one. "Stop it!" she commanded herself aloud. "You're just gettin' plain nervous. Get a grip!" She took a deep breath and concentrated on keep the cattle bunched and moving.

When she heard a horse coming up behind her at a fast pace a few minutes later, she felt her throat tighten. Leaning down, she pretended to straighten her stirrup and glanced under her arm.

She breathed a sigh of relief and turned as Daniel rode up. "You scared me," she told him. "I thought you were the mysterious rider."

Daniel laughed. "Nope. Just your old cousin Daniel." Then his smile disappeared. "I saw Anders talkin' to you. Did he tell you about the tracks?"

"Yes." Amy nodded.

"I found more tracks. I think there's at least two following us. I'm convinced of it now. Something is going on."

"Do you think it could be rustlers?" Amy asked.

Daniel groaned. "I hope not. You've had enough trouble with guys like that."

Amy shrugged. "I guess we wait and see."

Daniel turned his horse. "That's all we can do. Let's hope it's someone with no ill intentions."

They rode for several more hours with no sighting of the riders. Amy was beginning to hope they had left when a movement attracted her attention. She fixed her eyes on the spot where she had seen the movement.

A few minutes later, a horse and rider had appeared in plain view on a hill not far away.

Amy turned in her saddle and waited until she caught Anders's eye, then glanced toward the hill. He nodded and rode over to Daniel. Amy watched them for a few minutes, and when she looked back toward the hill, the horse and rider were gone. She did not see them again, but she felt uneasy.

They made camp earlier than usual that evening. Amy felt tense and nervous. Clint put the cattle and cavvy near each other and placed extra men around them. He started to help set up camp but soon rode off alone.

When he came back, his face was grave. Amy, Anders, Tye, and Daniel waited to hear what he had seen.

"I don't know what to think. The men say their horses keep looking around and acting nervous." He was silent a moment, thinking. Then he straightened. "Daniel, you're a good tracker. I want you to find these men and trail them. See what you can learn. I'd go myself, but I need to stay here. Be careful," he warned.

"Sure, Uncle Clint," Daniel agreed.

"Can I go with him?" Anders asked quickly.

Clint thought a moment, then nodded. "All right. Daniel may need help."

Amy packed some food in their saddle bags and waved as they rode off. Then she joined her dad by the wagon.

He leaned wearily against it. "I hope this isn't another case of rustlers," he told her. "I've had enough of that. I wish this country was more open. It would be easy to sneak in here. Too easy." He was silent a moment, then levered himself away from the wagon. "I'm going to do a little scouting around. Be back soon."

Amy watched as he rode away. *Dear Father, please help all this to turn out all right, and please keep everyone safe.*

Amy busied herself helping Grubby get supper ready. She gathered wood, hauled water, and mixed bread dough. When she had finished everything he needed her to do, she sat on the wagon tongue to oil her bridle while she waited.

As the shadows deepened and the sun slipped below the horizon, she glanced anxiously in the direction the men should come from.

Finally, Anders rode in. His horse was lathered and breathing hard. Amy tossed the bridle aside and ran to meet him. "I'm so glad you're back!"

"Where's your dad?" he asked as he dismounted.

"I don't know. He rode out just after you left and hasn't been back since," Amy told him. "Where's Daniel?"

"I don't know. We separated to follow different sets of tracks, and when he didn't show up at our meeting place, I came back. Figured I'd better get your dad to help me look."

"What did you find?" Amy asked.

"I followed a trail for a ways and came upon a log cabin in the woods. The tracks I followed led straight there, but there were also fresh tracks leading away. I wish your dad were here." Anders set his saddle on the ground, then leaned against his horse, staring into the distance.

"Did there seem to be any one home?" Amy asked.

He shook his head and led his horse away. When Clint rode in ten minutes later, Anders told him about the tracks and the cabin.

"I'm worried about Daniel. He didn't come back to the spot where we'd agreed to meet," Anders told him.

"Why did you separate?" Clint asked.

"The tracks split and went in different directions. Daniel said we could cover more ground before dark if we separated," Anders explained.

Clint shook his head. "Next time, stay together. It's more important that you stay safe than to cover more ground."

"Yes, sir." Anders nodded.

Clint sat down on the wagon tongue and rested his chin in his hand.

"Aren't you going after Daniel?" Amy asked.

Clint looked up at her. "No, it's too near dark, and there's no telling what's happened. If he isn't back in an hour, I'll get the men together, and we'll go out. He probably went farther than he thought, so I'll give him some more time to get back."

"Okay." Amy was worried, but she knew that if her dad was really worried, he'd go out and try to find

Daniel right away. *Keep Daniel safe, Lord*, Amy prayed as she settled down to wait.

When Daniel rode in half an hour later, Amy hurried to meet him.

"What happened to you?" she gasped as he dismounted and limped toward her. His clothes were torn and muddy, and he was scratched and bruised.

He grinned. "I was riding across a creek when my horse slipped and fell." He rubbed his knee. "I think it struck a rock."

Clint stepped from behind Amy. "Glad you made it back, Daniel. We were gettin' worried. Did you find anything?"

Daniel shook his head. "Nothin' much. From the looks of the tracks, he's been hangin' around camp." He shrugged. "I couldn't tell much more than that. What did you find, Anders?"

He listened thoughtfully as Anders told about the cabin and fresh tracks.

"There might be some connection," Anders said as he finished his story. "Maybe it's their hideout or something. I did find one spot where whoever it was had dismounted. The footprints were small, like a boy. If they are young, they may try something foolish tonight. Maybe we can set a trap. Hopefully it's just a curious youngster."

Clint nodded. "Let's hope you're right. We don't have much time to set anything up. Let's put our heads together and think of something."

Several hours later, Amy crouched behind a bush not far from camp. She could see the flickering light of the fire dancing on the wagon cover. The deepening shadows moved eerily with the breeze, and the wind whispered among the bushes with a lonely sound.

Amy waited tensely. A coyote howled in the distance. She jumped, then laughed at herself for letting her imagination run away with her.

Then she listened more closely. *Something sounded suspicious about that coyote*, she thought. When the coyote howled again, she was sure.

It's a signal. Amy whistled softly.

Daniel, who was to her left, whistled back. He had heard it, too.

Amy leaned forward and scanned the horizon. The silence seemed to stretch on forever. Then she heard a rustle to the right and slightly behind. Slowly she turned her head. A large shape appeared against the sky. It appeared to be a horse, but she could not distinguish a rider.

Suddenly there was another noise to her left. She turned and saw a crouching figure silhouetted against the starry sky.

Quietly, she crawled toward it. The figure began moving slowly toward camp. Amy noted that whoever it was, was small. *Either a very short man or a kid like Anders suspected*, she thought.

The figure was heading straight for the camp. Amy followed him, being careful not to make a sound. The person had circled around to approach the camp from behind the wagon. Amy laid flat on her stomach behind a boulder at the edge of the camp. She held her breath. Now there were two figures discernible against the sky.

Grubby and Arty were sitting near the fire, talking and laughing.

Amy watched as the two figures moved steadily till they were next to the wagon. She caught a movement out of the corner of her eye and quickly swung her head around. Two tall figures followed the first two. Crouching low, Amy followed. She reached them just as Clint's voice rang out. "Stay right where you are."

The first two figures froze. Clint and Daniel leaped forward and pushed them into the circle of light. As Arty and Grubby rose to their feet, Anders and Tye appeared from the other side of the clearing. Amy walked around the corner of the wagon, then stopped short in surprise. *They aren't any older than me!* Curious, she stepped closer.

Daniel had one boy by the arm, and Clint had the other. The boys looked pale and frightened.

"Why were you sneaking into our camp last night and following us today?" Clint asked sternly.

The taller one answered, "We live in a cabin south of here with our mother and sister."

Amy glanced at Anders. Maybe it was the cabin he had found earlier.

"You didn't answer my question." Clint frowned. "Why did you follow us?"

The boy shrugged. "Somethin' to do. We've been traveling."

"What's your names?"

"I'm Tyler, and he's Brent."

"Your last name?" Clint asked.

Tyler looked sullen. "White."

"How old are you?"

"I'm fifteen, and Brent is fourteen."

"What were you going to do at our wagon tonight?" Clint asked next.

"Just lookin' around," Tyler answered.

Clint didn't look convinced. "How far is your cabin?"

"About a day's ride," Tyler answered.

Clint was silent a moment. "Since you're here, you might as well stay the night ... on one condition," he added as Tyler's eyes began to dance. "You behave yourself."

The boys nodded, and Tye struck up a conversation with them as Clint drew Amy, Anders, and Daniel aside. "I want you to keep an eye on them," he said in a low tone. "I don't believe they are telling the truth, and I don't trust them. That Tyler is a sly one. Keep an eye on him."

When Daniel and her dad had gone, Amy turned to Anders. "What do you think of our visitors?" she asked. "I don't think they were doing it just for fun."

Anders shook his head. "I don't think so either." He shrugged. "Just keep an eye out. It wasn't their cabin I found, either, if they're telling the truth about the distance."

They were both silent a moment, then Amy grinned. "Hey, Anders."

"Hey, what?"

"I know someone who thinks they're an owl."

"What?" Anders stared at her. "Who?"

"I guess that makes two people!" Amy laughed.

"Aw, Amy."

"Got ya!" Amy chuckled.

"Quit yer braggin'." Anders grumbled. "And don't you tell anyone!"

Amy chuckled. "You've enjoyed yourself at my expense before," she reminded him.

Anders grinned. "I guess so."

They joined Tyler, Brent, and Arty by the fire.

"Decided to join us?" Arty asked with a smile.

"I reckon sorry company is better than none." Amy grinned.

The boys chuckled. "Where are you headed next?" Tyler asked Arty.

Arty jerked his head in Amy's direction. "Ask her. She's the boss's daughter."

Tyler looked expectantly at her.

"We're on our way down south," she answered evasively. She felt hesitant about telling him too much.

"Mexico?" he asked.

Amy shook her head. "Texas."

"Where in Texas?"

Amy hesitated. "I'm not sure of the town." *Well, that was the truth. I wonder why he's being so insistent.*

Later that evening, Amy showed Tyler and Brent where they were to sleep. Anders and Daniel were going to take turns watching them.

"Better you than me stayin' up all night," Amy told them.

"Huh. Just 'cause I'm a guy I get to lose sleep!" Anders grumbled.

Amy laughed. "Well, I think you'd much rather lose sleep than have me watch them, right?"

"Absolutely," Anders agreed. "If they did try anything, you'd probably scream or something and mess everything up."

"Boys." Amy shook her head. "Will I ever understand them?" As she crawled into her bedroll after reading her Bible by the light of the fire, she thanked the Lord for helping them to catch the mysterious riders.

Please help us to find out what they are up to and keep everyone safe, she prayed.

Chapter Twelve
Lurking Shadows

After breakfast the next morning, Anders pulled Amy aside. "You'll never guess what happened last night," he said excitedly.

"What?" Amy asked curiously.

"I took first watch, and around midnight, Tyler and Brent got up and snuck out of camp. I woke Daniel and we followed them. They stopped about a quarter mile from here and crouched down behind a boulder. They seemed to be waiting for something ... or someone. Anyway, Daniel and I waited and watched. Not too long later, we heard horses coming. Tyler stood up and whistled. A few minutes later, three men rode up and dismounted. Tyler greeted them, and they sat down together." Anders paused a moment. "We managed to get a little closer and could hear what they were saying. One of the men spoke.

'Now boys, here's the plan. There's goin' to be good money in this for you if you do it right. In the morning, you leave the camp. Make up some excuse. Follow them all day and don't be seen. We'll be watching to make sure you do it right.' His voice was mean and from what we could see in the dim light, his features were hard and cruel. He went on.

'When they've made camp and have the cattle off grazing, sneak in as close as you can get without being seen and start shooting and yelling. We want the cattle to scatter and run. We'll be waiting not far away. As the cattle run away, we'll gather them up. Meet us at the usual place. We'll settle up then.'

'All right,' Tyler told him.

'Now get back to camp before you're missed.'

"Boy, did I want to laugh at that!" Anders chuckled. "The three men rode off, and we followed the boys back. We both went to sleep then because it was obvious they weren't going anywhere."

"Wow! Sounds like you had a full night." Amy shook her head. "Did you tell Dad?"

Anders nodded. "Yep, we told him. We'll be passin' through Red River City about noon today and he's goin' to get the marshal to help tonight."

"But if the rustlers see him talkin' to the marshal, they'll get suspicious and either hightail it or do something desperate." Amy frowned.

Anders grinned. "Nope. That won't happen. The marshal's office is in the back of the general store. Your dad is goin' to act like he's there to get supplies, which he is, but he'll also be talkin' to the marshal."

"But what about when the marshal comes to camp?" Amy asked.

"Your dad's gonna have him act like a traveler just passin' through, and he's gonna ask if he can spend the night with us."

"Smart!" Amy smiled.

"Sure, it's smart. Your dad thought it up ... with a little help from me!" Anders grinned.

"You scamp!" Amy laughed. "But wait a minute, how did he know about the marshal's office?"

"I gave him that valuable piece of information. My uncle lives in Red River, and he took me with him when I was visiting once. He had to see the marshal on business," Anders told her.

They talked for a few minutes, then Anders left to saddle his horse, and Amy went in search of her dad. He was talking to Tyler and Brent.

"I guess we'll be on our way," Tyler was saying as Amy walked up.

"All right." Clint nodded. "But let me warn you, other people would not be so tolerant. Be careful who you choose to play your game with."

A hint of a smile flitted across Tyler's face. He nodded to Amy, and then the two left to get their horses.

"Hi, Dad," Amy said when they were gone.

"Oh, hi, Amy. You're so little I didn't see you," her dad teased.

"I'm not that small!" Amy protested.

"Almost." Clint smiled. "Did Anders tell you about last night and our plan?"

Amy nodded. "Uh-huh."

"Pretty smart, isn't it?" Clint asked with a twinkle in his eye.

"Sure." Amy grinned. "Has to be if you thought it up!"

Clint grunted. "Smart aleck!"

Laughing, Amy turned away to see Tye walking toward her, leading Bannie. He was groomed and saddled. "Thank you, Tye. You didn't have to do that." She gave him a smile.

"That's okay, Amy. I was glad to do it." He handed her the reins and walked quickly away. Amy adjusted her stirrups and stepped into the saddle. Bannie tossed his head and pranced around.

"Feeling good after a day off, huh?" Amy patted his neck. She turned Bannie around and headed for the herd. She leaned forward and let him run. It felt good to feel the wind whipping through her hair. Bannie squealed and gave a buck. Amy laughed and grabbed the saddle horn.

Suddenly, she heard a shout. Tye and Anders came galloping up beside her.

"Race you to that rock!" Anders shouted.

"I'll beat you there!" Amy shouted back.

"Yeah, right."

Amy raised herself up in the stirrups and dug in her heels as Tye gave a cowboy yell that spurred the horses on.

Slowly but surely, Bannie pulled ahead. Amy whipped past the rock a full length ahead of the others. Gently she pulled on the reins to slow Bannie down. As the boys drew their horses in, Amy grinned in triumph. Anders raised his arms in mock surrender.

"Say it." Amy grinned.

"Say what?" Anders asked.

"You know what," Amy told him.

"All right, all right. Bannie won." Anders shook his head.

"Come on, guys. They'll be waiting for us," Tye reminded them.

As Amy rode up to the herd, Daniel called to her. "Did you hear what happened last night?"

She nodded. "Anders told me."

"Did he or Uncle Clint tell you the plan?"

"Just the part about the marshal."

Daniel rode closer. "Uncle Clint thinks the best way to do it is to let them get the cattle and hightail it. Then we'll follow them to their hideout and get them. No one should get hurt that way."

Amy nodded. "That sounds good."

"Well, got to get on the job." Daniel waved as he rode away. Amy helped herd the cattle to a waterhole to drink, and then they pushed on. Several hours later, Amy was surprised when the herd stopped and began to circle. She strained to see up ahead, trying to figure out what the problem was.

"Amy!" Daniel called to her. "Uncle Clint wants you."

Amy waved to let him know she had heard and wheeled Bannie around. "You wanted me?" she asked when she reached her dad.

"The boys will stay with the cattle. You're coming into town with Arty, Grubby, and me," he told her.

"Okay." Amy could see the chuck wagon in the distance, already heading for town. She whistled for Rio, and he bounded up beside her.

After a few minutes, Amy said, "It was kind of quiet this morning."

Clint chuckled. "So you like it when there're rustlers around, eh?"

"Well, not exactly." Amy smiled. "I just like it when there's something unusual going on."

"Just like your mother. She was the kind of woman who loved adventure. If something wasn't happening, she'd make something happen. I think other people thought she was a little strange, but that was the part of her personality I loved. Never was a dull moment around her." Clint's eyes held a faraway look. "There never was an ordinary day for her. Every day was special. Each day was a treasure." He looked over at Amy. "You are like her in that. Just after she died, I couldn't stand to watch you doing anything. You are that much like her." He smiled. "Now I'm thankful for that part of you. It brings her memory closer to me."

Amy smiled back. "I'm glad I'm like her."

When they reached the town, Amy tied Bannie to the hitching post and helped Arty down from the wagon. He slowly made his way toward the store with the aid of his crutches.

Clint joined them just outside the door. "Grubby is going to get the supplies we need while I go talk to the marshal. I'd like you two to stay by the door and watch for anyone suspicious coming in."

"Okay," Amy agreed. There was a chair on the boardwalk just outside the door, and Arty seated himself on it while she leaned against the wall.

"Nice little town, isn't it?" Arty commented.

Amy nodded. "Yep, it's a real Western town, that's for sure." she pulled something out of her pocket and held her hand out toward him. "Let me see your hat, Arty."

"What for?" he asked as he pulled it off and handed it to her.

"I made you a new stampede string," she explained. Expertly, she slipped the old one off and put the new one in place. "It's out of horse hair. The black is from Bannie, the white from Renegade, and the red is from Kalila, Tye's horse," she told him as she handed his hat back.

"Thanks a lot, Amy." Arty grinned as he pulled his hat back on. "I've been needing a new one."

Amy tipped her head and studied him. "Looks good on you," she commented after a moment.

Arty blushed and ducked his head.

Amy had just finished helping Grubby load up the supplies when her dad walked out. He was in a hurry to get back to the herd, so he and Amy rode ahead of the wagon.

"So it's all worked out?" Amy asked once they were out of town.

Clint nodded. "He'll bring two deputies with him and make out like he's a traveler passin' through. When the action gets going, we'll need all the hands, but I want you, Anders, Daniel, and Tye to stay together."

"Okay," Amy agreed. They rode up a small hill and the herd came into sight.

"Go tell the boys that," her dad instructed her as he rode away with a wave of his hand.

Amy headed for the wagon first. "Got any jerky, Grubby?" she called as she drew alongside.

"Sure." Grubby handed Arty the reins and reached beneath his seat, drew out a paper sack, and tossed it to her.

Amy caught it and stuffed it in her saddlebags. "Thanks!" she called over her shoulder as she rode away.

She found Anders and Tye together riding drag. "Dad said to give you a message," she said, tossing them each a piece of jerky.

"What would that be?" Anders asked around a mouthful of jerky.

"Mind your manners, young man!" she scolded, giving him a playful shove. "He said that when things get going tonight, he wants the three of us and Daniel to stay together."

"Oh, I see." Anders nodded. "He figures I'm the most responsible and he wants me to look out for you two."

Amy turned Bannie around. "Since you insist on insulting me ..." she said, laughing.

"Did you give Arty the stampede string?" Tye asked before she could leave.

Amy turned back and nodded. "I gave it to him while we waited for Dad at the store. He really liked it."

"Good." Tye bit off another piece of jerky.

The cattle were restless that afternoon, and the men had their hands full keeping them bunched and moving.

"Someone is following us. The cattle are so nervous and keep trying to run away. Sure wish I had their sense of smell. Maybe then we'd know what it was and where it is," Anders commented to Amy.

Amy laughed. "You'd better watch what you wish for; you just might get it, along with their looks!"

"I'll take your advice. I'm homely enough as it is!" Anders grinned.

"You're not homely." Amy chuckled."On the contrary ..."

"Knock it off!" Anders interrupted, embarrassed.

That evening, Amy rode into camp with a calf across her saddle horn. The little fellow was too young to keep up, so her dad was going to sell him in town the next day.

Amy tied the calf to the wagon while she unsaddled Bannie. She heated some water over the fire and stirred in a can of powdered milk. As she passed with the pail of milk, Arty called, "There goes the milkmaid!"

Amy made a face and continued on her way. She was struggling to make the calf understand that his supper was in the pail and not on her fingers when Anders walked up.

As she turned to say something to him, the calf butted the pail, and Amy was instantly covered in warm milk.

"Ugh!" she sputtered, stepping back quickly.

Anders chuckled as he took the pail from her. "I'll feed him while you clean up." he offered.

"Thanks." Amy didn't leave immediately but stood watching as he approached the calf. Dipping his fingers into the milk, he let the calf suck on them while he lowered them into the milk. Soon the calf was sucking the milk hungrily.

"It's the calf whisperer!" Amy declared. "You'd think I would have known how to do that, living on a ranch!"

Anders chuckled but said nothing. Amy swiftly changed her clothes and washed the dirty ones in a pail of warm water.

After she rinsed them several times, the milk smell finally disappeared, and she spread them on a rock to dry.

She joined the others by the fire just in time to hear her dad say, "Everything must go on as usual. We can't give the rustlers any reason to suspect anything. Not a word to anyone about what is really going on."

Amy filled her plate from Grubby's large dutch ovens and found a place to sit.

"Are you ready for your adventure?" Daniel asked as he seated himself next to her.

Amy nodded. "I just hope no one gets hurt."

A little while later, Amy was sitting on the wagon tongue, oiling and cleaning her saddle, when there was a noise just outside the circle of light. Amy leapt to her feet as three men on horses appeared out of the darkness.

"Howdy," one of them said as he dismounted.

Clint stepped forward to greet them. "Howdy yourself."

"We were just passin' through and saw your fire," the first man said. "We wondered if you'd allow us to stay the night."

"That's the marshal," Anders whispered to Amy.

"Certainly," Clint told the man. "I'll show you were you can put your horses."

Amy giggled as her dad led the men toward the corral.

"What's funny?" Anders asked.

"Listening to them talk like that when we know it's just an act," Amy told him.

Anders chuckled. "Yeah, I guess it is funny."

"Why do they have to talk like that?" she asked.

Anders shrugged. "I guess in case any of the rustlers are nearby listening."

"But they're all out by the cattle," Amy said.

Anders grinned. "That's where they said they'd be, but how do we know that whole speech last night wasn't a trick to get us to let down our guard?"

Amy nodded. "I see what you mean. Maybe they were trying to throw us off as to their whereabouts so we'd be less cautious."

"Right. It always pays to be careful."

After the men had cared for their horses, Grubby served them the food he had been keeping hot. Amy listened as they talked to Clint.

"Where you headed?" one of the deputies asked.

"Ranger City, Texas," Clint told him. He explained about the rustlers that made the journey necessary.

The men continued to make small talk. The conversation seemed a bit strained.

Amy noticed the men looking around, their eyes darting about nervously. *I wonder why they look nervous. Surely they've done things like this before*, she thought, puzzled by their actions.

As Amy prepared to go to bed a little while later, Clint called after her. "Don't forget you have second watch."

"I won't," she called back. *I'm going to saddle Bannie, but not for second watch*, she thought to herself.

She slipped under the rope of the makeshift corral and whistled softly. Bannie nickered and nuzzled her pocket. Amy chuckled as she pulled out the apple she had deposited there. She saddled him and fastened on his nose bag.

Leaving him tied to the wagon, she crawled into her bedroll. The frosty night air had a nip to it. Amy pulled her blankets up to her chin. Rio snuggled close. Amy giggled when a warm, wet tongue reached out to lick her face. "Cut it out, Rio," she scolded. "I'm trying to sleep."

She lay awake for a while thinking of the coming events. She prayed for the safety of everyone involved, and then she drifted off to sleep.

Chapter Thirteen
Treasure Hunt

"Wake up, Amy," a voice whispered urgently. Amy sat up and rubbed her eyes. "What's going on?" she asked bewilderedly.

"It's me: Anders. Get up and follow me."

Amy was instantly wide awake. Throwing back her blankets, she slipped on her boots, shivering in the cold air. The wind had picked up, and it moaned as it swept through the rocks and trees.

Amy followed Anders as he crawled out from under the wagon and crouched in its shadow. She could see Bannie and Sky Blue tied a few feet away.

"Just a few more minutes," Anders whispered.

Amy nodded, then realized Anders couldn't see her in the dark. "Right," she whispered back. She was tense and watchful.

Tye appeared out of the darkness and crouched down beside her. The whole camp was dark and appeared empty, but Amy knew the marshal and his men, along with Clint and the hands, were waiting in readiness.

Suddenly shrill yells and gunshots shattered the silence.

Anders leapt up, pulling Amy to her feet. Tye ran for his horse while Anders swiftly untied Bannie and held him steady while Amy mounted. Then he swung into his own saddle and took off at a gallop, Amy and Tye right behind him. Amy felt rather than saw the presence of the other men as they galloped along. She pulled Bannie up short as they neared the riders and what was left of the herd.

For a few minutes, all was confusion as riders with bandanas over their faces charged through the herd, firing their guns into the air and yelling. Amy struggled to control Bannie as he plunged and bucked, trying to run. Desperately, Amy held on until the noise subsided and the horses began to calm down.

"Is anyone hurt?" Amy asked as Daniel appeared at her side.

In the dim light, she saw him shake his head. "Doesn't look like it. They got away with most of the herd."

"Aren't we going to trail them?"

"Listen!" Daniel told her. "Uncle Clint is explaining now."

"We can't let the rustlers know we're on their trail. Grubby, Arty, and Derek will stay at camp to make it appear that we are there. The rest of us will wait here a while, then we'll track them."

Derek immediately headed back to camp. Grubby had already made a large fire, and Amy could see him moving around.

"I'm hungry," Anders announced a moment later.

"That's no surprise." Amy pulled a sack out of her saddle bags and handed a sandwich to him, Tye, and Daniel.

"Oh, thanks. You're always well prepared, aren't you?" Anders bit into his sandwich.

"I have to be because you aren't!" Amy teased.

Anders chuckled. "We make a great pair. You're organized, sensible, sweet, pretty, and smart ... all the things I'm not!"

Amy laughed. "You're funny, Anders. Did you know that?"

He shrugged. "It's true."

"I agree with Anders," someone said out of the darkness. Clint appeared beside them. "You're very humble, Amy."

"I agree," Anders said with his mouth full.

"All right, all right. Quit gangin' up on me!" Amy laughed.

"All right, kids. We're getting ready to leave. Stay together and out of trouble!" Clint reminded them.

"Have no fear, sir. I will take the best care of the lady," Anders said, grinning.

Amy swatted him. "Come on, Mr. High and Mighty. I'm rarin' to go."

Amy tingled with excitement and anticipation as they wound their way through the trees and rocks. *Keep us safe, Lord, and help us to catch the rustlers and get the cattle back. In thy name, Amen*, she prayed.

The path was steep, and Amy had to concentrate on staying on Bannie. The trees grew close together, and she struggled to ward off branches that slapped her face and pulled at her hair and clothes. It was a dark, windy night, covering up any noise their horses' hooves made on the rocky ground, but it made for difficult riding. Their progress was slow but steady.

An hour later, Amy pulled Bannie up and listened as her dad gave directions. The men spread out and surrounded the small clearing in which the rustlers' cabin stood.

Amy tied Bannie and joined Daniel, Tye, and Anders behind a clump of bushes and watched as her dad, the marshal, and the three deputies surrounded the cabin.

The clearing was silent except for the moaning of the wind. No light showed from the windows, and it seemed to be void of life.

As she waited, a sudden thought came to Amy. *I wonder how the marshal knew where this cabin was*, she wondered. *It's in such a remote place; why would he know where this was? And how did he know the rustlers would be here? He didn't seem to be following tracks. It was more like he was following a well-known trail.*

She tucked that away for further consideration at a later time and turned her attention back to the men by the cabin. The marshal stepped up to the door and struck it with the butt of his rifle.

"Come out with your hands up!" he called.

Amy could hear angry shouts from the men inside. A light appeared in the window, and then the door opened. Three men stepped out, followed by Tyler and Brent, their hands held over their heads. Tyler had a six-gun strapped to his waist. The marshal stepped over and jerked it from the holster.

"You won't be needing this," he told him, handing the gun to one of his men. The marshal searched the men, then handcuffed them and turned them over to his deputies. Clint turned toward the trees and waved his arm.

"That's our 'okay' signal." Amy got to her feet and hurried toward the cabin. By the time Amy reached her dad, the marshal had taken a lantern and was searching the cabin.

"Why is he doing that?" she asked him.

"There was a bank robbery in town last month. Grubby heard about it as he was getting supplies earlier and suggested this may be the same gang. I suggested that the marshal should check it out," Clint explained.

Amy nodded. "May I go in and look around?"

"Sure, if you stay out of his way," Clint agreed.

Anders and Tye followed her inside.

"What are you doing?" Anders asked.

"Just lookin'," she told him.

The cabin was smaller inside than it looked. Along the right wall were three bunks. A large, stone fireplace was on the back wall. A cupboard was along the left wall. Some shelves held provisions.

"They must have been staying here for quite a while," Amy thought.

Three canvas bags were lying in front of the cupboard. A rough table and four chairs were in the middle of the room. Three rifles and two six-guns lay on the table. Amy walked along the walls, tapping them every few feet.

Nothing hollow there. She checked the cupboard and floor.

As she knelt to look under the bunks, she heard the marshal say, "Looks like they're either innocent or have spent the money already. Let's get them back to town."

"Wait!" Amy cried.

The marshal frowned and turned around.

"I think I found something," she told him.

"Really?" he came over slowly and knelt beside her.

"There's a board sticking up under here." She wriggled forward on her stomach. "I need some light."

The marshal pushed a lantern toward her. Amy pulled the board up and stuck her hand in the hole it revealed. She felt something touch her hand. She grasped it firmly and pulled it up into the circle of light. It was a canvas bag.

The marshal took it and opened it. "Yep, it's the money." His voice sounded dry. He stood and started for the door.

"Wait a minute." Clint stepped forward. "According to what Grubby heard, there should have been four bags total."

The marshal hesitated. "I only heard there was one," he said finally. "But go ahead and look."

Amy reached back into the hole and pulled up one, two, three bags.

As she crawled out from under the bunk, Anders cheered, "Way to go, Amy!"

The marshal looked the money over. "Looks like it's all here," he grunted. "Nice job, young lady. I believe there's a reward attached to this money." He counted out two hundred dollars and handed it to Amy.

Amy stared at him. "Two hundred dollars?" she asked in amazement.

"Are you goin' to let me borrow some?" Anders asked.

"Anders! You amaze me!" Amy scolded.

"I'm kidding, I'm kidding!" Anders held up his hands.

While they were talking, the marshal hauled the bags of money outside. When he finished, he held his hand out to Clint. "Thanks for your help. We've been after this gang for a long time."

Amy thought she heard one of the deputies snicker, but when she turned to look at them, they all wore serious looks.

"Thank you." Clint shook the marshal's hand firmly.

The marshal nodded to Amy, then turned and walked outside.

Clint turned to Amy. "I still can't believe you found that money when the marshal couldn't."

"That's what bothers me. He didn't seem glad I found the money." Amy frowned. "He didn't do a thorough job in the first place, then he seemed upset when I found it. And I can't really believe he didn't know how much money there was supposed to be."

"He probably just didn't like being outwitted." Anders chuckled.

Clint frowned. "Something does sound suspicious, but we really don't have anything to go on. He was probably just upset that you found the money."

Amy shrugged. "You're probably right." Then she grinned. "As always! What am I going to do with all that money, anyway?"

"Give it to me!" Anders grinned.

"We'll put it in the bank in Durango as soon as we get home. In the meantime, I'll keep it for you." Clint said.

Amy handed him the money, and they started for the door.

"The marshal was happy to catch those men. They've been terrorizing the area for months. Well, let's head back to camp and get some sleep," Clint said.

"Will we move on tomorrow?" Amy asked as they joined Daniel and Tye and the hands by the horses. The marshal and his men had already left.

Clint shook his head. "I have some errands to run in town tomorrow, and we're all tired. Let's get the cattle and get back to camp."

The sun was just peeping over the horizon when they rode into camp. Amy glanced at her watch. *"5:00 AM. I've been up since midnight. Only two hours of sleep. No wonder I'm draggin'."*

Wearily she slid to the ground and started untacking Bannie. He tossed his head and pranced about when she removed his bridle. "You've still got some energy left," she remarked.

Grubby handed her a plate of hash browns and bacon and a cup of coffee when she reached the wagon.

"Thanks, Grubby." She smiled as she took it from him. She ate it slowly, staring into the fire.

"Amy?"

Amy shook her head to clear her thoughts.

Her dad was smiling at her from the other side of the fire. "You've been stirring the food around on your plate for the last five minutes. I think you need to go to bed." Amy smiled. "I guess I do." She told him goodnight, handed Grubby her plate, and crawled into her bedroll.

Home, sweet home, she thought with a chuckle. *Under a wagon. A lot of people in the world would be glad for even a wagon over their heads. I'm fortunate to have so much.*

She snuggled down under the blankets, shifting around to find a comfortable spot. The sounds around the fire died down, and once again the camp was quiet.

*****

Amy sat up and rubbed her eyes. *How long did I sleep?* she wondered. The sun was up and shining brightly. She slid out of her bedroll and reached for her watch.

"Ten o'clock!" she exclaimed. "I haven't slept that late in a long time." As she pulled on her boots, she was startled by Anders's voice.

"Lazy bones lie abed!" He was hanging over the edge of the wagon, grinning at her.

"You're such a tease, Anders." Amy rolled her eyes at him. "Where is everyone?"

"Your dad rode into town with Grubby, Arty, and Tye. Daniel is sittin' beside me—"

"How did Arty go with his cast?" Amy interrupted to ask.

"He doubled behind your dad. Back to what I was saying before I was so rudely interrupted ..."

Amy heard Daniel chuckle.

"And the rest of the hands are doctoring some of the cattle and doing odd jobs." Anders swung to the ground, and Daniel followed him.

Amy rolled up her bedroll and joined them. "Any grubs around, or do I have to starve?" she asked.

Anders grinned. "You might if I get to the pot first!"

"Oh, no, you don't!" Amy gave him a playful shove.

Anders stumbled against a saddle lying on the ground, fel, and came up sputtering. "All right. Let's lay our enmities aside and eat. I'm too hungry to get revenge!"

"Fine by me!" Amy laughed. "Let's call a truce."

"Sure." Anders agreed.

"I don't think that will last long." Daniel chuckled as he followed them to the fire. "You'll stop long enough to eat. Then, well, I think you can imagine the rest."

After eating, the three hauled the dishes down to the creek. Daniel washed, Amy rinsed, and Anders dried.

They were almost finished when Amy glanced at Anders just in time to see a grin flit across his face.

He's up to something, she thought to herself.

A few minutes later she handed him a cup to dry and turned back to her rinsing.

Suddenly Anders dipped the cup into the creek and threw the water at Amy. Amy grabbed another cup and retaliated. Daniel got his share of the soaking, as did the previously dry dishes.

Treasure Hunt

As Amy and Anders flopped onto the ground ten minutes later, laughing breathlessly, Daniel grinned at them triumphantly. "I told you it wouldn't last long." He picked up the towel Anders had dropped and began re-drying the dishes.

Amy shrugged, grinning. "We were just having fun."

Just as they finished drying the last dish, Tye joined them. "What happened here?" he asked, noting the wet, muddy clothes of the three. Without waiting for an answer, he said to Amy, "Your dad wants you."

Amy tossed him her dishtowel and went to find her dad. Clint was nowhere to be seen when she got back to camp. Amy asked Grubby if he knew where he was.

"I think he went out to the herd," he answered.

"Thanks." Amy went to the corral and whistled. Bannie threw his head up and charged toward her, scattering the other horses right and left. The big gelding lowered his head for the bridle, and then Amy hopped on bareback.

"Amy Susanna!" Clint shook his head in disbelief as Amy rode up to him. "I thought you had learned your lesson about doing daft things like that!"

Amy was standing on Bannie's back, holding the reins in her teeth and balancing as he walked.

She grinned as she dropped down. "Guess I haven't, Dad. You wanted to see me?"

"Yes, I did. You, Anders, Tye, and Daniel are going with me to see Tyler and Brent's mother."

"Why are we going there?" Amy asked curiously. "Do you know where she lives?"

"The marshal asked me to tell her of Tyler and Brent's arrest. Go get the boys, and a saddle, too!"

"Sure thing!" Amy laughed. Half an hour later they were on their way.

"Are you sure you know where you're going?" Amy asked as they rode single file up a rough trail. "We just keep going around and around and around!"

Clint chuckled. "The marshal told me to keep following this path until we come to a small cabin in a clearing. I guess it's the only house along this path unless you go past it."

"Okay, but it's your fault if we get lost!" Amy warned.

Clint raised his hands. "I'll take the blame!"

They had been riding for two hours or more and Amy was just about to tease Clint about getting them lost when the group rounded a curve in the path and a small cabin came in sight.

"Hello!" Clint called as they rode up.

A tall woman appeared in the open doorway. "Hello. What brings you up this way? We don't usually get visitors."

Clint dismounted and stepped forward. "I'm Clint Kentworthy, and I've come to talk to you about your sons, Tyler and Brent."

The woman looked at him a minute in silence, then said softly, "Please come in."

As Amy tied Bannie to the hitching post, she remarked to Daniel, "She's beautiful, isn't she?"

Daniel grinned. "Sure, but she can't hold a lantern to you!"

Amy gasped and blushed. "Hush, Daniel!"

Daniel laughed. "You are way too modest, Amy. You really are pretty."

Amy shook her head at him. "You shouldn't flatter people, Daniel."

"I'm not flattering you. I'm serious," he insisted.

"Well, you can stop complimenting me or whatever you want to call it and follow the others," Amy told him.

As they entered the cabin, Amy noticed a young girl sitting in the corner with some sewing in her lap.

"This is my daughter, Hannah, and I'm Jessica, Jessica White," the woman introduced herself.

"Nice to meet you both," Clint said.

"I'll get you something to eat." Jessica turned toward the cupboard.

"Please, don't bother," Clint said quickly. "We won't stay long."

"It's no bother," Jessica assured him. "And I know the nature of the trail you had to come up to get here."

She bustled about the little cabin, getting them coffee and biscuits.

"Thank you, Mrs. White," Amy said as Jessica handed her a plate.

"Oh, just call me Jessica, dear, and you're very welcome." Jessica smiled warmly at Amy, and Amy smiled back.

Once they were all served, Clint cleared his throat. "I'm afraid we haven't come on a pleasant errand, Mrs. White," he began.

"Please, call me Jessica," Jessica broke in.

"Well, then, Jessica." Clint cleared his throat. "We have met your boys. I guess there is no way to put this tactfully: they were arrested for rustling last night."

Jessica did not show any emotion, but Hannah gave a little gasp. "Please tell me everything," Jessica said quietly.

Clint told the story very simply. "I'm sorry, Jessica."

"Thank you for coming to tell me, Mr. Kentworthy. I—"

"Clint, if you please."

"Very well. Thank you, Clint, for coming to tell me. I've been expecting something of the kind for quite a while. Ever since their father died, well, I just can't keep them in hand." Jessica sighed.

"How long ago was that?" Clint asked.

"Well, let's see." Jessica thought a moment. "Hannah was two then, so about ten years ago."

"Why do you still live here alone, Jessica? It's so far from anyone. Not near any help."

Jessica smiled. "My late husband loved this place so much, I just haven't found it in me to sell it yet. As for being far from anyone, it is, but I trust in God to protect us and send help when we need it."

"You're a Christian?" Clint asked.

Jessica nodded. "I have been for many years. And you?"

"Yes, we are Christians, too." Clint nodded. "I guess the covering should have given it away."

"Yes, I should have noticed that as well. Now, enough about me, are you new here? I don't recall seeing you before," Jessica asked curiously.

Clint explained about the cattle drive and why it was necessary.

"And it was you, Amy, who heard the noise and went for help? How wonderful! Sometimes I wish I was a girl again," Jessica exclaimed. Then she addressed Clint, "And your wife? Did she stay on the ranch?"

Clint shook his head. "My wife passed away five years ago."

"Oh, dear. I'm sorry I asked. Perhaps, Amy, you would like to write to Hannah and me. It does get a little lonely up here sometimes." Jessica smiled.

"I'd enjoy that." Amy nodded.

Jessica wrote down her address and handed the paper to Amy as Clint got to his feet. "We'd best be going. It's a ways back to camp, and it's getting late."

"Thank you again for stopping by. We'll go to town tomorrow and see about the boys." Jessica offered him her hand.

Clint took it. "My pleasure," he assured her.

As the group rode away, Jessica and Hannah waved from the doorway.

Amy waved back until they rounded a bend in the trail and rode out of sight.

Clint was silent on the ride back to camp, and Amy smiled to herself.

I think I know why Jessica gave me that address, and I'm pretty sure I know what is on Dad's mind right now. Jessica seems sweet, and I think Dad is lonely without Mom. And Jessica's a Christian, too. That's something. You don't find women like that all over the place. I wonder if Dad would actually write to her. What would it be like to have a mother again? Not to say, two brothers and a sister. It would take some getting used to for sure. I'll just have to pray that God works it all out His way. Your will, not mine, Lord. If this is right for me and Dad, then I'll be happy with whatever happens. She prayed as they rode down the mountain path.

Chapter Fourteen
The Dust Storm

Three weeks later it dawned a bright and clear Sunday morning.

Amy went humming and whistling about her chores with Rio tagging along at her heels. She was in a hurry to get finished before it was time for church.

They were going to have church right out in the open, just as they had been doing for several weeks. They had stopped at a ranch house to buy some eggs and flour the day before, and the rancher, Joe Atwell, had offered the use of his pastures and corrals. Men and cattle alike were enjoying the day off. Usually even on Sundays the men had to take turn herding the cattle, but today everyone would be able to attend the service because the Lord had provided them with pasture for the cattle and horses.

It was almost time for church to begin when Amy finished her work. Clint had invited Joe and his family to join them, and they readily accepted. Amy seated herself next to Daniel on the ground in the shade of the wagon. It was a hot day, and Amy was glad they didn't have to travel in the heat.

"Let's start with a couple of songs. Anyone have a suggestion?" Clint asked, looking around.

"Amazing Grace," Anders suggested.

The group lifted their voices in praise, the music blending with the sounds of nature.

They sang several more songs, and then Clint stood up to preach. "Let's turn to James chapter one, verses five and six to start with."

When the rustle of pages stopped, he read the verses aloud. "If any of you lack wisdom, let him ask of God, that giveth to all men liberally, and upbraideth not; and it shall be given him. But let him as in faith, nothing wavering. For he that wavereth is like a wave of the sea driven with the wind and tossed. For let not that man think that he shall receive any thing of the Lord." He paused a moment, then explained the verses. "I think this first verse is saying that we should not hesitate to ask God for help and wisdom. If we are uncertain about what to do in a certain situation, God is clearly saying that He will give us wisdom if we ask for it. It says here 'that giveth to all men liberally.' If we ask for it, He will give it liberally. But in verse six it says that we must ask in faith, nothing wavering, meaning that we should ask believing that He will do as He promised. Verse seven says that that man, meaning the man whose faith wavereth, shouldn't expect anything of the Lord. The Lord wants us to trust and believe in Him. Let's read verse eight now."

When the service was over, Amy stood up stiffly and went to put her Bible in the wagon. As she did so, she heard her dad inviting the Atwells to join them for lunch. *I hope they'll accept,* she thought. *Their children are so cute.*

Joe thought a moment. "All right. Thanks for the offer."

His wife, Sara, took the four towheaded children to the house to wash up, and Joe joined Clint and the other men under the willow trees by the creek.

Anders walked up beside Amy. "You know what I'd like?" he asked.

"What?"

"Some of your chocolate chip cookies, ice cream, and light fluffy bread. I'm getting tired of the heavy stuff Grubby makes."

Amy nodded. "I have to admit I am, too, but it's hard to make nice bread and other stuff in the little stove we brought. You'll have to endure it for a little while longer."

"Come'n get it!" Grubby called.

Amy watched as Sara helped the children get their food. "Aren't they cute?" she asked Anders as they waited their turn.

Anders shrugged. "Whatever you say."

Amy shook her head. "You like children better than that. I know you do," she told him.

Anders just grinned and shrugged. After getting her food, Amy joined the others under the trees. Joe was commenting on the dry weather as Amy seated herself.

"We've been having small dust storms about once a week. Not real big ones, but it's enough to cause a lot of problems. Cattle have been getting dust pneumonia. Been droppin' fast." He shook his head. "Hope it rains soon. I won't have enough feed for winter if this keeps up."

"How many head have you lost?" Clint asked.

"About twenty. Mostly the calves, but I noticed a few older steers wheezing yesterday." Joe sighed. "I'm not a big rancher. I can't afford to lose a lot of cattle or to buy feed."

"We'll be praying for you," Clint told him. "I'm sure there's other ranchers' hurting too."

Joe nodded. "There are. Quite a few. I'd appreciate the prayers."

When everyone finished eating, Joe made an announcement. "Since you invited us to eat with you, we'd like to treat you all to some ice cream. If you will come with me, Clint, we'll carry the things out here."

"Thank you, Joe," Clint said. "I hardly expected this. It will be a nice treat."

Amy nudged Anders, who was sitting next to her. "Looks like you'll be getting your wish sooner than you thought."

"Guess so." He grinned.

Clint and Joe were soon back. Clint was carrying a hand-crank ice cream maker, and Joe had a large box. When the men set the things down, Sara poured the mixture of cream, sugar, and eggs into the metal cylinder and filled the area around it with the ice and salt.

The Dust Storm

Tye took the first turn cranking and turned it over to Anders when his arm got tired. Daniel and Amy helped too. Half an hour later the ice cream was ready. Amy helped Sara dish it up, and then she joined Anders, Tye, and Arty by the creek.

She took a bite of the thick, creamy treat as she sat down. "Mmmm!" she closed her eyes, savoring the rich flavor. "This is so good! It's been so long since I had ice cream."

"I've only had it once before in my entire life. That was when my parents were living." Arty licked his spoon. "Pa took us to town and treated us. Ma had to convince me to eat it. I thought it was snow."

"My uncle is really rich and his family have ice cream every night after supper," Tye put in.

"Every night?" Amy stared at him in disbelief. "I can't even begin to imagine that!"

"We only get it at birthdays or special events because it takes so much sugar and takes so long to make," Anders said. "Boy, would I love to have it every night!"

After they'd finished eating, Amy took their bowls back to the wagon, then returned to the boys.

Daniel joined them by then and was chatting with Anders.

Amy listened to them for a few minutes, then suggested, "The creek looks mighty inviting, boys. How about doing some wading?"

"Yeah, Amy!" Anders cried. "Come on, Arty. I'll help you down to the bank. You can have at least one foot in."

With Daniel on one side and Anders on the other, Arty managed to get down the steep bank. Amy was the first one in because she had already been barefoot.

"No fair!" Anders yelled as she leaped into the creek and promptly threw a handful of water at him. He yanked off his boots and slid down the bank. Daniel and Tye joined them, and soon all four of them were engaged in a water battle.

Arty took his share of the splashing, but his pant leg kept his cast reasonably dry.

After playing in the creek for a while, Amy got a book and read to Arty while Daniel dozed nearby. Anders and Tye decided to explore down the creek a ways.

Soon Arty dozed off, and Amy shut her book. Quietly she got to her feet and went back to the wagon where Grubby was starting supper. He looked up as she approached.

"Where is everyone?" she asked looking around.

"Your dad and the hands went with Joe to look over the stock, and Sara went to the house with the children. Want to help?" he asked.

"Sure." Amy caught the bowl he tossed her.

"Mix some biscuits then." Amy put her book in the wagon and got out the sourdough starter.

Grubby watched her as he peeled the potatoes. "Don't beat them so hard," he told her. "You've gotta stir 'em just enough to mix 'em or they don't taste right."

Amy mixed the batter until everything was blended, then handed the bowl back to Grubby.

"Now wash your hands and round up them pesky youngsters, wherever they are."

Amy grinned as she walked away. She knew that was Grubby's way of getting rid of her so he could make supper the way he wanted to. It was a long-standing feud between them. He appreciated her help, Amy knew, but preferred to do things his own way.

Supper was a jolly time. The mouth-watering smells drifted on the breeze from the huge dutch ovens. Grubby had made steak, bacon, biscuits, hash browns, and coffee, and the Atwells had promised more ice cream.

After eating her supper, Amy sat on the wagon tongue and finished her ice cream, watching as the sun slowly began to sink below the mountain peaks. The sky was streaked with gold and purple and pink.

That'd make a pretty picture, Amy thought.

She stood up and climbed up into the wagon, then pulled a thin package out of a box.

When she climbed back out, she found Anders sitting on the wagon tongue.

"Took my spot, did you?" she asked, giving him a gentle push.

Anders laughed and slid to the ground. "What ya got?" he asked.

Amy pulled a sheet of paper and a pencil out of the package. "Drawing stuff. I'm going to draw the sunset," she told him.

Anders looked surprised. "I didn't know you could draw."

"My mom taught me. She loved to draw." Amy drew a few lines on the paper. "I haven't done it in a long time. Guess it reminded me too much of her. For the first little while, Dad didn't like to see me draw, so I kind of stopped. I brought this stuff along 'cause I figured I might want to start using it again."

"Hmm." Anders watched as the picture took shape. Amy's pencil moved busily across the paper, drawing the mountains, sunset, creek, and camp.

When it was finished, she held it up for Anders to see.

"That's really good." He took the paper and studied it. "That's really good, Amy. You could probably sell some of your drawings."

"Oh, I don't know about that." Amy shook her head.

Anders still held the drawing. He seemed reluctant to give it back. Finally he asked, "May I keep this, Amy?"

"Sure." Amy gave him a puzzled look, but Anders tucked the picture away without saying anything.

Just then, Daniel called to them. "Come on, guys! We're going to do some singing. Get your guitars."

Amy put her drawing things away and got her guitar out of the wagon.

The others had gathered around the fire. Joe had his fiddle, Daniel had his banjo, and Anders and Amy had their guitars.

"Anyone have a song?" Clint asked.

"'The Master's Call,'" Daniel suggested.

"That'll be a solo, Daniel," Anders told him.

"Sorry, not happening."

Joe led out on the fiddle, and the rest joined in.

The evening passed quickly, the frogs and crickets adding their voices to the music. The firelight danced, and the creek gurgled nearby. They sang "Cattle Call," "Old Cowboy's Lament," "Riding Down the Canyon," "I'd Like to be in Texas," and many more. When they finished singing, Clint closed the evening with a chapter from the Bible and prayer. Then the Atwells said goodnight and returned to the house while the others began getting ready for the night. Amy saw her dad heading out to check on the cattle, so she walked out to join him.

"Been a nice day, hasn't it?" he remarked as she walked up.

She nodded. "Sure has." She leaned on the fence and stared out over the herd.

"It was a blessing not to have to herd the cattle today. The Atwells were very generous to let us use their pasture and to treat us to ice cream." Clint grinned down at her. "I think the boys were especially glad about the ice cream part."

Amy chuckled. "Yep. They sure were."

They talked for a while more, and then Clint turned toward the wagon. "Well, let's go back. Everything looks fine out here. We'll be heading out early tomorrow."

*****

Everyone was up bright and early the next morning. Breakfast was hurried and the men had the cattle bunched and ready to go while Grubby was still packing up. Amy was helping him harness the mules when she noticed Sara coming across the lawn.

"Good morning, Sara." Amy greeted her warmly.

Sara returned the greeting, then shyly handed her a small package. "To remember us by," she said. "We enjoyed yesterday very much."

Amy opened the package and pulled out a small, tatted doily. She knew enough about tatting to know that it was very well made.

"Thank you very much, Sara. I will keep it always. Maybe we will meet again someday?"

Sara understood Amy's meaning and nodded her head. "Yes. Perhaps not on this earth, but we will surely meet again."

Amy smiled. "I'm glad, Sara. Thank you again." She waved as Sara returned to the house, then tucked the doily into the wagon and went to saddle Bannie. The black gelding was full of spirit after his day off.

"Settle down, Ban. I can't tighten the cinch with you dancing around like that," Amy told him.

Bannie whinnied and tossed his head.

"No backtalk. You're as bad as a kid!" Amy gave the cinch one last tug and swung into the saddle.

The hands were pushing the cattle toward the gate, but Tye and Anders sat talking on their horses a little ways off. Amy suddenly grinned mischievously and stepped Bannie up into a lope.

When she got close, she let out a whoop and galloped Bannie straight at them.

Anders grabbed his saddle horn with a surprised yell as his horse leapt to the side, then bolted after the black gelding. Tye had seen her coming and was ready for his horse's reaction.

When Amy and Anders managed to stop their horses, Tye loped up behind them.

"That was so funny!" Amy leaned over her saddle horn, laughing.

"What's the big idea, Amy?" Anders sputtered as he struggled to keep his excited horse still.

Amy grinned. "You've done the same thing to me before. Besides, you looked half-asleep so I had to wake you up for the day."

"Uh-huh. Good excuse for just plain meanness," Anders grumbled.

Tye broke in. "It was pretty funny, Anders, you have to admit. You looked hilarious grabbin' for that horn! I'd have done the same thing Amy did if I'd have thought of it."

Anders opened his mouth to reply, hesitated, then shut it again and rode off.

"He's not really mad is he?" Tye asked when Anders was out of earshot.

Amy laughed and shook her head. "No, he's just pretending. By lunchtime he'll be so hungry he'll forget everything else."

"Good." Tye looked relieved. "I thought maybe we'd gone a little too far that time."

"Believe me, he's done the same thing to me I don't know how many times."

Someone called Tye's name and he rode off. Amy pulled her bandanna over her nose and mouth as she rode toward the pasture where the cattle were filing out of the gate.

Seven hundred head of cattle stirred up a lot of dust, especially when the weather had been so dry. It was early in the morning, but it was already getting hot. Heat waves rippled across the ground.

Amy fanned her face with her hand. The cattle filed slowly out the gate and onto the road. Amy followed them, then turned back to wave to the Atwells. Soon they were out of sight, and Amy turned her attention back to the cattle who were plodding steadily along, well accustomed to the constant walking. It was almost noon when Clint stopped the herd at a river so the cattle could drink.

As Amy stopped Bannie and swung to the ground, glad for the chance to stretch her legs, she noticed that the cattle were acting nervous and skittery. The horses seemed nervous, too. Rio whined softly as she led Bannie to the creek and dropped his reins.

"What's the matter, Rio?" The dog pressed himself against her. Amy patted his head, then pulled her canteen off her saddle and took a long drink. *Wonder why the cattle are so nervous*, she thought. She groaned as she remembered what had happened the last time the animals had been nervous. *It had better not be rustlers or wolves again.*

Suddenly she heard a shout.

Quickly she swung around, her heart pounding with apprehension.

"Look at the sky!" someone shouted.

Amy turned, and what she saw made her gasp.

A threatening black cloud loomed on the horizon and was rapidly approaching.

"A dust storm! No wonder the animals were nervous" Amy flung her canteen strap over the saddle horn and grabbed Bannie's reins.

The Dust Storm

"Amy!" Her dad suddenly appeared and pulled his horse up sharply beside her. "Dip your bandanna into the water and tie it over your face!" he had to shout to be heard above the increasing roar of the wind. "Take Bannie and get behind those bushes! They'll protect you some from the sand." He turned his horse and started to ride off.

"What about the cattle?" Amy cried.

"They'll have to fend for themselves—" The wind flung the rest of his words away.

A moment later, the storm hit with all its fury. Bannie bucked and plunged, fighting to be free, but Amy held on and pulled him away from the river.

Coughing and choking, she managed to get her bandanna over her mouth and nose. Through the swirling sand, she could see the shadowy forms of the men and horses.

"Lord, keep us safe!" she cried. Panic welled up in her throat. She stumbled and fell. Shoving herself to her feet, she laid a hand on Bannie's trembling neck and tried to get her bearings. It was impossible in that swirling world of sand. The wind shrieked and moaned. Amy flattened herself against Bannie, letting his body shield her from the stinging sand.

Finally, after what seemed like hours, the wind finally died down, and the sun began to shine through the dark clouds. Amy levered herself away from Bannie and pulled her bandanna off her face. Sand poured off of her. Bannie snorted and tugged on the reins.

"Still a little nervous, huh, boy?" Amy rubbed his neck to sooth him, then started toward the wagon, wading through the sand. To her relief, she saw dusty, dirty men coming from all directions. After a quick count, she saw that everyone was accounted for.

Something still feels funny, like something's missing. She thought hard, then, as she glanced around again, it hit her.

"Where's the cattle?" she asked her dad anxiously as he walked up beside her.

"Who knows?" he said grimly. "They ran when the storm hit." He ran his fingers through his hair with a weary gesture. "It's no use running after them like a chicken with its head cut off. Let's see if there's anything left to eat that isn't full of sand and come up with a plan."

"I'm going to wash up." Amy turned toward the river, then stopped abruptly.

Clint laughed at the look on her face.

"On second thought ... maybe I won't!" Amy made a face.

The water had turned a muddy, murky brown.

Rio trotted over to it, sniffed, then walked away. Amy returned to the wagon and tied Bannie to the corner.

Arty grinned at her from his perch on the wagon seat. "You're a sight, Amy."

"I'm sure I am." Amy rubbed her hand over her face. "Any better?"

Arty laughed. "Yeah. Now you've got a bunch of dark streaks across your face."

"I give up!" Amy shook her head. "You don't look much better." She held out her hand to him. "I'll help you down, then we can see if Grubby has anything for lunch."

Grubby did manage to find a few things that were still edible. The men ate hurriedly and in silence.

When they were finished, Clint told them to saddle fresh horses and spread out to look for the missing cattle.

Amy switched her saddle to Buck and strapped a six-gun to her waist before mounting. It was best to be prepared in rough country. Rattlers and wild cats abounded in the rocky hills. Her dad had taught her to shoot before she was ten years old. Buck was prancing about as Amy mounted. "Settle down, boy," she told him. "We've got some long miles ahead of us."

For several hours, Amy rode along the river, gathering up the drifting cattle as she found them. She relied on Rio and Buck to tell her where the cattle were hidden. There were many places for the cattle to hide out of sight. She could ride right past and not see them.

It was hot, tiresome, frustrating work. The cattle were still nervous and kept trying to break away. It was a difficult task for a long rider.

By the time Amy reached camp with the cattle she had gathered, she was very hot and tired. Anders and Tye greeted her as she rode up.

"You look just wonderful!" Anders teased as he helped her drive the cattle toward the rest of the herd.

"Thanks," she said shortly. "I feel just about as great as I look." She scanned the herd. "Looks like some are still missing."

Anders nodded. "Yup. It'll take a while to gather them all." He grinned at her. "Cheer up, girl! I don't think I've ever seen you so disgruntled!"

Amy sighed. "Sorry." She reined Buck around and rode away. It was very late when all the cattle had been gathered up and accounted for. Amy had never been so tired in her life.

"I hope nothing like this happens again for a long time," Amy said to her dad as they untacked their horses.

"Listen to the adventure lover!" Clint chuckled as he pulled his saddle off the horse.

Amy smiled wearily. "I think I've had enough adventures for a while."

"Well, you won't get away from them until this trip is over," Clint told her.

"I know. In the meantime, you'd better stay away from me for a while. I'm feeling grouchy!" Amy jerked the stirrup down.

"Oh, boy! I'll be sure to keep my distance! Your mother used to get grouchy once in a while and whoo-whee!" Clint chuckled. "I learned to leave the chocolates on the table and stay in the barn!"

Amy laughed. "Maybe I'd feel better if I had some chocolates!"

"Sorry, no store out here!" Clint grinned.

"That's all right. I think a good night's rest, without an adventure, is the cure," Amy told him.

"I agree." Clint gave her a loving look.

Chapter Fifteen
Finally There

For seven long weeks they continued their journey, crossing streams, rivers, and mountains; going through towns; and encountering many different people and situations.

One night, in early September, as they sat wearily around the campfire, Clint announced, "Two more days should see us to our destination, Lord willing. I don't know about the rest of you, but I'm ready to sleep in a real bed for a change!"

The men chuckled appreciatively.

"It has been a lot of fun, but also a lot of work," Amy said. "Sleeping on the ground, getting wet, cold, or hot by turns gets pretty old after a while. And no offense to you, Grubby, but I'm ready to eat something other than refried beans!"

There was a murmur of agreement from the men.

"Well, lassie, I have to agree with you." Grubby wrapped his hands around a steaming cup of coffee. "Bein' bounced around in the wagon all day doesn't agree with my old bones. Those mules don't pick the smoothest places to walk either."

"Maybe if you'd stay awake you could persuade them to take a smoother route," Arty said with a twinkle in his eye.

"Look here, laddie, I thought we had an agreement. Don't you go telling all my secrets or the boss might get the idea I've been slouchin' off." Grubby shook his fist at him.

Arty laughed easily. "I'm not scared to tell what I know now that I'm not ridin' with you anymore." Arty had gotten his cast taken off when they passed through the last town three weeks before, and now he was back to riding.

Later that evening, Clint and Daryl sat on crates by the wagon talking in low tones while Amy cleaned her saddle by the light of the fire and Anders mended the mules' harnesses.

"I'm so glad this trip is almost over," Amy remarked to Anders. She sighed. "But then we have to ride all the way back! I'm really tired of this drive, Anders. I just want to go home and sleep in my own bed!"

"Oh, cheer up!" he told her. "At least we won't have to drive seven hundred head of cattle. We'll be able to go faster then. And be thankful you don't have to live this way. There are some people that do, you know."

"I know. I'm sorry I complained." Amy put away her saddle oil and stood up. "Well, goodnight."

"Night." Anders grinned up at her and winked. "You'll have a smile for me tomorrow, right?"

Amy chuckled. "Sure."

Rio snuggled close to Amy as she curled up under her blankets. The September nights were beginning to get chilly, and Amy was glad for his warmth.

I am so glad this drive is almost over. It was a good experience and like Dad said, it helped me appreciate how hard my ancestors had to work. Anders is right: I should be thankful I don't have to live this way. I guess I was griping about it. There is something special, though, about waking up every morning outside, listening to the world wake up around you. You can really see God through the animals and plants that surround you. Thank you, Lord, for this opportunity to learn to know You in a new way.

*****

The next morning, Amy shivered as she threw back her warm blankets and rolled out from under the wagon into the gray, chilly dawn.

Still half asleep, she struggled into her coat and boots and put her bedroll into the wagon. As she crowded close to the warmth of the fire, Grubby handed her a cup of coffee.

"A brisk morning, eh, lassie?" he greeted her. "This ought to warm you up."

Amy grinned. "I sure need warmed up this morning. It hasn't been this cold for a while."

Clint was in a hurry to leave, so Amy grabbed some jerky and hurried to saddle Bannie.

As she led him out of the corral, she noticed he was unusually jumpy and excited.

"Settle down," Amy muttered. "I don't have time for this."

She finally got him saddled and started to swing up. The next thing she knew she was lying on the ground staring up at the sky and Bannie was standing several feet away, reins hanging.

"Are you okay?" Clint's concerned face appeared above her.

Amy sat up and flexed her shoulders. "Yeah, I'm fine," she grinned. "I think the only thing hurt is my pride."

Clint chuckled. "Maybe that's a good thing!"

Amy laughed. "Yeah, I guess so." She pushed herself to her feet but gasped as she took a step and grabbed her dad's arm.

"What's the matter?" Clint asked.

"Guess I did something to my ankle," she told him.

"Which one?"

"The left one."

Clint knelt beside her and his gentle fingers probed the sore ankle.

"Ouch." Amy winced.

"It's not broken, thankfully," Clint said as he straightened up. "Just sprained. I'll wrap it up, then you can ride with Grubby at least for today."

Amy groaned. "Do I have to?"

Clint chuckled. "Yes, you do. It won't be that bad."

"I can't believe this happened, and on the last day, too," Amy said as her dad helped her to her feet. She hopped to the wagon on her good foot and sat silently as Clint wrapped her ankle.

Anders rode up and grinned at her. "Look at the queen! Riding in the wagon while the rest of us have to ride in a saddle!"

"I assure you, I'd much rather be in your position," Amy told him.

Anders bowed. "That is quite an honor, my lady."

"Oh, stop!" Amy told him. "Did you happen to see exactly what happened? One minute, I was almost in the saddle, and the next staring at the sky."

Anders shook his head. "Nope. I didn't see what happened, but all the horses seem a little jittery this morning. Maybe it's the crisp air, or they could be looking forward to a barn!"

"Silly!" Amy chuckled.

Clint helped her onto the wagon seat, and then he and Anders rode away and Grubby climbed up beside her.

"So you decided to keep me company today, eh, lassie?" he asked with a twinkle in his eyes. "That's right kind of you. I get kind of lonesome now that the laddie's well and back to ridin'."

"Aw, Grubby, you know I'd rather be out there. My saddle's a lot more comfortable," Amy told him.

Grubby chuckled. "I don't blame you none, lassie. There was a day when I would have picked a saddle over the wagon seat, but now," he shook his head, "my ridin' days are over."

Amy limped around camp that evening. It really wasn't a bad sprain, and she pleaded to be allowed to ride the next day.

"It hardly hurts at all, Dad, and I'll be careful and keep it wrapped up," she told him.

Finally Clint relented. "Oh all right. You're as stubborn as your mother. Just don't come whinin' to me when it starts hurtin'," he said goodnaturedly. "We should reach the ranch by early afternoon, so you won't have to ride all day. By the way, did I tell you that Devon has a daughter your age?"

Amy shook her head. "No, you didn't tell me. What's her name?"

"I believe he said Roseann. But no boys!" he added with a grin as Anders joined them.

"Rats!" Anders rolled his eyes. "Guess I'll have to hang out with the horses if I want good company!"

"That's quite a compliment, Mr. Archer. No gentleman could have better manners," Amy said sarcastically.

Anders bowed. "Thank you, Miss Kentworthy. You flatter me."

Clint shook his head, laughing. "All right, you two, come along. Supper's ready."

*****

Daniel greeted Amy as she sleepily crawled out from under the wagon the next morning. "Hey, Amy. Looking forward to sleeping in a real bed tonight?" he asked.

Amy smiled. "Sure am." She limped over to the corral and whistled for Bannie, who came bucking and squealing to greet her.

"Come on, you old lug." She slapped him affectionately and slipped on his bridle. "Don't you make me fall again today you hear? Sure wonder what spooked you. Or maybe you were just acting up, huh?"

She saddled him and lead him to the wagon, then tied him to the corner of it.

Grubby handed her a cup of coffee and a plate of hash browns and bacon as she walked up.

"Last day of this fare for a while," Amy observed.

"Now, lassie, you insultin' my cookin'?" Grubby asked.

"Of course not, Grubby." Amy pretended to look shocked. "Merely stating that I'm ready for a change of diet."

Anders walked up beside her, and Amy grinned at him.

"Have you tired of the horses' company already?" she asked.

He tipped his head to the side and studied her. "Well ..."

"Just admit it. You know I'm much more interesting than them."

"Well ...," he said again, a smile playing around his lips.

"Oh, all right, I lose." Amy threw up her hands in mock surrender.

"Again." Anders grinned.

Someone chuckled behind them. "If I ever get bored I know where to come for entertainment!" Clint said.

"Thanks, Dad. I'm sure that's something I want to be remembered for." Amy rolled her eyes.

Clint chuckled. "Your mother always wanted to be remembered for that. She could find fun and laughter in almost any situation." He turned away. "Hurry and finish. I want to get going."

A few minutes later, as Amy was preparing to mount Bannie, Tye suddenly appeared beside her. "Maybe you'd better let me hold him while you get on," he suggested.

"That's a good idea," Amy agreed. "Thanks."

Tye held him firmly, but Bannie behaved himself and stood quietly as she got on.

As she rode out to the herd, Arty rode up beside her. "So you got a taste of what I did for six weeks." He slouched in his saddle and twiddled his thumbs.

Amy laughed. "Yep. I can sympathize with you now. I was sick of it after one day."

The rest of the morning went smoothly. They did not stop for lunch as Clint was in a hurry to get to the ranch before dark and they still had some miles to go. Most of them had prepared for this by stowing jerky in their saddle bags, but Anders, as usual, had not thought ahead, and Amy was obliged to share her jerky with him.

At about two o'clock, they passed the town of Ranger. Clint rode over to Amy. "We've got about ten miles to go. How's your ankle?"

"It's doing okay." She looked around. "This looks different than what I was expecting."

"Oh?" Clint raised his eyebrows. "How is it different?"

Amy shrugged. "I guess I was expecting to see less people and ranches."

Clint nodded. "I was here a long time ago, before I married your mother. It was sparsely populated back then. It certainly has changed. Lots more people have migrated here from other areas."

Several miles later, they stopped to water the cattle at a small creek. They hadn't passed water since early that morning, and the cattle were thirsty. Amy reined Bannie up the creek where the water hadn't been stirred up and slipped the bit out of his mouth, hung the bridle over the saddle horn, and bent to refill her canteen.

Without warning, Bannie suddenly waded into the creek and laid down.

"No, Bannie!" Amy cried.

Bannie rolled around and splashed the water with his nose, obviously enjoying himself.

"You brat! You're getting my saddle all wet!" Amy leapt into the water and grabbed the bridle, then looped the reins around his neck. By tugging insistently, she got him to his feet and led him out. On the bank, he shook and sent water spraying everywhere, then looked at Amy as if to say, "What did I do?"

"Oh, Bannie!" she groaned. "Now I've got to ride in a wet saddle and wet clothes."

With a sigh, she retrieved her canteen, slipped on his bridle, and swung into the saddle, grimacing as she felt the wet leather.

"What on earth happened to you?" Daniel exclaimed as she rode up. "Decide to take a bath or something?"

"Bannie decided to go swimming, and I had to wade in to get him. Did you know that wet leather feels terrible?" Amy sighed.

Daniel laughed. "Trust you to get into some sort of trouble on the last day. Bannie looks rather pleased with himself."

"No doubt he's thrilled to have gotten the better of me," Amy said dryly.

Thankfully, there was a pleasant breeze, so Amy and Bannie were both fairly dry when her dad announced that they had only one mile to go.

Bannie caught Amy's excitement and pranced about as she eagerly scanned the horizon for the first glimpse of the ranch. Someone shouted behind her and Amy turned to look.

Anders yelled something she couldn't hear and pointed up ahead.

She turned back and immediately spotted the tops of ranch buildings. A smile spread across her face. *We're finally here!* she thought excitedly.

Clint shouted Amy's name and motioned her upfront. Amy waved her hand to show she understood, then dug in her heels and galloped to the front of the herd, Daniel following her.

As they rode up, several cowboys from the ranch came out on horseback to meet them, and together they worked to turn the herd into the ranch yard where other cowboys joined them and helped drive the cattle into a small pasture. When the last cow walked through the gate, Amy joined her dad, and a moment later, a tall, light-haired man rode up on a dark bay horse.

"I'm Devon Henderson." He offered his hand with a smile.

"Clint Kentworthy." Clint shook the offered hand. "Nice to meet you." He motioned to Amy. "My daughter, Amy."

Devon shook her hand. "I have to say I was surprised when your dad told me you were coming along," he told her. "But you seem to have come through all right."

A slim, pretty girl walked up beside him. "This is my daughter, Roseann," Devon told them. "Roseann, this is Clint and Amy."

"Glad to meet you, Roseann." Amy smiled at her warmly.

Roseann just stared at her, then turned and walked back to the house.

Devon stared after her with a frown. "I'm sorry about that, Clint. Ever since my wife left, Roseann has been different. I don't mean to excuse her rudeness, but she has been having a hard time lately. I'll show you where you can put your horses and supplies."

"Thanks." Clint and Amy followed him.

As Amy was unsaddling Bannie in the barn a few minutes later, Anders appeared beside her and leaned against the barn wall. "So what do you think of Roseann?" he asked.

Amy shrugged. "I'm not sure. She didn't say anything when I said I was glad to meet her. Mr. Henderson said his wife left and that Roseann has been different since then. Maybe she was a nice girl before."

Anders grinned. "Maybe you'll be hangin' out with the horses, too. She seemed to me like one of those pasty-faced girls who never stick their nose outdoors."

"Well, let's not jump to conclusions," Amy told him. "She could be a very nice girl underneath that tough shell."

Anders shrugged but said nothing.

Roseann did not join them at supper that night, which was served under one of the few trees in the ranch yard.

"Probably didn't want to spoil her fair complexion," Anders muttered to Amy.

Amy rolled her eyes at him as she took a bite of Johnnycake.

After supper, everyone, excluding Roseann, gathered in the cookhouse. The night air was chilly, and steaming cups of coffee were passed around. Amy listened as the men swapped exciting stories.

Devon's men sure can spin a yarn twice as tall as they are, she thought with a chuckle.

After a while, Clint came to sit beside her. "I've arranged to stay here for a week. We need some time to rest and our equipment and horses need looking after. That'll be plenty of time for you and Roseann to get acquainted." He grinned.

"Aw, Dad!" Amy moaned.

"Yes, I know, not exactly your type, but remember, you're a Christian and she's not. She's had some trouble lately too. Show her Christ's love," he told her.

Amy nodded. "Yes, Dad. I'll remember."

"By the way," Clint said as he stood up, "you're to sleep in her room. Devon said he didn't think a bunkhouse was the proper place for a young lady, and I agree. Roseann probably isn't too happy about it, so be extra considerate."

Amy nodded, then grinned. "What did you think of the boys' yarns?"

Clint chuckled. "Some pretty tall tales if you ask me. They're fun to listen to as long as you know what's fact and what isn't. Some greenhorns would probably fall for it."

Amy laughed. "Probably."

At nine o'clock, Amy said goodnight to her dad and walked over to the house. Roseann was sitting on the porch, absently flipping through a magazine. She did not look up as Amy climbed the steps.

"Hi," Amy spoke uncertainly.

Without a word, Roseann tossed the magazine to the side and stood up. Brushing past Amy, she entered the house. Amy followed her through the living room and down a hallway. The room they entered was obviously a girl's room. Painted a bright color, it seemed a cheerful place.

"What a pretty room!" Amy exclaimed.

Roseann stared at her for a moment, then turned away.

Half an hour later, Amy gave up trying to draw Roseann into a conversation. She flopped on her bed and pulled her Bible out of her bag. *How nice a real bed feels*, she thought as she opened her Bible to First Colossians.

A few minutes later, Amy was surprised when Roseann asked, "What are you reading?"

"*The Bible*," Amy answered with a sweet smile.

Roseann laughed contemptuously. "That old book? What do you want to read that boring thing for?"

"Well, the Lord gave it to us to help us live for and serve Him. It has some interesting stories in it."

"Really?" Roseann asked sarcastically.

Amy turned the pages of her Bible until she found the story of David and Goliath and began to read aloud.

Glancing up once in a while, she saw that Roseann was becoming interested in spite of herself.

When Amy finished the story, Roseann was staring at her. "Goodnight," Amy said and turned over.

Roseann blew out the lamp without replying.

Amy smiled to herself. *The seed is planted. Lord, help it to sprout.*

Chapter Sixteen
A Trip to Town

When Amy woke the next morning, Roseann was still sleeping.

There were sounds of activity outside, so Amy dressed and slipped out, leaving her Bible on her bed. *Maybe Roseann will read it if I'm not there*, she thought hopefully.

Anders, Tye, Arty, and Daniel were standing outside the bunkhouse when Amy stepped onto the porch.

Anders noticed her and waved her over.

"Ready for some good company?" Anders asked as she joined them.

Amy laughed. "At least you'll talk to me!" She related what had happened the night before. "I guess all we can do is pray for her. I get the feeling that she is one unhappy little girl inside. I hope she reads my Bible," she finished.

Anders nodded. "I bet you gave her a pretty big shock. Of course, that isn't unusual, but—ow!" he yelped.

"You think you're so smart, Anders Archer!" Amy planted her hands on her hips.

"Come on, Amy, give me a break!" Anders held up his hands.

"She just did!" Tye chuckled.

"Sure feels like it," Anders muttered, rubbing his arm.

"Quit gripin', Anders, and take your punishment like a man. I'm heading for the feed trough; is the whiner club going to join me?" Daniel asked over his shoulder as he opened the bunkhouse door.

"What did you say?" Amy asked.

"Oops! That didn't include you, Amy." He chuckled.

"Better not have!" Amy grinned. "Or you'd be in big trouble!"

Clint was waiting in the bunkhouse for her.

"Morning, Dad," Amy greeted him.

"Morning, Amy. Have a goodnight's sleep?"

"Best in a long time!" she grinned.

While they ate, Amy told him about her evening. "I plan to read a little from the Bible out loud every night. Maybe it will get through to her."

Clint nodded. "That's a good idea. What were you planning on doing today?"

"I was about to ask you the same thing," Amy told him.

"I'm going to get started getting ready for the return trip. I doubt Roseann wants to entertain you all day. I'm sending Grubby and Caleb into town for supplies; would you like to go along?" he asked.

Amy nodded. "Sure. Can I ride in?"

"Yes, but take Buck. I noticed Bannie got a cut on his leg yesterday. You shouldn't stress it today by riding him. He's been working pretty hard the last while; he needs a break."

"Okay. When are they going to start?" she asked.

"Right away, I think. Here comes Grubby now."

While her dad talked to Grubby, Amy slipped back into the house for her spurs. Roseann was sitting in a chair reading a book when Amy walked in. Amy noticed the Bible was moved from where she had left it.

"Good morning!" Amy greeted her cheerfully.

"Morning," Roseann mumbled.

"My dad is sending some men into town, and he said I could ride in with them. Would you like to come along?" Amy invited.

Roseann hesitated. "Well ... I suppose. I don't have anything else to do."

"Good." Amy smiled. "It's too pretty a day to stay inside. I'll wait out on the porch while you get ready."

Roseann came out a few minutes later dressed in a riding skirt.

"My saddle and bridle are hanging in the tack room, and I ride the white mare," she said, seating herself in a rocking chair.

Amy was a bit taken back, but she understood what Roseann was implying. "Sure, Roseann, I'll be happy to saddle your horse for you. Should I bring her to the porch when I'm ready?"

"If you like."

When Amy reached the barn, out of Roseanna's hearing, she burst out laughing.

"What's so funny?" Anders asked, coming up behind her.

"Oh, Anders, you won't believe what just happened!" She related what had just passed between them.

"You're a wonder!" Anders exclaimed when she finished. "Anyone else, including me, would have been offended, and you just laugh it off!"

"Well, I suppose if I took offense at every little thing, I wouldn't be a very nice person to be around. Anyway, I honestly think she doesn't know any better or how silly she sounds. So I guess I'll have to show her there is another way," Amy told him. "I'd better get going."

It didn't take Amy long to saddle the two horses. The white mare was small; Buck towered over her, but Amy noted the smooth, clean legs and deep chest of the little mare.

"Bet you're a speedy little thing," she murmured as she buckled the breast collar. At the last minute, Amy invited Arty to go with them, then led Buck and the mare to the house.

"You sure took long enough." Roseann stood and walked slowly across the porch.

"I'm sorry," Amy said sweetly. "I talked to my friend for a few minutes." She handed Roseann the mare's reins, then mounted Buck.

Arty joined them, and they followed the wagon out to the road. "Let's get ahead of them," Arty suggested. Amy turned to Roseann "How 'bout it?" she asked.

When Roseann nodded, Amy dug in her heels, and Buck leapt ahead.

They cantered along the road for about a mile. The horses seemed to enjoy the brisk gait as much as the riders.

They came upon a large mesquite bush, and Amy suggested they stop and rest the horses in its shade. Though it was still early in the morning, it was already hot and dusty.

Roseann said nothing, but Arty agreed, so he and Amy turned off the road, and Roseann followed in silence. The three dismounted and loosened the cinches. Amy lifted her saddle to let the slight breeze blow over Buck's sweaty back, then did the same for Roseann's mare. The three horses stood with heads hanging, swishing the pesky flies away with their tails, taking full advantage of the rest.

When she was finished with the horses, Amy flopped down beside Arty and waved her hat hand in front of her face. "Whew, is it hot!" she said.

After a moment of uncomfortable silence, Roseann asked abruptly, "Why do you wear that silly scarf on your head?"

"Because the Lord asks me to, Roseann. He says so in Second Corinthians, chapter eleven. It says that if a woman doesn't have her head covered when she prays or prophesies, which means teaches Biblical truths, then her head should be shorn. The covering is a symbol of submission," Amy explained. "Just as it says a woman shouldn't have her head *uncovered*, it says that a man should not have his head *covered* when he prays or prophesies."

"Oh," Arty said. "Is that why your dad and the other men take their hats off when we pray before a meal or at church?"

Amy nodded. "Yes, that's why."

"Hmph." Roseann snorted. "That's silly!"

"I don't think it is," Arty said. "It makes perfect sense."

"Here comes the wagon." Amy stood to her feet. She tightened her cinch and Roseann's, then swung into her saddle.

"How much farther to town?" she asked Roseann as they rode back onto the road.

"About three miles," Roseann answered.

They rode the last few miles in silence, each busy with their own thoughts.

"Give me wisdom how I can help Roseann, Lord. She is so unhappy, and her need of You is great. Show her Your love, Lord, and help me to be a good example."

The town of Ranger was a small, close-knit community of businessmen and ranchers. It had a row of small businesses on Main Street and a few scattered houses. It was the type of town where everyone knew everyone and strangers always created a stir. There had been rumors about an outfit coming on a cattle drive from Wyoming, so of course a crowd gathered around the group as they rode into town.

"My, aren't we famous!" Amy remarked to Arty.

He chuckled. "I don't think I've ever had this much attention in my life!"

"Just remember: it's only because you're with me!" Amy told him.

A Trip to Town

Arty just rolled his eyes.

They dismounted in front of the general store. Roseann dropped her mare's reins and disappeared into a small ice cream parlor down the street. Amy and Arty exchanged looks. With a shrug, Amy picked up the discarded reins and led both horses across the street to the livery stable, and Arty followed with his horse.

After watering the horses and turning them loose in a corral, Amy turned to Arty. "How 'bout we join Roseann? My treat."

Arty grinned. "Could a fellow turn down an offer like that?"

The cool air of the little shop was a welcome contrast to the sweltering heat outside. As she and Arty headed for the counter, Amy spotted Roseann sitting with several young people in the corner and after getting their ice cream, Amy and Arty joined them.

"Good, cold ice cream sure hits the spot on a cold day like this," Amy remarked as she sat down.

"It certainly does," a pleasant-looking, dark-haired girl agreed. "Did you come in with the outfit from Wyoming?" she asked.

"Yes, I did. Arty came with us, too," Amy replied.

"I didn't know they brought a girl with them. I suppose I should introduce myself. I'm Julie Myler," the girl said, extending her hand.

"And I'm Amy Kentworthy. The cattle we brought with us were found on my father's ranch, and he is the one heading up the drive," Amy explained, accepting the offered hand.

Julie nodded. "I see. Did you have a good trip?"

Amy laughed. "Quite an adventuresome trip, but yes, it was a good trip."

"What happened?" Julie leaned forward eagerly.

"Let's see …." Amy counted them off on her fingers. "Wolves, stampede, rustlers, dust storm, and perhaps a few more minor things."

"My goodness!" Julie exclaimed. "You'll have to tell me all about it. Let's go sit outside."

"Sure." Amy agreed. "Just let me tell Arty where I'm going."

Roseann had disappeared with some other girls, and Arty was talking to a young man at a table nearby. He looked up with a smile when Amy tapped him lightly on the shoulder.

"I'm sorry to interrupt, Arty," Amy said. "I'm going outside with Julie. Let's meet outside the livery stable at two o'clock, okay?"

"Sure, thanks for letting me know."

Julie had already gone out. Amy spied her perched on the hitching post as she walked out the door.

"So tell me everything that happened," Julie said as Amy walked up.

"It might take a while." Amy smiled.

Julie grinned. "I've got all day."

Amy described the trip in detail, Julie interrupting occasionally to ask a question.

When Amy finished, Julie shook her head. "Do you know what a lucky girl you are? What I wouldn't give to be in your shoes. You must have had so much fun!"

"Yes, I did, but it was a lot of work, too."

"I'm sure it was. You should write a book," Julie told her.

Amy chuckled. "Well, maybe someday. I'm not sure how good I would be at it."

"I love to write," Julie said. "I write little stories for the fun of it. Nothing much, but a few of them have been published in the newspaper."

"Really? Good for you." Amy shook her head. "I doubt I could ever write anything anyone would want to read. I like to draw though."

"I can sketch a bit, but I like writing better," Julie informed her.

"Well," Amy said with a chuckle, "if you ever decide to publish your little stories, I'll be happy to illustrate them for you!"

Julie laughed. "Okay, it's a deal!"

They were silent a moment, then Julie said, "We've been sitting here for a long time. How 'bout I show you around town?"

"You bet." Amy nodded, standing to her feet. "I want to see every nook and cranny of this place."

The rest of the afternoon passed quickly as Amy and Julie went from one shop to another.

"1:45!" Amy exclaimed, glancing at her watch. "I've got to get to the livery stable. Arty will be waiting."

"I'll come with you. I've got to get home, too." Julie followed her along the boardwalk. Arty was waiting by the corral when Amy and Julie walked up. Roseann was with him.

"How'd your afternoon go?" Amy asked him.

"Great. I met a guy named Adam. He's the one I was talking to in the ice cream parlor. Seemed to be a nice fellow."

"Adam is nice," Julie spoke up. "His father's ranch borders ours, and Adam comes over now and then to lend a hand."

"Glad you had a good time," Amy said to Arty. She turned to Roseann. "How about you?"

"It was fine." Roseann said shortly.

Amy was turning toward the corral when Julie asked, "May I ride with you? I live about four miles past the Rocking H."

"Sure," Amy agreed quickly. "That'll be fine."

Julie's horse was in a stall in the barn. Buck and Roseann's mare were in the corral. Amy saddled them out while Julie saddled her horse.

In a short time they were ready to go. Amy looked admiringly at Julie's horse as she led him out of the barn. A tall, dark-colored gelding, he was very flashy. He held his head high, but his eyes were gentle and intelligent. He had the stocky, muscular build of a well-bred cowhorse.

"He's a looker," Amy commented.

Julie smiled. "Thanks. My grandpa gave him to me for my birthday. He's only five, but Grandpa spent a lot of time training him, and Dad says he's the best horse on the ranch."

Amy nodded. "My dad gave me mine for my birthday, too. He's four. This is my dad's horse I'm riding now. Bannie has a cut on his leg, so I didn't ride him today. What's your horse's name?"

A Trip to Town

"Rocket." Julie patted the horse affectionately. "And with good reason. He always starts off like a rocket!"

Amy chuckled. "Mine's full name is Black Banner, Bannie for short. He's solid black with a white star." She turned to Roseann. "What about your horse, Roseann? I don't believe I've heard her name yet."

"Little Lady," Roseann replied without looking at Amy.

"Little Lady," Amy repeated. "That fits her. She certainly is little."

The time passed swiftly as they rode back to the ranch. Amy, Arty, and Julie chatted together, but Roseann kept to herself, thwarting Amy's efforts to draw her into the conversation. When they reached the ranch, Amy, Arty, and Roseann turned in the lane while Julie continued down the road. Amy watched as Julie leaned forward and dug in her heels. The gelding leapt ahead and streaked down the road and out of sight.

"She sure picked the right name for him," she commented to Arty. "He's a quick starter all right."

Arty nodded. "He sure is. I prefer a slower starter myself. They usually have more stamina."

Amy nodded agreement. "That's true. A slower, steadier horse is best, Dad always says."

They dismounted by the barn, and Roseann promptly headed for the house. Arty rode out to help Anders, Daniel, and Tye, who were moving some cattle from one corral to another, while Amy unsaddled Buck and Lady.

She had just finished when Anders rode up. "Was the princess any more amiable today?" he asked as he dismounted.

"Not much. I met a nice girl in town, though, and we had fun. I don't know who Roseann hung around with. Arty found a friend I guess." She chatted while she groomed the horses, then headed for the house.

Roseann was nowhere to be seen when Amy entered her room. Amy took off her spurs, straightened her covering, then went back outside.

She spied her dad talking to Devon and Daniel by the horse corral and started toward them.

"Have a good day?" Clint asked as she walked up.

"Yes, I did, thank you," she smiled.

"What'd you think of the town?" Devon asked.

"I thought it was very nice, Mr. Henderson," Amy replied. "Everyone was very friendly."

"I'm glad you enjoyed it." One of his men called him and he hurried away.

"How's Bannie's leg?" Amy asked her dad.

"It's better. You could turn him loose with the other horses tonight."

"Good," Amy replied. "He was getting antsy being cooped up." She promptly headed for the barn.

Chapter Seventeen
Disaster in the Night

After supper that night, everyone gathered in the bunkhouse. Though it was hot during the day, the September nights were chilly, and Amy was glad for the warmth of the woodstove.

It was a jolly evening. Bowls of apples and nuts were passed around along with steaming cups of coffee. Amy helped herself, then went in search of the boys.

She found them gathered in the corner. A loud roar of laughter greeted her as she joined the circle.

"What's the joke?" she asked as she seated herself on the bench Anders offered her.

He seated himself on the floor as he replied. "Arty just dumped a handful of nuts down Daniel's back."

Daniel stood to his feet and shook his shirt. Nuts clattered to the floor. Amy chuckled.

"Thanks, Amy," Daniel growled. "I thought I'd at least get some sympathy from you."

"Out of luck, Daniel." Amy grinned.

"Guess what I found out, Amy." Arty's eyes twinkled.

"What?" she asked curiously.

"Your dad invited Adam and Julie over tomorrow and gave all of us, including Daniel, the day off to go riding around the ranch in the hills."

"Oh, good," Amy exclaimed. "That'll be lots of fun. I'll have to remember to invite Roseann to come along." Then she paused, frowning. "How did he know about Julie and Adam? I didn't tell him yet."

"I told him," Arty told her. "He had Daryl ride over to their ranches and invite them."

At nine o'clock, Amy made her way over to her dad. He was sitting by the wall, listening to the men talk. He smiled when she sat down beside him. "I suppose Arty broke the news?" he asked.

"He sure did." Amy grinned.

"And you're here to tell me you're heartbroken and want me to cancel, right?"

"Aw, Dad." Amy gave him a playful shove.

Clint chuckled. "I suppose you're ready for bed, huh?"

"Yep." Amy yawned.

"All right. Off you go. Don't forget to do your devotions."

"I won't. Night, Dad."

"Night, Amy."

Amy shivered as she stepped out into the starry night. A soft breeze was blowing, bringing the night sounds to her ears.

She stood for a moment, listening to the night creatures and the rustling of the horses in the nearby corral. "What a beautiful night," she breathed. "Thank you, Lord, for creating this world for us to enjoy."

Roseann was sitting by the window sewing when Amy entered the room.

"Hello, Roseann." Amy sat on the edge of her bed.

"Hi," Roseann returned.

Well that's progress, Amy thought. *At least she answered me.*

Amy got ready for bed, then picked up her Bible. "Would you like to hear another story?" she asked.

Roseann shrugged her shoulders.

Amy took that as a yes and turned to the story of Daniel and the lion's den. Roseann listened with wide-eyed interest, her sewing lying forgotten on her lap. When she finished the story, Amy silently held the Bible out. Roseann took it and slowly turned the pages.

Amy smiled to herself as she snuggled down under the covers and drifted off to sleep.

*****

Hours later, Amy sat bolt upright, her heart pounding. It was still dark, but a strange orange glow poured in the window. She leapt out of bed and ran to the window.

What she saw made her gasp. *The barn is on fire!*

The flames leaped high in the sky and gave it an eerie glow. Men were running and shouting; horses were screaming with terror.

"Roseann, the barn is on fire!" Amy shouted.

"What?" Roseann scrambled out of bed.

Amy waited only long enough to get dressed, then tore out of the house.

Tye was the first person she came to. His face was black with soot.

"Tye!" Amy cried. "What's going on? Where's Dad? Is he okay?"

"He's helping to get the horses out of the barn." Tye had to shout to be heard. "Stay away from there. You could get hurt," he warned her.

"There's still horses in there?" Amy could hear heartrending cries from the trapped horses.

"'Fraid so. They got six of them out, but there's still a few more in the back corner."

Amy didn't wait for him to finish. She started running toward the barn.

She was almost there when someone leapt out of the shadows and grabbed her arm.

"Let me go!" she cried, struggling to free herself.

"Hold on, Amy." She recognized Anders's voice. "You can't go running toward a burning building like that."

"I've got to find Dad, Anders. Now let me go!"

"He's fine, Amy." Anders still held on. "Calm down and think, or you could get hurt."

Amy stopped struggling. "I won't do anything foolish, Anders, but I've got to find Dad."

"He's fine." Anders said again as he released her.

Amy turned and ran toward the barn again, wincing at the frantic calls of the trapped horses. Anders followed her closely.

Anxiously she scanned the crowd of shadowy figures. For several agonizing minutes, she ran through the crowd of men, looking for her dad's familiar form.

"I don't see him anywhere!" she shouted over her shoulder to Anders and would have dashed into the smoke filled barn but Anders grabbed her arm and swung her around. Gripping her shoulders so tight it hurt, he looked into her eyes.

"I just saw him a few minutes ago, Amy, and he was perfectly all right. You've got to think straight or yer gonna get hurt!" His voice rose with every word until he was nearly shouting.

"I've got to find him," she said stubbornly. "I have to see for myself he's okay. Let me go!"

"I won't until you promise not to go into that barn!" Anders said fiercely. His fingers dug into her shoulders. "Promise me or I'm taking you back to the house!"

Amy stared at him in shocked surprise. Anders had never spoken to her like that before. At first she felt defensive and angry that he would speak to her as if she were much younger, but then she realized he was speaking out of concern for her safety, and her anger melted away.

"I promise, Anders," she said quietly.

As Anders let her go, a man ran up to them with two pails in his hands. "Help get water," he shouted, shoving the pails into their hands.

Anders grabbed a pail with one hand and Amy's arm with the other. "Come on!" he called. "We've wasted enough time!"

"Why aren't they fighting the fire?" Amy shouted as she followed him to the pump, noticing the men were leaving the barn and going to the other buildings.

"They can't save the barn, but if we wet the other buildings down, it'll keep the fire from spreading," he shouted back.

Arty was working the pump, and Amy shoved her bucket under the stream of water. As soon as it was full, she ran for the bunkhouse because it was closest to the burning barn. Sparks were falling dangerously near it.

She was running back to the pump when a hand was placed on her shoulder. "Dad!" she cried as she recognized the familiar figure.

Clint smiled, his teeth showing startlingly white in his blackened face.

"Are you all right?" Amy asked.

Clint nodded. "I'm fine, Amy."

"You didn't get all the horses out, did you?"

Clint shook his head. "Daryl's horse, Bandit, was in there, and two of Devon's."

"Oh, no!" Amy groaned. "Bandit was Daryl's favorite."

Clint nodded. "I know, but there was nothing we could do. It's too dangerous to go back in. Thankfully there were only a few horses in there. The others are all out in the pasture."

For the next hour, they worked to save the other buildings. Finally, all that could be done to save them had been done. Now they had to let the fire burn itself out. The frantic calls had ceased, and Amy knew the horses were no longer suffering.

Anders came to stand beside her. "Did you hear about Bandit?" he asked.

Amy nodded, staring at the burning barn.

Anders sighed. "Daryl's pretty upset. He raised Bandit from a colt, and he was going on fifteen."

Amy shook her head. "It must be hard to lose a horse like that."

Anders shifted uneasily and stared at his feet. "Uh, Amy, I'm sorry I was so rough with you. I hope you understand. I was worried you were going to run into the barn. Will you forgive me?" His voice was low and pleading.

Amy was touched. She had been hurt when he had spoken to her so curtly, but she knew he had been afraid for her. He had been thinking of her well-being, and she could appreciate that.

"Yes, Anders. I forgive you. I'm not angry," she assured him. "I was angry at first, but I realize you were worried about me and didn't mean to come across the way you did."

Relief showed in his blue eyes. "Thanks, Amy. I didn't realize until afterwards how I must have sounded. I was hoping you would understand."

Roseann appeared beside them. "Where's my dad?" she asked anxiously.

"I don't know." Amy told her.

"Did they get all the horses out?"

Amy shook her head. "Two of your dad's horses were still in there. I don't know which two they were, though."

The sun was just beginning to rise when the last flames died out and the men gathered around the ruins. They were exhausted, and their clothes and faces were black with soot.

Daniel was standing next to Amy. He leaned down and whispered. "I bet Uncle Clint offers to stay and help rebuild."

Amy nodded. "I'm sure he will. Does anyone know how the fire started?"

"Devon thinks it was arson, and I agree. That seems to be the only logical explanation. The fire started on the south side of the barn, the side away from the other buildings, perfect cover if someone didn't want to be seen. The men are all sure no one left a lantern burning. We'll probably never be able to prove it, but I have a hunch those rustlers had something to do with it."

Amy nodded. "That makes sense."

A little while later, while they were eating an early breakfast, Clint did offer to stay, but Devon shook his head.

"Thanks a lot, Clint, but you need to get home. The winter storms will be starting soon. We can manage the rebuilding."

"Well, if you're sure, Devon," Clint said. "I'd be more than happy to help. We might as well help you with the cleanup while we're here at least."

After breakfast, Amy wandered outside. She was standing by the corral looking at the barn ruins when her dad joined her.

"You'd better get the horses tacked up," he said.

Amy looked at him in surprise. "I didn't think we'd go now."

"There's nothing for you to do here. You might as well go."

"Okay, if you're sure we won't be needed."

"I'm sure." Clint assured her.

Amy informed the boys that their plans hadn't changed, then went to the house. Roseann was sitting on her bed brushing her long hair when Amy entered the room.

"Julie and Adam are coming over to go riding with us; would you like to come along?" Amy asked.

Roseann thought a moment. "All right. When are you leaving?"

Amy shrugged. "I'm not sure. Whenever Julie and Adam get here, I guess." She grabbed her spurs and saddlebags and headed out the door.

Anders was standing by the chuck wagon when she came out. "Good thing your saddle was in the wagon or you'd be goin' bareback," he said as she walked up.

Amy nodded. "It was only in the wagon because I was cleaning it last night and forgot to put it back. I'm glad it didn't burn; I sure wouldn't want to be going bareback all the way home."

Tye and Arty were already in the corral getting their horses when Amy and Anders got there.

Little Lady nickered and bumped Amy gently with her nose as she stepped through the gate. Amy scratched her ears. "You're an affectionate little thing, aren't you? I'd saddle you up for Roseann, but I think her side saddle and bridle burned last night. I wonder what she'll use." The last was addressed to Anders.

Anders shrugged. "Maybe since we're not going to town, she'll ride astride."

"Maybe." Amy busied herself saddling Bannie. "Sure am glad you weren't in the barn last night, boy," she murmured.

She had just finished with Bannie when Roseann appeared with a saddle and bridle over her arm. She was dressed in a divided skirt suited for riding astride.

"Where'd you find tack?" Amy asked.

"My grandpa gave my dad this saddle a while ago, but Dad likes his old one better. It was in the bunkhouse, and there's always an extra bridle hanging in the shed," Roseann said.

Amy was surprised at this flow of words. She hadn't been expecting an answer at all. "Well, I'm glad you have something to ride in." She took the tack, slung the saddle over the fence, and, carrying the bridle, opened the corral gate.

A few minutes later, Julie rode in on Rocket, followed shortly by Adam. Amy greeted them, then headed for the bunkhouse. Daniel hadn't come to get his horse yet, and she wanted to see what was taking him so long, and Grubby had promised to pack them lunch.

The smell of freshly baked bread greeted her as she stepped inside. "Mm! It smells good in here." Amy sniffed appreciatively. "Do you have our lunch ready, Grubby?"

"Yes, lassie," and he handed her a sack containing jerky, Johnnycake, and cookies.

Amy thanked him and went in search of Daniel. She found him behind the bunkhouse talking with some of the men. "Aren't you coming?" she asked when she got his attention.

Daniel shook his head. "Some things came up and I need to stay here. If I get finished in time, I'll join you later."

"All right." Amy was disappointed. *I hope he'll still be able to come later*, she thought as she stepped outside. She always enjoyed spending time with her cousin. Amy went back out to the horses and put the lunch—along with a coffee pot, plates, and cups—into her saddle bags.

"'Bout time you got here. We've been waiting all morning," Anders teased.

"You just hold your horses, young man," Amy scolded.

"I am holding him," Anders said in an innocent manner.

"Uh-huh, smart alec!" Amy rolled her eyes.

"Thanks for the compliment!" Anders grinned.

"Drop it!" Amy exclaimed.

Anders promptly dropped Sky Blue's reins.

Everyone laughed. "If you're going to act this way all day, I'll leave you behind!" Amy threatened.

"I'll be good as gold, my lady," Anders replied meekly. "Where's Daniel?"

"He can't come now, but he might be able to join us later," Amy explained.

"That's too bad. I was counting on him to keep you in line!" Anders ducked behind his horse as Amy threw a handful of dirt at him.

Julie rode Rocket over to Amy. "Is he always this funny?" she asked.

"You bet." Amy chuckled. "You'll hear lots more of that kind of thing before the day is over."

Julie shook her head. "How does he think of all that?"

Amy shrugged. "I'm sure I don't know."

Clint came out to see them off. "Be sure to be back in time for supper," he told them.

"I don't think you have to worry about that." Amy laughed. "We only packed enough food for lunch. Anders's hollow leg won't let us stay away!"

Clint chuckled. "With four boys along, I think you're right, Amy. Now off with you and have fun!" He slapped Bannie on the rump, and the boys let out a cowboy yell.

"And they're off!" Daniel shouted as they galloped past the bunkhouse.

Chapter Eighteen
Adventure on the Bluff

Once they were past what was left of the barn, heading onto the range, Amy asked Roseann where would be a good place to stop for lunch.

Roseann thought a moment. "There's a creek with a few small trees. If we take our time, we'd get there about lunchtime," she offered.

"That sounds nice. Let's go there," Amy suggested, and the others readily agreed.

"Why don't you lead since you know the way, Roseann?" Amy suggested.

Roseann smiled smugly and trotted Little Lady to the front.

Anders caught Amy's eye and made a face. Amy frowned and reined her horse closer to him; she spoke in an undertone, "Behave yourself and be polite, Mr. Archer."

He bowed. "Yes'm."

Amy laughed. "So long as you're that polite to me, I may excuse your faults and breaches in manners."

"In that case …," he said teasingly as he reached over and slapped the unsuspecting Bannie, who snorted in surprise and gave a buck.

"Hey!" Amy pulled him up sharply. "You tryin' to get me piled?"

Anders yelped as Amy smacked him with the ends of her reins.

Anders tried to grab her reins away, but Amy dodged and galloped off.

They chased each other around for a few minutes, then rode back, laughing and breathless.

Amy rode over to Julie. "See what I mean?" she asked.

Julie chuckled. "Seems to me it wasn't only Anders!"

Amy flashed her a grin. "My, how observant you are!"

As they were riding along a few minutes later, Anders's horse, Sky Blue suddenly dropped to one knee. Anders was flung into the saddle horn and nearly fell off.

"What happened?" Amy asked as he regained his balance and Sky Blue got to his feet. "Did he stumble?"

Anders shook his head. "No, he was bowing."

"Oh, did you bump his spot?"

Anders nodded. "Yep."

"What do you mean?" Julie asked curiously. "Is he trained to bow on command?"

"Yes." Amy nodded. "Anders has taught him all kinds of tricks. Come on, Anders, show us what you and Sky Blue can do."

"Aw, Amy!" he groaned. "I thought this was my day off."

"Come on, Anders," Amy pleaded.

"Oh, all right. Just for you."

The others stopped their horses as Anders rode out in front and swung the blue roan gelding around to face his audience.

"Bow to the ladies!" Anders said.

Sky Blue promptly dropped to one knee. Anders bowed and tipped his hat.

Then Sky Blue got to his feet and began to sway from side to side.

"He's dancing!" Julie cried.

Suddenly the horse reared straight up. As he dropped back down, Anders slid out of the saddle and stood in front of the horse and bowed. Sky Blue bowed back.

"How old are you?" Anders asked.

Sky Blue pawed the dirt one, two, three, four, five, six, seven times.

"Correct!" Anders grinned. "Are you a good horse?"

Sky Blue nodded.

Anders patted him on the neck and remounted.

"Boy, how'd you do that?" Arty asked.

Anders shrugged. "I've had him since he was a colt. I've just said the same things the same way for so long that, well, it just happened. My dad took me to a fair once when I was little, and I asked the trick guy how he did it, and he showed me. Amy helped me train him too. When he went down on his knee a few minutes ago, I had accidentally bumped his shoulder with my foot, which is his cue to bow."

"Wow!" Julie exclaimed. "I wish you lived here so you could teach me and Rocket."

"Well, we could teach you a little bit. Amy can help," he offered.

"Oh, good, that'll be fun."

They spent the rest of the morning exploring the ranch, following the winding, twisting cattle trails and visiting the old Indian burial grounds.

It was almost one o'clock, when Amy suggested they head for the creek.

"My stomach says lunch is late," Anders declared.

Amy shook her head. "Your stomach would say it was late no matter what time it really was. Besides, you're the one who wanted to keep looking for arrow heads. How much farther, Roseann?" she asked.

"See that bluff?" Roseann pointed. "The creek is just to the right of it. It empties into a water hole."

"Beat you there!" Amy yelled, digging in her heels, and Bannie leapt forward.

"No fair!" Anders shouted after her.

Amy raised herself in the stirrups and urged Bannie on. She loved the wind whipping through her hair and feeling the powerful muscles rippling beneath her. She let Bannie gallop for a few minutes, then eased him down into a steady lope. By the time the others caught up, she had Bannie staked on his picket rope under one of the scattered trees by the small creek and was unpacking her saddlebags.

"You cheated, Amy," Anders complained as he dismounted.

Amy grinned. "Bannie would have won either way."

"Would not!"

"Would to!"

"Would not!"

"Would to!"

"Amy, are we going to eat today?" Arty asked.

"I suppose." She chuckled. "Anders, could you please fill the coffee pot with water?"

"After what you said to me?" Anders folded his arms.

"Do you want a cookie?" she asked without turning around.

Anders picked up the coffee pot. "Anything else I can do while I'm at it?" he asked sweetly.

"I knew that'd get you!" Amy laughed.

Fifteen minutes later they were seated around the fire ready to eat.

"Would you pray, Anders?" Amy asked.

"Sure."

The boys removed their hats, and they all bowed their heads. Amy noticed Roseann watching them thoughtfully.

Anders thanked the Lord for the food and asked for protection for the rest of the day. When he finished, Amy poured the coffee, and everyone helped themselves to the Johnnycake, jerky, and cookies.

"Anders!" Amy exclaimed, catching sight of his loaded plate. "We're going to have to make you jog home!"

Anders shrugged. "Oh, well," he grinned, taking a big bite of cookie. "Yuck!" His hand flew to his throat and he stumbled to his feet, choking and coughing.

"Anders!" Amy cried. "Have you no manners?"

Anders gulped down his coffee, his face red. "Whew! What'd you put in those cookies?" he finally gasped.

"Anders, if you're foolin'—"

"No, Amy, try one!" he insisted.

Amy picked up a cookie, took a bite and gagged instantly. Grabbing her cup, she took a long drink. "I must have used salt instead of sugar!" she exclaimed. She picked up the rest of the cookies and dumped them beneath a tree. Rio trotted over and licked one. Everyone laughed as he drew back in surprise and sat down, staring at the cookies with a puzzled expression. Amy made a face as she seated herself. "Those were terrible!" she said as she took a bite of Johnnycake. "I've got to wash that taste out of my mouth!"

"So what are you going to give me now, Amy? Seeing as your cookies aren't any good!" Anders asked, smiling archly.

Amy thought a moment. "I'll give it to you after we do the dishes," she told him. Anders appeared satisfied and went back to eating, not noticing Amy wink at Arty and Tye.

Later, when they were finished eating, Amy suggested Julie and Roseann wash the dishes while Anders dried. Adam put the fire out, and Arty and Tye helped Amy clean up.

"What's your plan, Amy?" Arty asked. "You winked at us. Are we supposed to help?"

Amy giggled. "Yep. I'm gonna need your help. You watch me, and when I nod my head, you grab Anders and throw him in the creek!"

Arty laughed. "Are you sure he won't get mad?"

Amy shook her head. "I don't think he will. He's usually a pretty good sport. It's a great day for a little swim anyway."

They quickly finished packing the food in Amy's saddlebags and went to stand near the dishwashers.

"Did you come to help, Amy?" Anders asked.

"Oh, I suppose I could." As she leaned down to pick up a dish, she nodded to the boys.

With a shout, they leaped forward and with one mighty shove, landed Anders in the middle of the creek.

He came up sputtering. "Amy Kentworthy!" he yelled, shaking water out of his eyes. "I got this instead of a cookie? Now I call that a raw deal!"

Amy was standing at the edge of the creek, and as Anders spoke, he lunged forward, grabbing her by the ankle and pulling her in.

Amy shrieked and hit the water with a splash. She came up laughing. "You might as well join us!" she called to the others. "Good thing it's not a cold day!"

Roseann stayed on the bank, but the others joined them in the water, and soon they were all soaked. Amy noticed Rio standing at the edge. "Come on, boy," she called. Rio jumped in with a happy bark, spraying water everywhere.

"Amy!" Anders yelled. "That was about as bad as you splashin' me yourself!"

"Like this?" Amy asked, tossing a handful of water at him.

Anders retaliated, and soon everyone was involved in the water fight. Half an hour later they stumbled from the water, dripping and laughing.

"Well, Amy, I can't believe I'm saying this, but thanks for the dunking! It felt pretty good." Anders grinned sheepishly.

"Any time!" Amy laughed. "And thanks for pulling me in! Except for the fact that I was wearing my boots!"

"I was, too!" Anders retorted.

"Uh huh. I know. Say, want to climb that bluff Roseann pointed out? That would help us dry off. By the way, Roseann, why do they call it a bluff? I thought a bluff was supposed to be flat on one side. That just looks like a hill."

"It's flat around the other side. There's quite a view from on top," Roseann told her.

"I'm game," Anders said. "I wasn't looking forward to sitting in my saddle all wet like this."

The others agreed, so they started walking across the open land that separated them from the bluff.

"Race you!" Anders yelled over his shoulder.

Amy sprinted after him. Tye quickly passed her and caught up to Anders.

As Tye shot passed, Anders grabbed his shoulder. Both boys lost their balance and fell.

Rio ran around them, barking hysterically. Arty ran past Amy and the two still rolling on the ground. Surprisingly, even with his bad leg, he beat them all to the bottom of the bluff. Large rocks dotted this side of the bluff, and they collapsed in the shade of one of them. Amy noticed that Roseann seemed to be enjoying herself.

"What'd you pull me down for?" Tye fumed to Anders jokingly. "I would have won."

Anders shrugged. "You would've done the same to me if you'd thought of it. Come on, I'm ready to climb."

"Beautiful day, isn't it?" Amy commented to Roseann as they climbed.

Roseann didn't answer. She was ahead of Amy and climbing slowly. The others were farther up the bluff.

Suddenly, Amy's head shot up. "Roseann!" she screamed.

Rustlers and the Texas Trail

Chapter Nineteen
THE ANGELS ARE SINGING

Amy covered the distance between them in a single leap. With one hand she shoved Roseann back as hard as she could, with the other she picked up a rock.

A large rattle snake was curled up just a few feet away on a flat rock. He was flicking his tongue in and out and angrily rattling his rattler.

Amy lifted the rock and waited.

Suddenly the snake struck, just missing her leg. Amy threw the rock, but it went wide.

A shot rang out. The rattler jerked and flopped around.

Amy looked up to see Anders' gun still smoking as he walked down to them.

"Are you okay?" he asked anxiously.

Amy managed a weak smile. "Yes, thanks to you."

Anders shrugged and put his gun back in the holster.

Amy turned to Roseann who was still cowering against a rock, looking pale and shaken. "Are you all right?" Amy asked.

"I ... I think so. Just shook up a bit," Roseann said, standing shakily to her feet.

"What happened?" Anders asked.

"I think the snake was sunning itself on that rock, and Roseann must have startled it," Amy told him.

"Let's kneel right here and thank the Lord for keeping you two safe," he suggested.

The seven knelt together and thanked the Lord for His protection. When they finished and stood up, Amy said. "Do you want to go back to the creek, Roseann? I'll go with you if you want. You look a little pale."

Roseann shook her head. "I'm okay now. Let's keep going."

Amy had expected her to make some biting remark after they prayed, but to her surprise, Roseann had remained silent.

Maybe something is getting through, she thought hopefully as they continued their climb.

Ten minutes later, they reached the top of the bluff.

"Wow!" Julie exclaimed. "What a beautiful view!"

"No kidding! This is great!" Adam agreed.

"I wish I had some paper and a pencil," Amy said wistfully.

"Maybe we can come back again before we leave," Tye suggested.

"That would be great! I'd like to take this image back with me." Amy gazed across the wide open space that stretched out before them. They looked around for a while more before they decided to head back to the creek.

The boys tried to slide down some of the flatter rocks on the way down but soon discovered that sun-baked rocks were not very comfortable to their backsides. Rio kept busy chasing pikas, prairie dog–like creatures that made their homes beneath the rocks, with the boys calling out encouragement.

"Ugh!" Amy shaded her eyes with her hand. "I'm ready for another dip in the creek."

"Yeah, me, too," Julie agreed. "It's hot today."

As they rounded the last boulder at the bottom of the bluff, Amy spotted a lone horse and rider riding slowly across the range.

"Hey, Anders, who do you think that is?" she asked.

Anders studied them for a moment. "I'll bet its Daniel coming to join us. Hey, Daniel!" he yelled and waved his arms.

The rider turned his horse and headed in their direction.

The seven young people started walking toward the rider, but as he drew closer, Amy studied him suspiciously. The rider was almost to them, when she spoke in a low tone. "Anders," she said slowly, "that's not Daniel."

"I was just thinking the same thing. Is it one of your dad's men, Roseann?"

Roseann shook her head. "No, I don't recognize him."

Suddenly Amy gasped. "Anders, look closely, quick! Don't you recognize him?"

The rider was quickly covering the ground that separated them.

"What, Amy?" Anders started to turn toward her, then his eyes widened. "Oh, no! It's one of the rustlers we caught a couple weeks ago!"

"Exactly what I was thinking," Amy said grimly. "If he recognizes us ... but none of the rustlers got a good look at us in the dark, so maybe he won't."

By now the rider was within speaking distance, and he reined in his horse. "Howdy, young folks. What are you doin' in this part of the country?" His tone was challenging.

"This is my father's ranch," Roseann spoke up. "Devon Henderson is his name."

"Well, you just take my word for it, you folks be mighty careful where you go wanderin' around if you don't want no trouble. Jist keep to your own territory."

"But this is my father's ranch!" Roseann protested. "We have a right to ride where we please."

"Jist don't go lookin' for trouble, that's all I'm sayin'. Adios!" He dug in his spurs and galloped off in a cloud of dust.

"Whew! What'd you make of that?" Anders asked as the man rode away.

"I say there's somethin' fishy goin' on," Amy said firmly. "Number one, we know he's been a rustler before, number two, he tried to scare us off for some reason; obviously he doesn't want us to find something out. Number three, he's supposed to be in jail, and number four, he rode off that way," indicating with her hand, "and from what I could see from the bluff, it's a barren desert out there. Perfect for a hideout, wouldn't you say?"

"Man, you ought to be a detective!" Arty told her.
"Thank you, but I'm a lady, not a man." she grinned.
"I say we head home and tell your dad about this," Anders suggested.
"Right." Amy agreed. "And watch our backs."
They hurried back to the creek where they had left the horses picketed, but to their surprise, the horses were nowhere in sight.
"He cut the picket lines and let the horses loose!" Amy cried after a moment of silence. She groaned. "And I'm not looking forward to walking all the way back. It'll be dark before we get there!"
"If the horses aren't far, wouldn't they come if we whistled?" Arty suggested.
"Good idea, Arty." Amy cupped her hands around her mouth and began whistling and calling. The others joined in and soon Bannie appeared, with the others following along behind.
"Praise the Lord," Anders said.
"We'd better get going. The more time we save the better." Amy grabbed her bridle as she spoke.
Once they were on their way, Amy had lots of time to think. *I wonder what that guy is doing down here. Obviously he escaped from jail. I think his name was Jack. I wonder if Tyler and Brent got out. That reminds me, I should write to Jessica. Maybe she'll have some news about the rustlers.*
She was jolted out of her thoughts when someone called her name. "What?" she asked.
Anders laughed. "Where were you, Amy? I said, a penny for your thoughts."

"For real?"

"No!" Anders rolled his eyes.

"I didn't think so." Amy chuckled. "I was just thinking about this rustler. I think his name is Jack, or something like that. He must've escaped from jail."

"Or never got there in the first place," Anders put in.

"What do you mean?" Amy asked curiously.

"Your dad just found out that the marshal was one of them. He was posing as a marshal in order to help them. Their plan was to, in time, overrun the town and use it as a sort of home base. I just remembered that your dad had told me that."

"Wait a minute, how'd he find that out?" Amy asked.

"He got a letter from Jessica."

"What! They're writing each other?" Amy exclaimed.

Anders stared at her. "You didn't know?"

Amy shook her head.

Anders shrugged. "Well, you do now. Anyway that's what she told him. Tyler and Brent were the only ones to reach jail."

"This may be worse than we think! I'll bet he didn't turn in that money either. He was probably involved in the robbery. Come to think of it, that's probably why he didn't find the money in the first place."

"Right," Anders agreed. "He was probably really disappointed when you found it."

"Oh, I'm sure!" Amy laughed.

She raised her voice so the others could hear. "I'm going to ask that you all not tell anyone about this man. Anders and I have been talking and this is more serious than we thought originally. Do not tell anyone except your parents, and please ask them not to tell anyone else. I'm going to tell my dad and Mr. Henderson and let them decide who to tell and what to do."

"Sure, I won't tell." Adam nodded.

"I won't tell," Julie agreed.

The others nodded their heads.

"Thanks," Amy said. "If this information gets out, whoever is involved in whatever scheme that man didn't want us to find out about could get warned and make a break for it before we have time to do anything."

When they reached the ranch, Amy dismounted by the corral, untacked and groomed Bannie, then scanned the yard, expecting to see Little Lady still saddled. To her surprise, Roseann was leading the untacked, groomed horse into one of the corrals. Wisely, Amy said nothing. She turned Bannie loose in the small pasture and went in search of her dad.

Devon was standing outside the bunkhouse talking with some of his men. "Did you have a good time, Amy?" he asked with a friendly smile as she walked up.

"Oh, yes, I had a lovely time. Do you know where my dad is?" she asked.

"He went to town earlier this afternoon. He should be back anytime," Devon told her.

"Okay, thanks." Amy headed for the house.

Roseann was standing by the window when Amy entered the bedroom. She turned around quickly when the door opened and said in a strange voice, "I need to talk to you, Amy."

"Sure." Amy replied.

"Should we go out to the porch? It's cooler out there." Roseann suggested.

"Okay." As Amy walked out to the porch, she wondered what Roseann could want. *She seems upset*, she thought to herself. *Maybe the incident with the snake has something to do with it.*

The two girls settled themselves on the porch swing. Roseann nervously fingered her dress. After a few minutes, she spoke. "I've been doing some thinking after what happened with the snake and ... and I want to thank you. You saved my life, you know, at risk of your own." She took a deep breath. "What I want to know is ... why? Why would you risk your life to save me when ... when I treated you so badly?" Tears welled up in her eyes and spilled down her cheeks. "I treated you so awful. When I learned you were a Christian, I made up my mind to hate you. I treated you like my slave or something, but you never complained. I didn't want anything to do with Christianity, but I've been miserable. It made me mad to see how happy you were, even when I mistreated you. Then you save my life." She looked down at her lap, her tears making a dark, damp spot on her dress.

Lord, give me the right words, Amy breathed. She cleared her throat. "Roseann." she began gently, "let me tell you of Someone who did give His life for you."

"You ... you mean Jesus, don't you?" Roseann asked, wiping away her tears.

Amy nodded. "Jesus died on the cross to save you from spending eternity in Hell and from your sins. If He hadn't died in your place, you would have had to die.

Let's take what happened today for an example. Let's say I was Jesus and you were ... you!"

Roseann gave her a small smile.

"By stepping between you and the snake, I took your place. Instead of letting the snake bite you, I chose to let it bite me. Thankfully, it didn't, but I knew I was ready to die and you weren't."

Both girls were silent for a moment, and then Amy pulled her Bible from her pocket. "There's a verse I want to read for you," she said, flipping through the pages. "When I got saved, just shortly before my tenth birthday, my mom used this verse to help me. Here it is. Isaiah 53:5: 'But he was wounded for our transgressions, he was bruised for our iniquities: the chastisement of our peace was upon him; and with his stripes we are healed.' Mom had me put my name in this verse," Amy explained. "But he was wounded for Amy Kentworthy's transgressions, he was bruised for Amy Kentworthy's iniquities: the chastisement of Amy Kentworthy's peace was upon him; and with his stripes Amy Kentworthy was healed.' Now put your name in where I put mine and read it again."

Slowly Roseann read the verse, inserting her name. "But he was wounded for Roseann Henderson's transgressions, he was bruised for Roseann Henderson's iniquities: the chastisement of Roseann Henderson's peace was upon him; and with his stripes Roseann Henderson was healed."

Her eyes were shining as she looked up at Amy. "I believe, Amy! I believe! How do I become a Christian?"

"Ask Jesus to forgive your sins and to come into your heart and be your Lord and Savior," Amy answered.

"Will you pray with me?" Roseann asked.

Amy nodded, and the two girls bowed their heads together while Roseann prayed. "Dear Lord, I know I am a sinner. Thank you for dying on the cross for me. I want you to come into my heart and be my Savior. In Jesus's name, Amen." Roseann lifted her head and looked at Amy, her eyes shining with hope and joy. "Thank you, Amy. Thank you for not giving up on me," she breathed.

Amy laughed joyously. "You're welcome, Roseann. This is an answer to my prayers!"

Roseann stood to her feet. "I'm going to tell my dad right now! Maybe now that I've become a Christian, he'll want to go back to church. He is a Christian but neither one of us has been living right. I think he's been bitter about Mom leaving, just like I was."

Roseann left to find Devon, and Amy went to greet her dad—who had just ridden in—joy and thankfulness in her heart.

"Did you have a good time?" Clint asked as Amy joined him.

"Oh, yes, but you'll never guess what happened!"

"Let me try," Clint grinned at her. "You ran into a rustler."

Amy's mouth dropped open. "How in the world did you know?" she asked in astonishment.

Clint chuckled. "I know everything. You should know that by now!"

"Dad!" Amy protested.

"All right." Clint leaned against the corral fence. "I ran into the marshal, and he knew about the group we caught in Red River. Turns out that the marshal there was one of the rustlers."

"I knew that," Amy said. "Anders told me."

Clint smiled. "Then I suppose you know that Jessica and I have been writing each other."

Amy nodded. "Why didn't you tell me?"

"I wasn't sure how you would take it. Kinda wanted to figure out if it was goin' anywhere first."

"You mean you want to marry her?" Amy gasped.

"Hold your horses! I've only known her a few weeks. Time will tell what happens. Anyway, back to the rustlers. Tyler and Brent were the only ones that made it to jail, and they've been released now. The marshal and his men cleared out of there soon after we did, and it seems they headed this way, to be closer to the border."

"But how did you know we'd seen a rustler?" Amy asked.

"Just a wild guess, from the look on your face," Clint told her. "Do you know which one it was?"

"Anders and I both recognized him as Jack." Amy told him about the rustler's menacing words and what she thought he meant by them.

Clint nodded. "Sounds like you're right. I think we've got another adventure on our hands!"

Chapter Twenty
The Hideout Hunt

"So what are we going to do?" Amy asked as they walked toward the bunkhouse together.

"Well, the first thing we need to do is find their hideout. Of course, a man would be suspected in a minute if he started looking around back there," Clint said thoughtfully.

"What if some of the hands just acted like they were looking for stray cattle or something?"

"Too risky." He glanced over at her. "Hm. I don't like the idea, but it may be our only option."

"We have to look for it!"

Clint nodded. "I don't like it, but I think it's the only way we can catch them. You can go on more trips to that bluff you were telling me about and try to get a look around without the men figuring out what you're up to. I'll have to talk to Devon about it, but I think that is the way to go. Just remember," his eyes twinkled, "your job is to *find* them, our job is to *get* them."

Amy laughed. She knew exactly what he meant. "Will we go tomorrow?"

Clint nodded. "Sure. Don't get into trouble, and take Rio along. He may be of some help. Well, I'm starved. We'll figure out the details later after I talk to Devon."

While they ate, Amy told her dad about Roseann.

"That's wonderful, Amy! I'm glad you were able to be a testimony. Maybe it'll help Devon." Clint gave her a smile that warmed her heart.

Thank you, Lord, for a father like mine. Amy prayed. Aloud she said, "Roseann was hoping it would help Mr. Henderson."

Devon came to talk to Clint then, so Amy went in search of the boys and found them outside sitting on the corral fence.

"What are you talking about?" she asked, climbing up to join them.

"Jack." Anders answered promptly. "Did you talk to your dad?"

Amy nodded and told them what she and Clint had discussed.

Anders's eyes danced. "Man alive! That ought to be lots of fun! Just think of how frustrated those guys will be!"

"Remember what Dad said?" Amy tilted her head to the side. "Our job is to find out where they are, not to catch them. I'm warning you, Anders, don't do anything daft!"

"Aw, Amy. I know better than that!"

"I hope so, or we could all get in a lot of trouble!"

Soon Clint and Devon came out and discussed the plan for the next day. Amy, Anders, Roseann, Tye, and Arty were to go back to the bluff and to see if they could see the rustlers' camp or hideout without drawing unnecessary attention to themselves. By the time they finished discussing the details, it was getting late, and Amy said goodnight and headed for the house.

"Sweet dreams!" Anders called after her.

"Thanks."

Roseann was sitting on the floor untangling some ribbon when Amy walked in, and she looked up with a smile. "I was wondering when you would come. What took you so long?" She got to her feet and put the ribbon away.

"I was talking to the boys. Listen to this." Amy leaned forward. "We're going back to the bluff tomorrow!"

"Why?" Roseann asked curiously.

Amy explained about finding where the rustlers were hiding out.

Roseann's eyes sparkled. "That'll be so much fun!"

Amy leaned back on her bed. "By the way, what did your dad say when you told him about you getting saved?"

"Well, he said he was glad that I'm happy now and that he knows he was wrong to be bitter at God for Mom leaving. He said he's been backslidden and wants to do better."

"That's wonderful!" Amy exclaimed. "See? The Lord used you to bring your dad back to Him."

Roseann nodded. "Maybe Mama will come back, too."

"I hope so," Amy said fervently. "Shall we read the Bible together tonight?"

"Sure."

After their devotions, Roseann asked Amy to tell about the cattle drive. Amy described the trip in detail. "But I was ready for a soft bed by the time we got here," she said.

Roseann chuckled. "I can imagine you were." She shook her head. "And here you are in the middle of another adventure! It seems to follow you everywhere!"

Amy laughed. "Dad says the same thing. I'm glad it does, though. I suppose I'd be lost without it." She yawned. "Well, I guess we'd better get some sleep. We'll need our heads to be bright and fresh tomorrow, I reckon."

"We sure will." Roseann blew out the lamp, and the room was cloaked in darkness.

Amy sighed contentedly as she settled down for the night. *Thank you for a wonderful day, Lord.*

*****

Amy awoke the next morning to someone shaking her and saying urgently, "Wake up, Amy. The calves are out!"

Instantly, she was wide awake. "The calves got out! Hey Roseann! I'm awake, quit jerking on me!"

"Sorry!" Roseann laughed. "Hurry up!"

Amy dressed quickly and followed Roseann outside into the early morning light. The frisky calves, delighted to be free, were running here and there. Several of the men were trying to round them up on foot, while others got their horses. Amy grabbed Bannie's bridle from the wagon as she ran past. He was standing at the corral gate and whinnied eagerly as she ran up. Slipping the bridle on, she led him next to the fence and used that to mount him bareback.

As she rode out of the corral, she noticed some calves heading down the road. She gave Bannie his head and galloped after them.

Several of them headed into the brush that lined the road, and as Amy followed them, a movement on the other side of the road caught her eye. She bent down, pretending to fix something on her boot, and looked beneath her arm.

A horseman was riding quickly in the opposite direction.

"That looks like Jack. What is he doing over here?" she said aloud. "I wonder if he let the calves out. But why would he do that? Unless ..." she sat up straight. "Unless it was to distract us while he does something else. But he rode off in the opposite direction of the bluff. Maybe their hideout isn't by there at all." She clucked to Bannie and started after the calves again.

Ten minutes later, she had them bunched and headed back to the ranch. As she rode up, Daniel opened the pasture gate.

"I was just about to go look for you," he greeted her. "Looks like they're all here now."

"Where's Dad?" Amy asked as she slid down and tied Bannie to the fence.

Daniel shrugged. "I don't know."

Amy found her dad saddling Renegade by the hitching post.

"Morning, Dad," she greeted him.

"Morning, Amy." He looked at her curiously. "What's the matter? You look like you've seen a rattlesnake."

"Almost." She told him about seeing Jack.

"Hm." Clint stroked his mustache. "I wonder what they're up to. Wish I knew why he came so close to the ranch. If he rode off the other way ...." He broke off his sentence. "We'll keep the plans for today, except I'm sending Daniel with you. Start right after breakfast, and be careful. I have a feeling those guys will have their eyes on you."

"We'll be careful," Amy promised.

She got her saddle from the wagon, then headed back to the corral where Anders was saddling Star, a palomino mare.

"Where have you been?" he asked without turning around. "You were gone long enough to round up every cow in Texas!"

Amy laughed. "Not quite that long, I'm sure. I was talking to Jack."

Anders swung around to stare at her. "What? You're kidding right?"

"Of course, but I did see him." She told him what she had told her dad and her suspicions that it was Jack who let the calves out.

Anders shook his head. "He didn't let the calves out, Amy. One of Devon's men said he forgot to latch the gate after he fed them last night."

Amy shrugged. "It was just an idea, but it still doesn't explain why he was riding over there." She indicated the direction with her hand.

Anders grinned. "Well, I guess that's somethin' for you to puzzle about."

Amy laughed. "As if I didn't have enough to do!"

Daniel walked up, leading his horse. "Ready, Freddy?" he asked.

"Yep, but I'm not Freddy." Anders gave one last tug on the cinch.

"My mistake. Catch, Amy." Daniel tossed her a paper sack. "Somethin' for lunch, I guess. Grubby wanted me to give it to you."

"Thanks." Amy tucked it into her saddlebags.

Arty and Tye rode up on their horses, and a few minutes later, Roseann joined them.

As she saddled Little Lady, she asked. "What direction are we heading today?"

"Back to the bluff, right guys?" Amy looked at Anders.

"Right." He nodded. "We didn't see anything there yesterday, but then we weren't looking for anything either. If we can't see anything from there, maybe we can ride a little ways beyond."

"And hope Jack or his buddies aren't around," Tye interjected.

"Right." Anders chuckled as he swung into the saddle.

As they rode past the bunkhouse, Clint called out, "Don't do anything daft. I need you back in one piece!"

Amy laughed and waved her hand to him. "I'll try to keep out of trouble! See you later!"

"Amy, did you pack cookies for lunch?" Anders asked as they rode past the corrals and headed onto the range.

"No salty cookies this time, I promise!" she assured him. "There are cookies, but Grubby made them."

"Whew!" Anders grinned. "At least we know they'll be edible!"

"Oh, come on, Anders," Amy protested. "That was a once-in-a-lifetime mistake!"

"Oh, yeah?" Anders challenged. "I'll catch you at it again someday."

"We'll see about that." Amy threw back her shoulders. "Just wait until I catch *you* doing something crazy!"

Anders chuckled. "All right, all right. I can see I'll have to watch my step from now on!"

A little while later, Anders sat up straight in his saddle and turned to Amy with a grin. "Say, Amy, I've got a joke for you. What's black and white and red all over?"

"A newspaper, silly. That joke's as old as the sun," Amy said.

"Seeing as the sun was made before man, I don't see how that could be," he teased.

"All right, Anders, I've got one for you," she said sweetly.

"Oh, no!" Anders pretended to be scared.

"Ready?" she asked.

"Ready!"

"All right, here it goes. I can make you say purple."

"How?" Anders asked curiously.

"What are the colors of the American flag?"

"Red, white, and blue."

"Correct!" Amy smiled.

"But you said you could make me say purple." Anders looked puzzled.

"Gotcha!" Amy laughed.

Anders groaned. "Rats!"

"That was a good one, Amy!" Daniel chuckled.

"The joke king gets bested at his own game!" Tye grinned.

"I have a feeling I won't live this one down for a long time!" Anders shook his head.

"Back home, no one ever gets Anders with a joke," Amy explained to Roseann. "It's usually the other way around."

The boys were laughing and joking, but Amy noticed Roseann seemed quiet and reserved. After a few minutes, she remarked, "You've been kind of quiet."

Roseann grinned. "I'm enjoying listening to you guys. Sometimes it's more fun to listen than to talk."

"I'm glad we're entertaining." Amy smiled. "I thought maybe something was wrong."

Roseann shook her head. "No, nothing's wrong."

"We're almost to the bluff," Tye announced

"I don't think we should leave our horses in the trees again. Maybe we should leave them at the bottom of the bluff where we can still see them," Amy suggested. "What do you think?"

"I think you worry too much," Anders grumbled.
"That's a good point," Arty spoke up.
"Which one?" Daniel asked, grinning. "That Amy worries too much, or that we should leave the horses where we can see them?"

Arty chuckled. "Well, maybe both, but I was referring to Amy's idea."

"I agree." Tye nodded. "We don't want to be left on foot with rustlers about."

"Then that's what we'll do," Amy said. "Let's race to the bluff!"

"And we're off!" Anders shouted. He reached over and grabbed her hat bandana as he raced past.

"Hey! Give that back!" Amy yelled.

*****

From a nearby hill, unfriendly eyes were watching.

"What'd you make of the kids bein' back, Jack?" The speaker was a dirty, mean-faced man with an ugly glint in his eye.

Jack scowled. "I dunno, Al. They could just be playin' around. I think the girl might've seen me this morning. I was down by the ranch lookin' around and the calves got out. She was roundin' them up on the road. I don't think I got away quick enough."

"What were you doin' down there?" Al asked harshly. "Thought I told you to stay away from there."

"I know, Al," Jack said patiently. "I was tryin' to gather information. Don't go gittin' mad at me. I'm not stupid. I know how to cover my tracks."

Al scowled. "I'm leavin' it to you to watch them kids and get rid of them if you can. Don't let me down or else!"

"I won't, Al. You can tend to your *other business* and leave this to me."

"Good. Now get goin', and don't let them out of your sight." Al stomped toward his horse, mounted, and galloped away.

Left by himself, Jack stared at the group down the hill. "I'm beginning to wonder what the meanin' of a life like this is," he muttered to himself.

He stood in silence for a few minutes more, then walked down the slope to his horse, mounted, and rode slowly away.

*****

The group reached the bluff and hobbled their horses. "Should we eat lunch on the bluff?" Amy asked.

"Probably'd be a good idea. It'd give us more time to look around." Daniel nodded.

Amy slung her saddle bags over her shoulder and started toward the bluff, then stopped and turned back. "There isn't any water up there." She let the saddle bags slide to the ground and dug out the coffee pot.

"I'll go get some." Tye offered.

"Thanks." Amy handed him the pot and picked up the saddlebags again. "We'll wait to eat until you get back."

"Of course!" He grinned. "You couldn't eat without coffee!"

Amy laughed. "Well, I could if I had to, but I'd rather not go without if at all possible."

Tye headed for the creek while the others started up the bluff.

"Do you think it's safe for Tye to go alone?" Roseann asked. "Maybe someone should go with him."

"I think he'll be all right," Daniel said. "We'll be able to see him most of the time from up here anyway."

Roseann shrugged. "Okay, I just hate to think what would happen if the rustlers should be hiding somewhere around here."

"Whew! It's really warm," she commented a few minutes later. "The rocks must give off radiant heat or something."

Amy nodded. "Probably. It'll be cooler on top. See? The grass is waving up there. Must be a breeze blowing."

"Hope you're right." Roseann wiped the sweat from her face.

It was cooler on top. A cool, gentle breeze was blowing. Anders and Arty gathered twigs and dry grass to build a fire while Roseann helped Amy unpack the lunch things. They had just finished setting everything out when Tye appeared with the water.

"I saw Jack," he announced as he set the coffee pot down.

"What? Where?" Amy exclaimed.

"He was riding just inside the trees on the other side of the creek. I don't think he saw me though. I ducked behind a tree until he was gone."

Anders shrugged. "He's probably watching us. We'll have to keep an eye on the horses."

"Maybe we should leave," Roseann suggested. "I don't like the idea of him watching us."

Rustlers and the Texas Trail

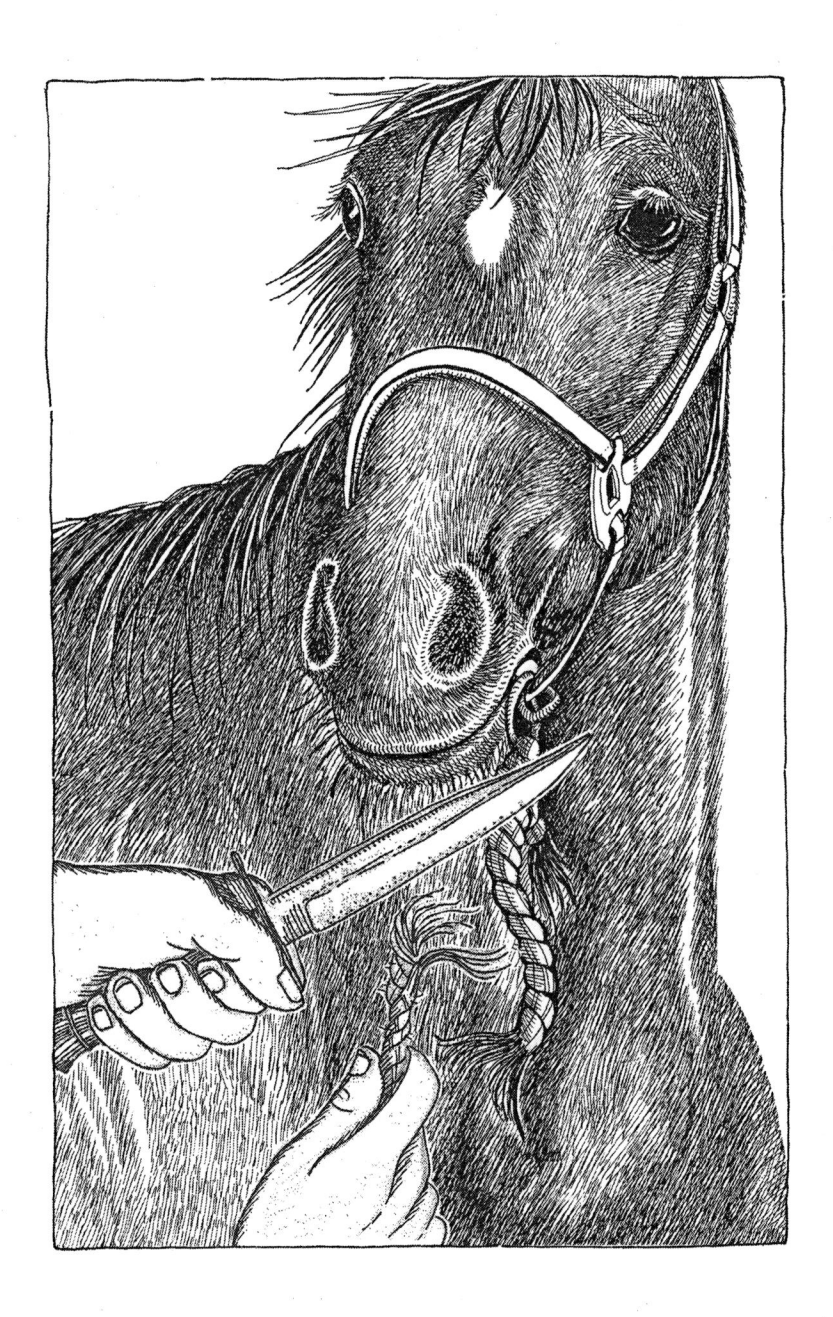

"If we go down now, he'll know something's up," Daniel said. "I don't think he'll come after us. Let's just act normal and eat lunch. Then we can ride around a little."

After Daniel asked the blessing on the food, they all found comfortable seats and studied the landscape while they ate.

"What are we looking for?" Arty asked.

"Anything unusual. Smoke from a fire, a campsite, riders, that kind of thing," Anders told him.

They were almost finished eating when Tye suddenly leapt to his feet. "Jack's down by the horses," he cried. "He's cutting the ropes again!"

Amy jumped up. "Come on! Let's get down there! Maybe we can stop him before all the horses get loose!" She started to run down the bluff, but Anders grabbed her.

"No, Amy," he said. "He's got a gun. Let him cut the horses loose; they won't get far. When he leaves, we'll go down and catch them."

"Ugh!" Amy stared down the slope. "I hate feeling so helpless."

"Quick, everyone! Sit down," Daniel said urgently. "We don't want him to know he's been spotted."

Amy flopped down and picked up her cup. "How long do we have to sit here?"

"Until he leaves," Arty answered.

Tye crawled over to one of the boulders and peered around it. After what seemed like hours to Amy, Tye reported that Jack was gone.

Instantly the others were on their feet.

"Let's get down there!" Amy said impatiently.

"Just hold your horses!" Anders told her. "The horses aren't going anywhere. They're too busy eatin'. We go runnin' down there, they'll spook and then we'll never catch them. Some of them aren't half-broke."

As they walked down the bluff, Roseann said, "I wonder why he didn't drive the horses off like he did before."

"He probably didn't want to draw attention to himself," Tye said. "If he'd made enough noise to spook the horses, we would have noticed him for sure. This way, he could get away undetected."

"Well, I'm glad he didn't spook them," Amy said. "It makes it easier to catch them."

Fifteen minutes later, they had the horses caught and back on new picket lines.

"Let's head back up the bluff," Daniel suggested. "We have to get our stuff anyway; we might as well look around some more."

"Sounds good to me," Amy agreed.

The six climbed back up the bluff and settled down to study the countryside below them.

After a while, Daniel leaned forward. "Unless my eyes are playing tricks on me, I think there is a group of riders coming this way."

"Can you see who they are?" Amy asked, straining her eyes to see the riders clearly.

Daniel shook his head. "No, they're too far away."

"I recognize Jack's horse," Arty said a moment later.

"Then he's not watching us?" Amy frowned.

Daniel shrugged. "Doesn't look like it."

Suddenly Tye burst out. "Look over there! Right next to that hill to the left. It's almost hidden. Do you see it?"

"A shack!" Arty exclaimed. "There are horses in the corral, and the riders are riding toward it!"

"That's got to be their hideout," Daniel agreed.

"We found it!" Amy cheered. "Come on, let's have some of these cookies to celebrate!"

Fifteen minutes later, Anders leaned back and patted his stomach. "The cookies were really good, Amy."

"Thanks and no thanks. You know I didn't make them." Amy rolled her eyes.

"You look so beautiful when you do that. Could you do it again in slow motion?" Anders teased.

"Oh, be quiet, Anders. Back to the rustlers." Amy said.

Anders stood up and turned around.

"What are you doing?" Amy asked, puzzled.

"You said 'back to the rustlers.'" Anders grinned.

Amy groaned. "Stop it, Anders."

Daniel spoke up. "I think, so we don't arouse suspicion, we should go down and ride around a while. The dishes need washed, so we'll go to the river first. Just remember: we weren't supposed to do anything more than to locate their camp, so our job is finished."

They quickly packed up and headed down to the horses.

"We'll take the horses with us," Daniel instructed. "We don't need them stolen or turned loose *again*."

The dishes were done amid much splashing and laughter. They were almost finished when Amy caught a movement in the trees and bushes behind them.

"Don't turn around, but there's a man watching us," she said out of the corner of her mouth.

Anders was drying the dishes beside her and was the only one who heard.

He turned to look at her. "Jack?" he asked.

Amy shook her head. "I only got a quick look, but I didn't recognize him."

"Come on, guys, we're ready to go," Arty called.

Amy picked up the dry dishes and dumped them into her saddle bags, scanning the surrounding bushes.

She caught another glimpse of the man as she mounted Bannie and noticed he was riding a pinto mare.

Quickly she suggested, "Let's ride over there," indicating with her hand. "Is there anything interesting to see there?" she asked Roseann.

"Depends on what you find interesting," Roseann replied.

Anders winked at Amy as he rode past. He knew why she wanted to ride in that direction.

They rode for an hour but saw nothing. Amy noticed some hoof prints, but that was all.

Finally, they decided to head home.

"It's so warm I'm getting sleepy." Anders yawned.

"Me, too," Amy agreed. "But every time I start to relax, I think about the rustlers, how they could be hiding behind a bush or rock, and suddenly, I'm wide awake!"

Anders chuckled. "Yeah, it is kind of creepy to think that someone could be watching us and we don't know it, but personally, I'm too tired to be worried!"

Chapter Twenty-one
Uncovering the Plot

Clint was sitting on the wagon tongue fixing a harness when the group rode in. He put the harness down and came over to meet them. "What'd you find?" he asked.

They took turns telling him the events of the day as they unsaddled their horses.

"Well, they picked a perfect spot to hide out," Clint said when they finished. He stroked his mustache thoughtfully. When he spoke again, his eyes twinkled. "Amy, I think you and I are going for a ride tonight."

"What are you talking about? Where will we go?" Amy asked, puzzled.

"Oh, just wait and see," he replied and quickly turned away.

Amy turned to the others with lifted eyebrows.

"Don't look at me," Daniel told her. "I'm as much in the dark as you are."

Amy shrugged. "He'll probably tell me right before we leave. Dad always did like being secretive and mysterious."

After they had taken care of their horses, Amy and Roseann went into the house. "I can't figure out what Dad's plan is." Amy flopped on the bed and folded her hands behind her head.

"You'll find out soon enough." Roseann seated herself in the rocking chair.

"I guess you're right." Amy sighed. "All the same, I wish he'd at least given me a clue."

Roseann smiled. "Patience is a virtue."

Amy laughed. "Listen to you! Our roles have reversed; now you're teaching me!"

Roseann chuckled. "I was just reminding you."

The girls talked for half an hour or so, and then Amy wandered outside and spotted her dad talking to Daniel by the corral.

When he caught sight of her, he motioned for her to join them. "We're going to eat supper in a few minutes," he said as she walked up. "I want you to have Buck fed and saddled."

"Okay." Amy stood staring after him as he and Daniel walked away, talking in low tones.

Guess I'm not supposed to know the plan yet, Amy thought as she picked up a halter and opened the corral gate. Buck was reluctant to be caught, and it was several minutes before Amy finally cornered him. She tied him to the fence and gave him a flake of hay and some grain to eat while she tacked him up.

Anders sauntered over and leaned over the fence to talk to her. "What do you know?" he asked.

"Nothing yet." Amy hefted the saddle onto Buck's back. "Dad just told me to saddle Buck. You got any ideas?"

Anders shook his head. "I figure it's got somethin' to do with the rustlers, but that's all."

Amy nodded. "That's what I'm thinking too."

Soon it was supper time. Amy expected to leave as soon as they finished eating, but to her surprise, her dad seemed to be in no hurry. Everyone gathered around the stove in the bunkhouse and talked away the evening hours. When it began to get dark, Clint motioned to Amy, and she followed him outside.

"Where are we going?" she asked.

"I want you to take me to the bluff. Can you find your way in the dark?" he asked.

"I think so. Why do you want to go there?"

"You'll see" was all he said.

Daniel had fed and saddled Clint's horse, Morgan, so they were soon on their way.

"Try to stay out of the open areas," Clint whispered to Amy.

"Okay," she whispered back.

When they reached the creek, Clint spoke again. "We'll leave the horses here. I think they'll be safe."

Amy dismounted and hobbled Buck.

"Take me to the top," Clint whispered as they approached the bluff. Amy led him on a zigzag course, dodging the many boulders and smaller rocks.

When they reached the top, there was just enough light to distinguish things clearly. Amy pointed out the shack.

There was light streaming from the windows, and Amy could just make out the shadowy forms of the horses in the corral. Clint was silent for several minutes, studying the terrain.

Finally he spoke. "Here's what I'm figuring to do. We're going to ride around that hill over there and come up behind the shack. Then we'll hobble the horses and sneak right up to it. Maybe we can hear something at the window. Got it?"

"I got it, but I'm not sure I want to," Amy said dryly.

"You can stay here if you want." Clint said.

"No way!" Amy shook her head. "Not by myself. It just seems foolhardy with just the two of us."

"I know," Clint told her. "But it would be doubly dangerous if there were more people. Besides, Daniel and Devon know where we are, and if we're not back by one o'clock, they'll come looking for us."

"Okay." Amy nodded.

"Let's pray before we go," Clint suggested as he removed his hat "Dear Lord, Give us safety as we try to find out what these men are trying to do. Give us wisdom and Your protection. In Jesus's name, Amen. Feel better?" he asked as they rose from their knees.

"Yes." Amy gave him a bright smile.

"All right." Clint laid his hand on her shoulder. "Let's go get the horses then."

Ten minutes later, Clint was leading the way around the bluff to the hill behind the rustlers' shack. The darkness of the night seemed to press in, and Amy shuddered to think what unfriendly eyes might be watching them.

Keep us safe, Lord, and give me courage, she prayed silently.

As they neared the hill, Clint whispered, "We'll just tie the horses to some bushes. We may need them in a hurry, and I don't want to deal with hobbles in the dark. Remember to keep your voice low. Sound carries easily on the night air."

Amy started to nod, then remembered that he couldn't see her. "Right," she whispered, and she swung to the ground and secured Buck's reins to a bush.

Her dad appeared beside her. "Hold onto my hand," he whispered. "I don't want to lose you in the dark."

"Thanks, Dad," Amy groaned. "I feel about three years old!"

Clint chuckled softly. "Sorry."

Together they climbed to the top of the hill.

When the shack came into view, Clint paused. "Let's wait here a minute." he whispered. A moment later, he gripped Amy's arm. Leaning close to her ear, he said, "Did you see that?"

"No." Amy shook her head.

"There was a bright spot of light, then it disappeared, like someone opened a door and shut it again. I thought I heard a horse a few minutes ago. Looks like they've got visitors. Let's get a closer look."

Silently they crept down the hill. About halfway down, Clint stopped so suddenly Amy bumped into him.

"We've got to circle around. We're downwind of the horses," he whispered.

They angled across the hill until the slight breeze was blowing in their faces.

Then Clint paused and drew Amy closer. "I want to hear what's going on in there and, if possible, get a look at the men. You can wait here or come with me."

"I'm not staying by myself," Amy said emphatically.

"Okay, then, keep down and follow me." Clint crouched low and walked slowly forward, Amy following closely. When they reached the shack, they crawled forward on their hands and knees until they were directly below one of the windows. It was open slightly. Clint raised a finger to his lips, and Amy nodded. She strained her ears to catch what was being said.

"Well, you sure took long enough to get here, Bart," a gruff voice was saying. "I'm gittin' mighty eager to git to the border. People are likely to git suspicious. We can't hide out forever. Someone's likely to find us."

"Calm down, Al." The smooth, quiet voice floated out the window to the listeners crouched beneath it.

Amy started. Reaching out her hand, she nudged her dad. He nudged her back, and Amy knew they were both thinking the same thing.

The quiet voiced man was the crooked marshal from Red River! He was speaking again and Amy listened carefully.

"I had a little 'business' to take care of. Don't worry about a thing. I've got everything ready, and it'll all go as planned."

"It'd better," Al growled. "I've done more than my share already. When are we gonna start gatherin' the cattle?"

"Tomorrow night," Bart answered. "We'll hold them down the river a piece. It'll take a few nights to gather them all, then we'll hightail it for Mexico! Just think of all the money we'll make, boys!"

A few of the men grunted.

"There's some nosy kids stayin' at Henderson's," another man spoke up, and Amy instantly recognized his voice.

"That's Jack," she whispered to her dad.

Jack continued. "You'd better look out for them. They're the same ones that tried to get us at Red River. I think they suspect somethin'. They were on the bluff yesterday, and I tried to run their horses off, but it didn't work. The girl's name is Amy, I think."

"Amy?" Bart echoed. "You bet we'd better look out for her. She's the one who found the money. She's a sharp one, all right. We may have to do something about her if she gets too curious." His voice was menacing.

Chairs scraped on the wooden floor as the men stood up.

"Tomorrow night," Bart was saying. "Meet me at the water hole at midnight, and we'll begin the raid."

Clint got to his knees and took a quick look through the window.

After a few seconds, he dropped back down, and pulling Amy close, he whispered, "Let's get out of here. Follow me."

Amy crawled along the ground as quickly and as silently as she could.

When they were far enough away, Clint stood to his feet and ran silently up the hill, Amy following.

About halfway up, Clint stopped and looked back at the shack.

As they watched, the door opened, and a man stepped out. He disappeared around the opposite side of the shack and reappeared a moment later, leading a horse. Stepping lightly into the saddle, he turned to speak to someone still inside the shack and as he did so, the light from the window fell across his face.

"It's him, sure enough," Clint whispered.

"Yep," Amy agreed. She could easily make out the features of the crooked marshal's face. "Wonder where he's goin'," she said quietly.

"I reckon he's stayin' somewhere else," Clint said as Bart swung his horse around and galloped away. "If the others get caught, he won't. He's the leader. There were six of them in there. I recognized three. Bart, Jack and one other one, I don't know his name."

While they were talking, they had been walking back to the horses. Morgan nickered softly as they walked up.

Amy ached all over, and she groaned as she swung into the saddle.

Clint grinned. "You look a little worse for the wear."

"I feel worse for the wear." Amy yawned. "I'll sleep good tonight."

"You'd better. We'll have a big day tomorrow."

They both fell silent as they began the long ride home.

It was nearing midnight when they reached the ranch. Nothing stirred as they rode in.

"Guess they gave up on us." Clint chuckled as he slid from the saddle.

"Guess so," Amy agreed.

Wearily she untacked Buck and gave him a good rubbing down. She fed him some grain, then headed for the house. Roseann was still awake, and she looked curiously at Amy as she entered the room.

"I'll tell you all about it in the morning, Roseann," Amy told her. "Right now, I need to turn in."

"I can see that." Roseann chuckled. "I can wait."

Amy quickly changed her clothes and stretched out on her bed. Roseann blew out the lamp and rolled over with a sleepy "Goodnight."

"Goodnight," Amy answered, and then all was silent.

*****

It was early when Amy awoke the next morning, and the sun was just beginning to peep over the horizon.

She slid out of bed and dressed quietly. Being careful not to wake Roseann, she slipped outside. The ranch yard was still and quiet. Amy walked along slowly, enjoying the beautiful, misty morning. She had just rounded the corner of a small shed when a shadow leapt out at her. Amy jumped back and gave a yelp of surprise. She let out a sigh of relief when she realized who is it was.

"Anders!" she scolded, crossing her arms. "That wasn't funny! I thought you were a rustler or something!"

Anders grinned and shrugged. "What are you doing up?" he asked, leaning against the shed.

"What are you doing up?" Amy retorted.

"Watching the sunrise," he replied.

"And?" Amy asked archly.

Anders groaned. "You're too smart! Take a look past the corrals, but don't make it too obvious."

Discreetly, Amy glanced in that direction. She could just make out a pinto horse and a man standing next to it, partly hidden by the mesquite bushes.

"I can't tell who it is," Anders said. "It's not Jack because he rides a bay."

"I think I recognize the horse, but I can't make out the man either," Amy said. "By the horse, I think it's the same man who was watching us at the creek."

"Should we get your dad?" Anders wondered.

"I don't know. He's not hurting anything. Just watching, looks like."

The bunkhouse door slammed in the early morning stillness.

"Sounds like they're getting up anyway," Anders observed.

Amy looked back toward the rustler. "He's gone," she said with disappointment.

"What happened last night?" Anders asked.

"Curious as a cat!" Amy teased. She told him about seeing Bart and described the rustlers' plan.

"Well," he said when she finished, "sounds like we'll be busy tonight."

Tye and Arty joined them then. "What'd you yell for, Amy?" Arty asked.

"You heard me, and it took you this long to come see what happened? I could have been being attacked by a rabid dog or a rustler or something." Amy shook her head in mock dismay.

"Sorry!" Arty grinned. "I figured you were big enough to take care of yourself! Maybe we should get a babysitter. Anders would do!"

Amy laughed. "I don't think that will be necessary. Anders scared me, that's all."

"Anders, you shouldn't scare little girls," Tye admonished.

"I'm not a *little* girl!" Amy retorted.

"You're shorter than me, so that makes you little." Anders grinned.

"Well, I may be little in stature, but not in other respects," Amy informed them.

"Hey! What's going on over here? Fight nicely, would you?" Daniel leaned against the shed, grinning. "Sounds like a pack of wolves. Your dad wants to see you, Amy. He's by the wagon."

"Thanks, Daniel. Maybe while I'm gone, you can talk some manners into these boys."

"I'll do my best, but I can't guarantee the results of my labors," Daniel said with a mock bow.

"You're as bad as they are," Amy called over her shoulder as she walked away.

Clint was sitting on the wagon tongue with a bridle in his hands. He looked up with a smile as she approached and motioned for her to sit beside him. "Did you recover from the terrors of last night?" he teased.

Amy smiled. "Yep, but I'm not sure if I've recovered from this morning." She told him about Anders scaring her and seeing the rustler watching them.

"Can you remember anything in particular about him other than his horse?" Clint asked.

Amy shook her head. "He was too far away. I'm positive it was the same one that was watching us at the creek yesterday though."

"Well, I don't think he's very important right now. I wanted to talk about our plan. The rustlers are suspicious about you showing up two days in a row and are getting jumpy. Just like we thought they would, they're speeding up their plan to gather the cattle and light a shuck for the border. Unless I miss my guess, they'll try to plan some sort of diversion to keep us busy so we can't go after them."

"You mean like make a fire or something?" Amy asked.

Clint nodded. "Something like that. I've talked to the marshal, and since we have evidence that these men have rustled cattle before, we don't have to catch them in the act. So, here's what we do. Tonight, at about nine o'clock, we'll head for the shack, taking a different route than before just in case we were being watched last night. We'll come up behind that hill, just like we did yesterday. They should all be there doing their last minute planning. Our men will surround the shack, and then we'll have them."

"Sounds like a plan to me." Amy smiled. "You think of everything."

Clint chuckled. "Not quite. You'll be going with us of course, so get together whatever you'll need. It's going to be a busy night. Maybe we'll be able to head home after this."

"That is the best thing I've heard in a long time." Amy sighed. "This trip has been exciting, adventurous, and a good learning experience. I've enjoyed it, but I'm very ready to head home and get back to a normal life."

"I definitely agree with you there." Clint slipped his arm around her waist. "You've done well, Amy, and I'm proud of you."

Amy laid her head on his shoulder. "Thanks, Dad. I love you."

"I love you, too, Amy."

Chapter Twenty-Two
Justice for All

The ranch was full of activity that day. News had come telling of bad storms in the mountains, and Clint didn't want to get caught in them on the way home, so they planned to leave the next day if all went well with the rustlers.

The change of plans added to the things that needed done in preparation for the adventure that night, and everything needed to be packed in the wagon ready to go, all the gear needed checked, and the horses needed shoed, ready to leave the next morning. Amy packed her things and stowed them in the wagon, then went in search of Roseann.

She found her sitting on the front porch, crying.

"What's the matter?" Amy asked with concern, sitting down beside her.

Roseann smiled through her tears. "Oh, Amy, I'm going to miss you so much!"

"I'll miss you, too, but we can write each other." Amy gave her arm a squeeze. She pulled a package out of her pocket. "Now, look what I have for you."

Roseann took the package and unwrapped the paper, revealing a small Bible. "Oh, Amy!" she cried, running her finger along the smooth binding. "Thank you so much! I'll read it every day."

"That is exactly what I want you to do." Amy leaned back in her chair with a satisfied smile.

"Where did you get it?" Roseann asked, flipping through the pages.

"Dad got it for me the other day when he went into town," Amy explained.

"Thank you again!" Roseann leaned over and gave Amy a hug. "Now come see what I have for you."

"I hope you don't feel you have to give me something just because I gave you something," Amy said as she followed her into the house.

"Not at all. This is a gift of appreciation for what you've done for me," Roseann told her. "Wait here."

She returned a few minutes later and handed Amy a thin, flat package wrapped in a piece of white cloth.

Amy unwrapped the cloth to find an embroidered sampler done in neat even stitches with the words "A Friend Loveth At All Times ..." surrounded by apple blossoms.

"You were a friend to me," Roseann said softly. "And you certainly did love me at all times. I've been working on it while you were out of the house, usually in the mornings."

"Thank you, Roseann." Amy gave her a hug. "I'll hang it on my bedroom wall as soon as we get home."

"Amy," someone called from outside.

"Coming," she called back.

Anders was standing on the porch steps when she came out. "Your dad wants you to mend the saddle blankets. Some of them are pretty torn up."

"Okay." Amy started down the steps, then turned back toward him with a twinkle in her eye. "Why don't you help me?"

"I think I've got something to do in the barn." Anders made a hasty retreat, to the amusement of both girls.

"I'll help you," Roseann offered. "We can do it here on the porch. I'll get my work basket."

Amy grinned. "I think you'll do a better job than Anders anyway. I saw how he tried to sew a ripped shirt once. Yikes!"

Roseann laughed. "Some men are good at mending, and others," she shook her head, "are hopeless!"

Amy found the pile of saddle blankets and carried them to the porch. "It's a good thing you're helping," she remarked to Roseann as she came outside with her sewing basket. "I'd never get them done alone."

"I'm glad to help." Roseann spread needle, thread, and scissors out on the table, then each girl picked up a blanket and got to work.

"It's only mid-morning, but it's already hot and muggy even though it is September," Amy commented after they had been working for a while.

"I'll get us some lemonade." Roseann place a saddle blanket on the growing stack of finished ones and stood to her feet.

"Mm!" Amy smiled. "That sounds great."

Roseann returned a few minutes later with a plate of biscuits and cookies and a pitcher of lemonade. "Do you think the boys would like to join us?" she asked.

"I never heard of a boy who could resist an offer like that." Amy chuckled.

Roseann smiled. "I'll get the glasses and you can invite them to our 'lemonade party'!"

Both girls giggled.

"They probably wouldn't come if you said tea party," Amy remarked. She stood up and stretched her aching muscles. "I'll go find them."

She spotted the boys as she came around the corner of the house. Anders was leaning against the pump with his back to her. Arty, Tye, and Daniel stood in front of him.

Hmm. I think I'll play a little trick on Anders in return for the scare he gave me this morning.

The three boys who faced her looked at her curiously as she approached. Amy put a finger to her lips and shook her head.

Arty gave her a wink to show they understood. Crouching down, she crept up quietly behind the unsuspecting Anders. When she was directly behind him, she stood up and gave him a push.

"Yikes!" Anders shouted, completely startled and almost losing his balance.

Amy leaned against the pump, laughing.

"Good grief!" Anders exclaimed when he saw who it was. "You sure do like to get a fellow back! Don't you have anything better to do?"

"Actually, yes!" Amy chuckled. "I came to invite all of you to a 'lemonade party' on the front porch with Roseann and me. Of course, if you have something else to do, we'll understand."

"I'm headin' that way this minute!" Anders laughed.

"We'd better hurry or Roseann will have eaten everything!" Arty chuckled.

"Double time!" Tye took off across the yard.

"You sure pulled a slick one on me." Anders admitted as Amy fell into step beside him.

Amy chuckled. "It wouldn't have worked if Tye, Arty, and Daniel hadn't kept quiet. They saw me coming in plenty of time to warn you. I just couldn't resist the opportunity to get you back for this morning!"

"Obviously." Anders shook his head. "Some friends that won't even warn a poor fellow!"

Just before they reached the porch, he asked. "Are you ready to head home?"

Amy nodded. "I'm getting homesick. I'm glad we're leaving early."

"Me, too." Anders agreed.

The rest of the day passed quickly as they finished up last-minute packing. By supper, everything was ready to go. Roseann joined them in the bunkhouse for supper, and the atmosphere was tense and excited.

"Sit still, Amy!" Anders complained. "You a bundle of nerves or something?"

Amy shrugged as she reached for another biscuit. "It's been a long day of waiting. I'm ready for something to happen."

"Me, too," Arty agreed. "Seeing as I missed out on the last rustler adventure, I'm excited about this one."

"We should be on our way just before dark," Tye put in. "And according to my watch, it should only be about two more hours."

"Think you can wait that long?" Roseann teased Amy.

Amy grinned. "I suppose I'll have to whether I like it or not."

Finally, just when Amy thought she couldn't wait another minute, Clint told everyone to head out and get their horses saddled. The horses had been rounded up earlier and were penned in the larger of the two corrals. Amy grabbed her tack from the wagon and made her way to the corral. Anders had already caught his horse.

"You better hurry up," he called. "Your dad might leave you behind!"

Amy slung her saddle onto the fence and hung her bridle on the horn. "You sound kind of hopeful! Don't worry; I know the way to the shack."

She stepped into the pen and held her hand out to Bannie. "Come on, boy, time to go to work." Bannie snorted and trotted to the back of the corral, wedging himself in between the other horses.

"He must think you work him too hard," Anders called out.

Ten minutes later, Amy gave an exasperated sigh. "All right, Ban, I'm going for my lariat. What's gotten into you?"

"He can't answer you," Tye informed her.

"Maybe that's a good thing." Amy's rope whirled through the air and settled smoothly over Bannie's neck. "He might say something he shouldn't if he could."

"What took you so long?" Anders teased as she led Bannie out the gate. "Everyone else is ready to go."

Amy rolled her eyes. "I would have been ready sooner if you would have helped me."

Anders laughed. "You know, Amy, I think that's the first time you've ever asked for my help. Ever since we were children, you wouldn't so much as allow me to pick up a toy you dropped."

Amy smiled. "Well, if I can do it myself, I'd rather not depend on anyone else."

Anders leaned against the fence. "Sometimes we have to accept the help of others, Amy. It's not good to rely solely on ourselves."

Amy looked at him in silence for a long moment. "Isn't it a good thing to be able to take care of one's self and not always depend upon others?"

Anders nodded. "Of course, but you can easily overdo that, Amy. There are times when you need to depend on others and be open to their help. I don't mean to preach at you."

Amy shook her head. "I know you aren't, Anders. You've given me a lot to think about." She glanced over at the others. "If I don't hurry, they'll leave me behind."

"Here, let me help you saddle up." Anders grabbed her saddle and swung it onto Bannie's back.

Amy laughed. "Okay, giving me a lesson in letting others help, eh?"

Anders grinned. "Guess so."

*****

Several miles away, the rustlers were crowded together in a small, dimly lit room, discussing the coming events over supper.

"Are you ready for the raid, boys?" Bart asked. His black eyes shone fiercely in the lantern light.

"Shore thing!" Al grinned wickedly. "Won't them ranchers have a surprise in the morning? Sure wish I could see that Amy what's-her-name's face when she realizes we're gone."

"We've got to be extra careful this time, Bart." Jack looked uneasy. "I've got a hunch they'll try to stop us somehow. Maybe not tonight, but they'll cause trouble for us before we're over the border."

"You may be right, Jack," Bart agreed. "Just keep a sharp watch out. Report to me anything that looks suspicious." He pushed back his plate as he rose to his feet. "My bridle needs fixin'. Don't want it breakin' durin' the raid. I'll be back in a jiffy." He disappeared outside, letting the door slam behind him.

He returned a few minutes later with the bridle in his hands. "It's a perfect night for this, boys," he said, lowering himself heavily into a chair. "It'll be light enough to see, but dark enough to give us cover. Nothin' should go wrong. We'll soon be rich men. By the way, I took a look at the Henderson place on my way here. There was an awful lot of activity. Looks like the group from

Wyoming is planning on headin' out soon. That should give you some peace of mind, Jack."

"I don't know about that," Jack said sullenly.

*****

Back at the ranch, Anders finished saddling Bannie, and then he and Amy mounted their horses and joined the others who were grouped around Clint as he gave last-minute instructions.

"The marshal is going to meet us at the bluff. We'll ride around behind the hill, then everyone except Amy, Roseann, Anders, Tye, and Arty will go down and surround it. All the rustlers should be inside, and it should be a fairly easy job. Lord willing, there will be no violence or bloodshed. Any questions?"

The group remained silent, so Clint reined his horse around and rode out of the ranch yard, the others following closely. They reached the bluff without incident, and the marshal was there as planned with his men.

"Let's hope this one's straight." Anders muttered to Amy. "If he isn't, we could find ourselves in a real fix."

"He looks fine," Amy told him.

"So did the last one," Anders retorted.

As they continued on toward the hill, Amy thought, *I'm sorry these men have to go to jail. I hope none of them have families, but they are stealing from honest ranchers, and I don't think they would have a problem hurting someone. Maybe they will learn their lesson this time.* She sent up a silent prayer for everyone's protection that night.

Justice for All

They rode silently to the back of the hill behind the shack and hobbled the horses.

"I'm not sure it was a good idea to come," Roseann whispered to Amy.

Amy smiled in the darkness. "You'll be fine," she whispered back. "Follow me. We'll go to the top of the hill so we can watch."

When they reached it, Amy and Roseann crouched behind a bush a few feet away from the boys.

"Just a few more minutes," Amy heard her dad whisper from nearby.

Peering around the bush, Amy could faintly make out the horses in the corral next to the shack. Light streamed from the windows, and she could hear rough voices and loud laughter. A movement caught her eye, and she turned to see her dad standing to his feet. The marshal gave the signal, and the men started toward the shack.

Walking in a crouch, the men paused at the bottom of the hill, and Amy could see the marshal waving his hand, directing who went where. The men melted into the darkness, and the moment of silence seemed to stretch on forever.

There was another wave of rough, unruly laughter from inside the shack, and the marshal's men took advantage of the noise. Amy could see faint moving shadows as the men drew closer to the shack.

Suddenly, a booming voice shattered the silence. "Come out with your hands up! You are surrounded!"

Amy couldn't see the door because it was on the opposite side of the shack, but she heard the scrape of chairs being pushed back. The door squeaked on its hinges, and in the dim light, Amy could see the rustlers file slowly out, hands held over their heads.

She watched as the men were searched and bound securely, then someone stepped into the light streaming from the shack window and waved his arm.

"That's the okay signal, guys!" Anders leaped to his feet and raced back toward the horses.

"Hey! Wait up!" Arty called.

Amy and Roseann helped unhobble the horses and lead them down the hill to the waiting men. Daniel met them and took his horse from Amy. "Thanks for bringing them down. Uncle Clint wants you to start saddling the rustlers' horses. Might as well let them ride in on them," he told her.

"All right." Amy headed for the corral.

Roseann followed Amy and offered to help.

"Sure," Amy agreed.

She opened the corral gate and slipped inside. The horses were huddled in the corner, their eyes wide and fearful. There was a three-sided shelter with a hitching rail in the center for tying horses and for hanging saddles, and there were pegs nailed into the walls for bridles and lead ropes.

Amy grabbed a bridle and slowly approached the nervous horses. Roseann followed her closely. Amy held out her hand, and a curious bay gelding stepped forward cautiously.

"Easy, boy," Amy murmured softly. She slid her hand down his neck, then slipped the bridle into place. Roseann caught the pinto mare, and together the girls tied them to the fence. Then Roseann began saddling while Amy caught the rest of the horses.

They had just finished saddling all the horses when the men finished searching the shack. They had found the stolen money and several rifles that had been stolen from a store a few towns away.

"Do you mind if I ask the men a few questions?" Clint asked the marshal.

"Not at all. Go right ahead."

Clint walked over the rustlers. "Who set fire to the barn on the Rocking H ranch?" he asked.

The rustlers stared at their feet in sullen silence.

Clint strode over to Bart. "I asked a question, sir."

"Jack did," Bart said through clenched teeth. "And that's about all he did."

"I told you burning the barn was a bad idea!" Jack shouted. "And you wouldn't have gotten this far if it hadn't been for me! It was my idea to get those kids to help us."

"Enough!" Bart hissed. "If you wouldn't have been so dumb we would be on our way to Mexico right now. Instead, look at us! We're caught, and it's all your fault!"

"More like all your fault, Bart!" Al spoke up. "You were so sure of yourself, and look what you got us! If you wouldn't have been such a knot head this wouldn't have happened! You got us into this fix. If it would have been up to me we would have skipped out after our pals got caught in Wyoming, but would you listen to reason? No! You insisted on trying again just so you could get revenge!"

"Be quiet!" Bart screamed. Although his hands were tied, he lunged at the smaller man, and both men fell to the ground.

Two of the marshal's men sprang forward and soon had the rustlers separated. Al looked unmoved by his boss's outburst, but Bart glowered at him angrily.

"So," Clint folded his arms. "The men we caught on my ranch in Wyoming and you are connected somehow. That's very interesting. And I suppose they gave us that story about heading for the railroad to throw us off the scent of you fellows down here in Texas. Thanks to those boys, Tyler and Brent, your little plan didn't work. Maybe a few months in jail will make you think twice about taking what isn't yours."

"All right," Jack spoke up. "I'll tell you everything if you'll go easier on me."

"Go on." Clint watched him closely.

"You were right: that group you caught up north was working with us. Bart was the ringleader, has been for years. When you caught our men up there, Bart took the job as marshal of Red River as a cover up. The rest of us stayed in that cabin while Bart kept his ears open for any likely lookin' chance to get some easy cash. Then he'd tell us, we'd slip into town, or wherever it was, take care of business, and slip away while Bart arrived on the scene and raised a ruckus about that thieving gang. When you caught on to us in Red River, we figured it would be better for us to let you get the cattle back and get away with our freedom. You had more than enough men to take us if you knew what our game was, so we pretended to go along with you and took the chance of being caught."

Bart had been silent up until this point, but he suddenly burst out. "That ain't true! Not a word of it. They made me take the job and would have killed me if I didn't! They're lyin'!"

"Go on, Jack." Clint ignored Bart's outburst.

"That's about all there is to tell," Jack said. "We'd only been there a few weeks when you came, and you know the rest."

"Not quite." Daniel stepped forward. "Why did you follow us here?"

"Bart was mad at the girl and him." He indicated Clint with a jerk of his head. "And he wanted to get back at them somehow. Besides, we wanted to be close to the border in case we had to get away fast. So we came down here and were gonna round up some cattle, makin' sure a good bit came from this ranch, then skip out. We pulled some smaller thefts on the way and got here two days after you did."

"Thanks for telling us that, Jack," the marshal said. "I'll see what I can do about a lighter sentence, but I'm not making any promises." He turned to Clint and shook his hand. "Thanks for tipping us off. This gang was causing some real problems, and I'm glad to have them caught finally, especially the ringleader. According to what I found out about him, he's been a real troublemaker for many years. He's got a list of offenses as long as your arm."

"Glad to help," Clint told him, accepting his offered hand.

The marshal's men tied the rustlers to their saddles, roped the horses together, and rode off into the darkness.

"That was hardly even exciting!" Anders remarked once they were on their way home.

"I think it went just fine," Amy said. "I'm glad things went so smoothly.

A brisk wind was blowing, and she shivered and pulled her jacket closer. "On nights like this, I can hardly believe I'm in Texas," she commented to Roseann.

Roseann laughed. "Contrary to what most people think, it isn't always warm and sunny. Nights can get very cold even if the days are warm."

They were nearing the creek, and Amy shivered again as she remembered the first day of the trip when Anders had poured cold water on her.

"Wouldn't some nice, cold water feel just dandy right now?" Anders asked with a grin.

Amy stared at him in astonishment. "How did you know what I was thinking?" she asked. "I was just thinking about the first day of the trip when you did that to me."

Anders grinned. "They say great minds think alike. I saw you look at the creek and shiver, and I figured I could make a pretty good guess about what you were thinking."

"What are you guys talking about?" Roseann asked.

"On our first day out, I was half-asleep in my saddle when suddenly, I was violently awakened," Amy told her. "Anders had found some nice, cold water in a creek and filled his canteen with it. Then he snuck up behind me and gave me a completely unexpected, freezing cold bath!"

Roseann shook her head. "I don't how you survive all his jokes."

"They aren't life threatening ... most of them anyway!" Anders protested.

"Maybe not, but they're enough to worry the life out of anybody," Roseann insisted.

"Yeah, maybe that's why Amy's so small!" Anders teased.

"There you go again!" Roseann shook her finger at him.

"I don't mind his teasing." Amy laughed. "And I don't think that's why I'm short."

When they reached the ranch, Amy untacked and groomed Bannie in the dim light of a lantern, and after turning him out with the other horses, she headed for the house.

Clint caught up with her as she crossed the yard. "Ready for bed?" he asked.

"Sure am." Amy nodded. "This whole trip has been exciting, but I'm ready for things to get back to normal. Or as normal as they get on a ranch." She flashed him a grin.

Clint chuckled. "You got that right. I'm ready to go home, too. See you in the morning."

Roseann was lying on her bed when Amy came in. "This will be our last Bible reading together," she remarked as Amy sat down.

"I guess so." Amy nodded. "But we can think of each other when we do our personal devotions."

Roseann nodded. "Yes, I will always think of you when I do my devotions." She held up the Bible Amy had given her and smiled.

Amy smiled back and opened her Bible. "Since it's our last night together, why don't we take a break from our regular pattern and just share a verse or two that are important to us?"

"That's a good idea," Roseann agreed. "Why don't you go first?"

"Okay." Amy turned the pages of her Bible. "I like Luke 18:16. 'But Jesus called them unto him, and said, Suffer little children to come unto me, and forbid them not: for of such is the kingdom of God.' It's comforting to think that Jesus takes time for even the little children. No one is too small for Him."

Roseann nodded. "That is a good verse. I like II Samuel 22:3: 'The God of my rock; in him will I trust: he is my shield, and the horn of my salvation, my high tower, and my refuge, my saviour; thou savest me from violence.' It's nice to know that God is my refuge, my high tower, He will shelter me from the storms of life."

"That's a great thought," Amy agreed, "to know that whatever happens, God is there and taking care of us." The girls shared several more verses, then prayed together and settled down for the night.

Thank You for protecting us throughout this trip and through all the adventures we have had, Amy prayed before she fell asleep. *Thank You for all the lessons You taught me. Help me never to forget them. Thank You for drawing Roseann and Mr. Henderson to Yourself. Please draw Roseann's mother back to You. Thank You for the friends we made. Give us safety as we travel home. In Thy name, Amen.*

*****

Everyone was up bright and early the next morning and rushed through chores and last-minute preparations.

After a hurried breakfast, Clint did one last check of the horses and equipment. The horses were saddled, the mules harnessed, and soon everything was ready to go.

"Why don't we have prayer before you leave?" Devon suggested.

The others bowed their heads as he prayed feelingly. "Dear Heavenly Father, thank you for the wonderful times of fellowship we have had these few days. Thank you for using Clint and Amy to draw our hearts back to you. Protect our friends as they begin their journey home. Bless them for all they have done for us. In Jesus's name, Amen."

Last goodbyes were said, and the group started out the lane.

"Write to me, Amy!" Roseann called after them.

Amy turned in her saddle and waved to Roseann and Devon one last time. "I will, Roseann, I promise!"

She waved until they rounded a bend in the road, and then she turned back, and a smile rested on her face.

She was going home!

Amy's Pancake Recipe

2 eggs
2 tbsp. sugar
2 cups milk
1 tsp. baking soda
2 cups self-rising flour
1/3 cup melted butter
1/4 cup cornmeal

Beat eggs with rotary beater until fluffy and light yellow in color. Stir in milk. Add mixed dry ingredients. Mix just until thoroughly dampened. Blend in melted butter. Spoon onto medium-hot ungreased griddle or lightly greased skillet. Turn when puffed and full of bubbles. Makes 16–20 pancakes.

Grubby's Biscuits

1 1/2 cups all-purpose flour
1/2 cup yellow cornmeal
2 1/2 tsps. baking powder
1/3 cup shortening or butter
1/2 tsp. salt
2/3 cup milk

Sift flour, baking powder, and salt into mixing bowl. Blend in cornmeal and shortening, then add milk all at once. Mix with a fork until blended. Knead gently about 1/2 minute on lightly floured board. Roll dough 3/4" thick. Cut with a 2" cutter and place on lightly greased baking sheet. Bake at 450 degrees 12–15 minutes. Makes 12 biscuits.

CPSIA information can be obtained at www.ICGtesting.com
Printed in the USA
LVOW08s1705290514

387787LV00002B/376/P